The gospel of Jesus Christ spread like wildf
precisely because it was true, powerful, and life-changing. The gospei
was and IS compelling! *Compelled By Love: Living and Sharing Your
Christian Faith* will take you step by step into the Good News of Jesus
Christ that will change your life and equip you to help others find the
truth they need and are looking for. Dive in…it's a good compulsion!

Dr. Pete Alwinson, FORGE MEN, Orlando, Florida

John has brilliantly simplified the fundamental truths of Christianity
without compromising depth, beauty, or mystery. Masterfully written
for both the new-to-the-faith and the well-versed believer, we are invited
on an adventure to discover what makes the narrative of God the foundation for a fruitful life. This is and will continue to be a go-to resource
for years to come.

Steven L. Barr, Founding Leader of Cast Member Church (Disney)
Orlando-Anaheim-Paris-Tokyo-Hong Kong-Shanghai

As one who came up in a non-liturgical, evangelical church, I was
never exposed to the Apostles' Creed until seminary. I remember
being asked by one of my professors what I believed. I wasn't sure
what to say other than I believed what the Scriptures teach. The
Apostles' Creed became a beautiful entry point into the richness of
historical Christian orthodoxy as it is revealed in The Great Tradition.

I have waited a long time for an accessible yet thorough treatment of this
beautiful catechetical tool. John has done a phenomenal job of inviting
us into his personal reflections upon these timeless truths. You are in
for a treat, a veritable feast of biblical exposition as it intersects the
missionary life we are all invited by The Holy Spirit to pursue. I plan on
using this resource everywhere I have influence.

The Rev. Foye Michael Belyea, Abbott of Anam Cara Life
Community & Canon Missioner for Missio Mosaic

If you're curious about the practical implications of faith in God for your daily life, I highly recommend diving into *Compelled By Love* by John Kimball. Through John's fervent exploration of the Christian faith, the book becomes more than mere words—it transforms into an actionable guide. Ideal for those newly ignited by their faith in the Lord yet lacking foundational biblical knowledge, this work promises to be a treasure trove of insights. Let it be the seed that, when nurtured with an open heart, blossoms into a bountiful harvest within and all around you.

Petr Činčala, PhD, Executive Director, NCD America, Berrien Springs, Michigan

John Kimball in his book *Compelled by Love* makes a biblical, historical, foundational case for recapturing authentic discipleship, the kind of discipleship Jesus practiced and commissioned the church to do. Anchored in the template of the Apostle's Creed we are given the essentials of the faith and a means to see people formed in following Jesus. This book offers a practical, insightful, thorough approach to discipleship in our modern world; a needed and necessary tool for everyone.

The Rev. Canon Jon Davis PhD, Rector / St. Mark's Episcopal Church – Palatka Florida, Mission Strategist / Trainer / Coordinator Fresh Expressions North America

Kimball offers us a scaleable and energizing tour of the foundation of faith. This is deftly crafted theological writing that calls us into a deeper life in God. The detail & pastoral weight here offer much in resource and realism.

There are many gritty and unavoidable implications for the depth and range of the creedal faith missing or manifest in the life of God's bride. Real belief is for everyone! And Kimball paints the beauty, flavor & goodness that "real belief has a recipe!" Real belief leads to salvation, and in our confessing, we are saved! This isn't knowledge so much as it is impartation. Deep to deep, spirit to spirit! Truly well worth your time!

Rev. Johnny Douglas, Vicar and Team Leader, St. Peter's Church Hextable & St. Paul's Church Swanley Village, England UK

Compelled by Love is a discipleship handbook and theology review all wrapped together around the wonderful framework of the Apostle's Creed. This Creed serves as such a unifying proclamation binding Christians across many different traditions, practices, and cultures. It articulates and outlines exactly what we believe, so it's brilliant that John would use it as a perfect framework and discussion guide for disciple making. What a tremendous tool for teaching and reinforcing key biblical truths! If you're looking for a resource to reboot your vision or a new approach to disciple making, you need to read this book.

Tim Gilmore, Wycliffe Bible Translators

This book will serve as a helpful tool for people who are devoted to be a faithful follower of Jesus and invite others to join them in the journey of discipleship. This teaching will deepen the faith of the readers as they explore the convictions set forth in the Apostle's Creed. It will also provide a foundation of faith that they can pass on to others who desire to learn and grow in their faith. The study guides are practical and help the reader personally engage with the foundational principles of the Christian faith.

Rev. Dr. Ron Hamilton, Conference Minister, Conservative Congregational Christian Conference, Lake Elmo, Minnesota

I believe everyone can benefit from this book no matter where they are in their Christian walk. Not only does John's book cement into place what we believe but it gives insightful ways to share our faith with children, teens and adults. Isn't that what disciple making is all about, raising up disciples?"

Kyle Holmes, Missionary to Spain and Missionary Sending Coach

Compelled by Love is a unique and needed resource for disciple-making. Its aim is both orthodoxy and orthopraxy. It grounds doctrinally while also guiding toward practical Christian living. The result is that it feels ancient and current at the same time. The best part is that Pastor John has written this resource to be utilized across the generational spectrum by including specific questions in each chapter for children, teens, and adults. I look forward to all of the people who will be challenged, encouraged, and equipped as disciples and disciple-makers of Jesus through this book.

Samuel Huggard, District Superintendent, New England District Association of the Evangelical Free Church of America

Dr. John Kimball writes a masterful book that is timely and a much-needed tool to develop sons and daughters of God. He writes with passion as a shepherd who longs to see the people of God thrive in their relationship with their heavenly Father. Kimball is a seasoned teacher who understands that education is more than just knowing something, it is the actual doing of it that makes true knowledge and wisdom. John writes prophetically, addressing the lack of biblical discipleship that reflects less the way of Jesus and the heart of our Father. This book is written by a genuine practitioner who does what he writes, and the fruit of that activity is evident in his family and ministry. You will want to read this book and use it as a tool to disciple others into their God-given identity and destiny.

Mike Chong Perkinson, Lead Pastor of The Lamb's Fellowship, Lake Elsinore, California; Director of Multiplication in the Southern California Conference of the Free Methodist Church of North America; Co-Founder and Senior Developer of The Praxis Center for Church Development; President and Dean of Church & Ministry at Trivium Institute of Leader Development

As a pastor, I'm always looking for tools that I can hand to others that will help them grow as disciples AND disciple others. John Kimball has produced a great tool for us. He does a wonderful job mixing theology, doctrine and practical discipleship using the Apostle's Creed as a framework. At the end of each chapter, he provides a study guide that will help you grow as a disciple and disciple others, including children and teenagers. This book will help you grow in your "wheelbarrow faith." It will help you understand the concepts and how to live it out with others.

Deryk Richenburg, Lead Pastor, Hope Community Church
Newburyport, Massachusetts

John's heart, as expressed in his book *Compelled by Love* is refreshing and timely. The Church suffered during a pandemic when it could have been an opportunity to thrive. Exploring and returning to the commands of Christ is a must if the Body of Christ is to flourish in this age. The basics of disciple making are unpacked in a way to provide laser focus on implementation. Be enlightened as you read, be enriched as you implement.

Rev. Todd E. Venman, Pastor, Wiltsie Community Church
Russell, Pennsylvania

COMPELLED BY LOVE

Living and Sharing Your Christian Faith

John R. Kimball

Forward by William Mikler

With Study Guide by Gayle Buford

Beaumeadow Group,
Oviedo, Florida

DEDICATION

This book is dedicated to my family. To my bride of 35 years, Kathryn, who has always been one step ahead of me in the spiritual formation journey; to my children – Lauren, Josiah & Sarah Beth, and Anna Jean – into whom I have loved investing over the years. You have no idea how much joy your love for Christ gives me.

And to the rest of my "kids" and grandchildren – both by blood and borrowed – may you always choose a fruitful life marked by personal transformation, an all-encompassing love for God, mission participation, and sacrificial service to His glory.

TABLE OF CONTENTS

ACKNOWLEDGMENTS

Compelled By Love is a nearly six-year labor of love, borne on the wings of a thirty-four-year pastoral career working with people from all walks of life. When I began praying about writing this text, I had no idea how many people would end up being a significant part of this journey. I am amazed and grateful for how the Lord brought all the right folks together.

First and foremost, I want to thank my family, and especially my bride Kathryn, for their patience and encouragement over the time it has taken to put this work together – weeks away on writing retreats, compiling research, and writing as part of a strategic three-month sabbatical, and then evenings sequestered in my office (even over holidays) putting the finishing touches on this manuscript. I am so grateful for their inspiration to write and their ongoing examples of the very heart of disciple making that are the foundation of this book.

I am also grateful for my co-laborers in ministry in the Palmwood Church family, so many of whom have taken Jesus' disciple-making mandate as a serious part of their Christian life. It is a blessing and a pleasure to be their pastor. I would also like to thank the national Church Development Team I lead within my denomination, a group of friends who believe that the Church is Jesus' primary plan for making disciples who make disciples. Their input and cheerleading along the way have been critical. And I would like to thank my colleagues, friends, and mentors, Tom Johnston and Mike Chong Perkinson, for their investment into my life and ministry that launched me on this journey so many years ago. All of these people have offered input, perspective, and encouragement as I wrote what you now hold in your hands.

There are a few people for which I am particularly grateful and without whom I could not have completed this particular work. First, I owe a great debt of gratitude to my theological review team – dear friends from many different theological perspectives who offered their time, insight, and meaningful critiques as they reviewed the manuscript: Dr. Ray Delaurier (Reformed), North Central Regional Minister, Conservative Congregational Christian Conference; Fr. Foye Belyea (Anglican/Charismatic), Abbot of Anam Cara Life Community & Canon Missioner for Missio Mosaic; Bishop Jayson Quiñones (Pentecostal), Lead Pastor of Core Faith Church & President of Oviedo Christian Ministers Association; and Dr. T.A. Powell (Baptist), Retired Pastor & Instructor with John W. Rawlings School of Divinity at Liberty University. Their input was invaluable.

Second, I would be very remiss if I did not thank my friend Gayle Buford, who employed her many years in public education and curriculum design to create the study guides you find at the end of every chapter. Theology is only as good as its application. Her guidance and suggestions make the truths of the Apostles' Creed very practical.

My gratitude to my friend Susan Moody for proofreading the final draft, making important suggestions, and helping me get the manuscript ready for publication. And finally, my long-time friend Kim Gardell of Gardell Design, who worked her artistic magic on my dauther Lauren's cover concept, formatting the chapters and pages and getting literally everything "typeset" and ready for printing. All of you have your fingerprints on this book, and I would not have it any other way.

Many prayers have been prayed while writing and subsequently for this tool that the Holy Spirit would use it to help folks make more and better disciples. I hope many are encouraged to begin the disciple-making journey because of this book. May God get all the glory, and may Jesus' kingdom expand!

FORWARD

The book you hold in your hands differs from most other books you and I have read. That's because most of those books were read for our own information or enjoyment, and reading them was a very private matter.

But this book is different. This book is one you will want to read with friends, talk about and discuss with them, and then compare notes on how its biblical content shapes and empowers the real living you do in this very real world our heavenly Father created for us.

Restaurant Row: Better than a Food Court

We've all been to a food court in a shopping mall that opens onto a collection of different kitchens and food choices. But this book opens onto something far more elegant than a food court. It opens onto Restaurant Row in the City of God, where some delicious feasting can be done.

Here is how this book does that: In each chapter, real-world pastor John Kimball uses a line from the Apostles' Creed as a doorway into a specific banquet hall of biblical truth. And he asks you to join him and feast.

Don't Dine Alone

Just as the choicest restaurants on Restaurant Row are best enjoyed with friends, find a table with some friends and enjoy the meal.

Where? That's up to you. Find a table in a coffee shop or a café. Meet in your dining room or kitchen or that of a friend. Gather in a classroom in your church, begging to be used more than one day a week. A porch or a patio will serve. Zoom if you have to. Talk on the phone. Get together. Read together. Talk about what you've read. Share what your reading did in and for you. Ask questions. Listen to your dining partners. Enjoy the meal *together*.

Dine Slow

Please don't rush your meals. The Bible isn't fast food. Take your time. Linger over each passage. (You might take a week, a month, or longer in some chapters of this book.) Think. Share. Wonder. Delight.

Then What?

Then what? Enjoy living out what you've learned. The fact is, I think you'll find that living what you learned will come naturally to you. The Bread of Life has that effect on people.

Summing Up

Word gets around about good restaurants, and you know the best restaurants on Restaurant Row by the long lines of diners waiting to gain entrance to them. As you and your friends feast on the chapters in this book, I have a hunch that word will get around. It'll get around in my circles among leaders I work with in Africa, Asia, Europe, and North and South America. We've needed a book like this for a long, long time.

Enjoy the feasts,

Bill
The Most Reverend William Mikler
Archbishop,
Communio Christiana Apostolate for the Nations
January 4, 2024 A.D.

PREFACE

There is nothing more compelling than the love God has expressed to us in Jesus Christ. That love compels us toward a deeper relationship with our Triune God. And it should also compel us toward a deeper relationship with everyone around us. This love also motivates us to participate passionately in Christ's mission of redemption. We live our Christian Faith, of course. But we must also *share* our Christian Faith with others. We are all called to be Christ's ambassadors – following the commission he has given us to be disciple-makers (Matthew 28:18-20). As the Father sent Jesus to us, so he sends us out into the world (John 20:21; Acts 1:8; Romans 10:11-17).

The title of this book reflects the words of Paul to the Christians in Corinth:

> *Since, then, we know what it is to fear the Lord, we try to per-suade men. What we are is plain to God, and I hope it is also plain to your conscience. We are not trying to commend our-selves to you again, but are giving you an opportunity to take pride in us, so that you can answer those who take pride in what is seen rather than in what is in the heart. If we are out of our mind, it is for the sake of God; if we are in our right mind, it is for you. **For Christ's love compels us**, because we are convinced*

that one died for all, and therefore all died. And he died for all,
that those who live should no longer live for themselves but for
him who died for them and was raised again.

So from now on we regard no one from a worldly point of view.
Though we once regarded Christ in this way, we do so no longer.
Therefore, if anyone is in Christ, he is a new creation; the old
has gone, the new has come! All this is from God, who rec-
onciled us to himself through Christ and gave us the ministry
of reconciliation: that God was reconciling the world to him-
self in Christ, not counting men's sins against them. And he has
committed to us the message of reconciliation. We are therefore
Christ's ambassadors, as though God were making his appeal
through us. We implore you on Christ's behalf: Be reconciled to
God. God made him who had no sin to be sin for us, so that in
him we might become the righteousness of God. (2 Corinthians
5:11-21, New International Version, **emphasis mine**)[1]

Our mission of reconciliation is something we should not only take seriously, but should truly love doing. Even when we find certain people
"unlovable," the love of Christ in us should overtake us. We are on
Christ's mission of reconciliation, wielding Christ's message of reconciliation (the gospel), as Christ's ambassadors – his commissioned,
authorized and empowered representatives. We are representatives of
the Redeeming King!

It's true that I was, in the same way, compelled to write this book. My
prayer is that it not only helps you fall more deeply in love with Jesus,
but that it also helps you fall in love with his mission. I pray that you
are *compelled by love* to invest your Christian faith into others so they
too can more deeply love our Savior.

–JK

---

1   *The Holy Bible: New International Version* (2 Co 5:11–21). (1984). Zondervan.

HOW TO USE THIS BOOK

Many parts of Western Christianity are in trouble. And, to be frank, most of the challenges we face are because we have stopped making disciples. Large portions of the Western Church have all but forsaken outreach, evangelism, and discipling people to maturity in Christ. And those who do focus on the next generations tend to make converts or believers rather than disciples. A believer *believes* something. A convert is *convinced* of something. But a disciple is quite different. I love Ray van der Laan's definition.

> "A disciple knows what the rabbi knows. A disciple does what the rabbi does. A disciple is just like the rabbi."[2]

A disciple *becomes* someone – there is a guided transformation to become more like Jesus. Further, disciples then go on to make more and better disciples. The local church that is used by God to truly transform hearts like this ultimately transforms its community.

The harsh reality for many Christians today is that they have never been taught how to do this – to make disciples. Some have even been told that the Great Commission is for missionaries, not "normal" church folk. But that is absolutely not the case. We are all Christ's

---

2   Ray van der Laan, *In the Dust of the Rabbi,* Discovery Guide in the series *That the World May Know,* (Nashville TN: Harper Christian Resources, 2006)

ambassadors (2 Corinthians 5:20). We have all been commissioned to fulfill his mission on the earth (Matthew 28:18-20). We are all supposed to be his witnesses in Jerusalem and all Judea, in Samaria, and to the ends of the earth (Acts 1:8). Christians today struggle with our disciple-making commission because so few have the simple training and tools to do it.

Compelled By Love was written for Christians just like this. It's designed to help someone who is new to disciple making do it well. By intent it is not overly theological – it's basically "Christianity 101." It's a fantastic place to begin – to grow as disciples ourselves and to invest in the next spiritual generations as we partner with the Holy Spirit to grow the Kingdom of God. There are other excellent tools available today we can employ for spiritual formation beyond the basics.[3] But for people who are just beginning on their journey of actually making disciples, this tool will lay a solid foundation on which to continue building.

In the Introduction, I explain my rationale for using the Apostles' Creed as my framework. Here, I will just say it helps us ensure we cover the essentials. We take the Creed stanza by stanza and unpack it in a way that even brand-new Christians can understand. The Study Guide at the end of each chapter will help the disciple maker consider various options for solidifying that chapter's content in the heart, mind, and life of their disciple.

SOME SUGGESTIONS

1. Don't Rush.

This book is not designed to be a curriculum but a road map. This is not a "study" to get through. This is a spiritual investment into someone's life. Take your time.

Every disciple is unique. They have a unique story – learn it. They have unique fears – talk about them. They have a unique calling – discover it. They have a unique learning style – employ it. The worst possible

---

3   Two of my absolute favorites are Ken Boa's *Conformed to His Image: Biblical, Practical Approaches to Spiritual Formation* (Grand Rapids MI: Zondervan Academic, 2001, 2020), and Diane Chandler's *Christian Spiritual Formation: An Integrated Approach for Personal and Relational Wholeness* (Downers Grove IL: InterVarsity Press, 2014). And there are others.

thing you can do with *Compelled by Love* is to use it as a typical "bible study" and only learn the topics academically. Western Christians love knowledge – but they are very poor at using that knowledge in a transformed life. Take your time. Every journey will be different. But if you think you can complete this book in 16 weeks (the number of chapters), you're doing it wrong. Again, it's a road map – not a curriculum.

2. Begin with Yourself.

There's an old saying, "You can't share what you don't have." Truth! The very fact that so many Western Christians have never made a disciple tells us that most of them were not discipled themselves. I have literally had *pastors* tell me that they have no idea how to disciple people. Begin by working through the process yourself before you take someone else through it.[4]

The first section of each Study Guide is *How Do I Live Out What I've Just Learned in My Own Life?* Start there. Read each of the scriptures referenced in that chapter multiple times. Pray through them devotionally. Listen to what the Holy Spirit is saying to you in that lesson, and then act on it. It's only when you can begin applying the content of that chapter in your own life that you can help others contextualize the material for theirs.

3. Find a Mentor.

In many of my seminars, I ask, "Who is discipling you right now?" The responses are interesting. Some people can name people who have invested in them in the past, but it is common for nearly 100% of the participants to admit that they are not *currently* being discipled.

Disciple making knows no term. You never "arrive." Even the most mature believers in Jesus need an ongoing investment.[5] Begin by asking the Lord to show you who your disciplers/mentors might be. Pay attention

---

4   The one exception to this suggestion is if you want to work through the material with your spouse. This is a great way to begin, and is also a wonderful investment in your marriage. It may also set you up to disciple another couple down the road as you learn together and see things from each other's point of view.

5   By the way, it's okay to have someone younger than you be your discipler. Chronological age does not always correlate to spiritual maturity. Look for people who are truly mature in the area where you need to grow. As a young pastor I discipled people twice my age. As a man nearing my 60s, I now have younger brothers and sisters helping me grow in key areas of spiritual formation.

to the people he brings to mind. Some may be people who can guide you holistically in your spiritual formation. Others may be his suggestions for a specific area of your Christian life.

As you consider the names of those who could guide you on this journey, give them a call – take them out for coffee or lunch – invite them over for dessert – and *ask* them. Be sure to tell them what you are asking them to do and why you have concluded they are the right person. Everybody needs multiple "Pauls" in their life.

4. Establish a Real Prayer Regimen.

Western Christians do not pray as they should. Again, this is the fruit of our need for authentic discipleship. You can make it simple. Start small and grow it over time. I tell folks to make it a goal to spend 10 minutes each morning in prayer – 5 minutes of quiet listening, 5 minutes of responding to God relationally in prayerful conversation.

One does not need a "prayer laundry list" for morning devotions. Prayer lists and prayer guides are helpful, but we must remember that we pray because of our relationship with our heavenly Father as his precious, beloved, redeemed children. We do not pray primarily to ask him for stuff – we serve him, not the other way around.

One of my favorite tools for prayer and devotion is the Daily Office. You can download apps for your tablet or phone that give you this tool. But be careful that you don't default to following the "outline" of such tools and miss the relational component. The primary focus here is a growing, loving relationship with your Father.

Trying to disciple another without a personal foundation of prayer is like trying to take a road trip without gasoline. Disciple making doesn't come from a text; it comes from a vibrant personal relationship with the Father in Jesus. Such a relationship is non-existent without life-giving prayer.

5. Keep it Relational, Not Academic.

We've already alluded to this, but the spiritual formation journey is not primarily about the information we learn. Information is required to grow, but we are always seeking the *transformation* produced. Our rational minds in the West love to learn – but learning without application is useless.

My mentor built his Doctor of Philosophy program on this idea. The Western education approach radically differs from the rabbinical approach Jesus used. The West is concerned with credentials, whereas Jesus seeks growth in character. The West is preoccupied with propositions and methodologies, whereas Jesus taught principles. The West teaches people how to do things, whereas Jesus taught people how to *live*. The West teaches knowledge to control, whereas Jesus teaches knowledge so we can become more obedient to the Father ourselves. Education in the West is anchored in knowing the universe, whereas Jesus' approach is anchored in knowing God – the Creator of the universe.[6]

To avoid becoming purely academic, stop after each section (in each chapter) and ask the Lord to show you both how you currently live out that truth and how he would have you grow in it. Don't just *learn* the facts and doctrines; seek to root them deeply into the way you think, speak, act, and live.

6. Take Time to "Stew" in the Related Scriptures.

One of the greatest challenges I have seen in my students of the past is their tendency to "skip" the scripture references in books they read. Many read the text but then gloss over the bible passages that anchor it. Don't do that!

Nearly every supporting scripture passage in this tool is written out for a reason. We want to make it as easy as possible for readers to actually *engage* God's Word (especially for new believers). There is a lot of Scripture in this book! It could not be written in any other way. Take the time to read each one. In fact, take the time to ponder each one as it relates to the topic at hand. Ask the Holy Spirit (the Spirit of Truth) to help you understand and apply those passages. Meditate on them.

I would suggest that you use many of the scriptures from the chapter you are on as the foundation of your devotional study for that week.

---

6   Tom Johnston, *Mentored Ministry: The Rabbinical Way of Jesus*, (Bedford NH: Praxis Center for Church Development, 2009).

Let the Word of God guide you. At times, you will likely end up on a beautiful "cross reference tangent" you didn't intend – which is a wonderful thing!

7. Use the Study Guide for Suggestions.

The study guide is just that, a guide. Don't attempt to use it rigidly. Some of my friend Gayle's suggestions will apply – others won't. Every journey is unique. But let the ideas she has written stir your imagination. The goal is to make the material in this tool as attainable as possible for each age group.

We've already talked about the first Study Guide section, but there are three others:

- *How do I impart what I've just learned to children?*
- *How do I impart what I've just learned to teens?*
- *How do I impart what I've just learned to adults?*

Our hope is that these sections will help you focus the content of each chapter in age-appropriate ways. While you can begin quite young with children, many of the suggested activities require them to be old enough to use art supplies like scissors and glue. In each case, it's best to familiarize yourself with the Study Guide before you begin. Several of the lessons for teens and children contain *suggested* online links to patterns or other tools. Over time, links change or break. Prepare ahead of time, and feel free to create or search for other such tools if needed.

Older teens may find the adult section more helpful. And we highly recommend using a journal for teens and adults – this can be a bound journal, notebook, or even an online tool like Evernote. Finally, don't feel bound by the Guide – be creative. We don't know your disciple(s) like you do. Make it applicable to them.

8. Make it Consistent.

Finally, be consistent. Disciple making is most fruitful in an ongoing, regular relationship. I've found that it is critical to put a *regular* date on the calendar to meet with my disciples. One meets with me every Monday, right after work, at 5 pm. I have another who joins me for lunch every Tuesday. I meet with one weekly over coffee. I meet three weekly online using web conferencing technology. The key is to make it consistent. Do that, and you'll be blessed by the relationship's fruitfulness.

I hope these ideas stir you! I've been a Christian since right after I graduated from my undergrad. I've now been a pastor for most of my adult life. I've been disciple making for most of that. I can promise you that there is nothing more fulfilling than being used by God to assist another precious soul grow toward maturity in Christ and begin fruitful ministry for his kingdom! Take the first steps and watch what God does to meet you on this journey. It's awesome!

INTRODUCTION
I Believe

When they returned to the other disciples, they saw a large crowd surrounding them, and some teachers of religious law were arguing with them. When the crowd saw Jesus, they were overwhelmed with awe, and they ran to greet him.

"What is all this arguing about?" Jesus asked.

One of the men in the crowd spoke up and said, "Teacher, I brought my son so you could heal him. He is possessed by an evil spirit that won't let him talk. And whenever this spirit seizes him, it throws him violently to the ground. Then he foams at the mouth and grinds his teeth and becomes rigid. So I asked your disciples to cast out the evil spirit, but they couldn't do it."

Jesus said to them, "You faithless people! How long must I be with you? How long must I put up with you? Bring the boy to me."

So they brought the boy. But when the evil spirit saw Jesus, it threw the child into a violent convulsion, and he fell to the ground, writhing and foaming at the mouth. "How long has this been happening?" Jesus asked the boy's father.

He replied, "Since he was a little boy. The spirit often throws him into the fire or into water, trying to kill him. Have mercy on us and help us, if you can."

1

"What do you mean, 'If I can'?" Jesus asked. "Anything is possible if a person believes." The father instantly cried out, "I do believe, but help me overcome my unbelief!" (Mark 9:14-24)

ALMOST BELIEVING

One of the most precious accounts in the Bible tells the story of a man who desperately sought out Jesus' disciples to free his beloved son from a demon. The disciples were still a bit "green" as they addressed the situation. It didn't go well, but it did provide an important teaching point as they all returned to Jesus together. Jesus quickly assessed the situation and tells them that, unlike some of the other demons they have encountered, this particular kind comes out only with prayer (some manuscripts also add "and fasting").

What makes this passage so precious, however, is Jesus' interaction with the boy's father. Exasperated and even more concerned about the disciples' failure, the father turns to Jesus and pleads, "Have mercy on us and help us, if you can." *If you can.* This is not only the language of desperation, but also of doubt. This dad has no real assurance that even Jesus can do it. This leads to a critical statement: Jesus tells him, "Anything is possible if a person believes" (Mark 9:23). The father's response is one of the most pure, most raw – most real – statements in the gospels.

The father instantly cried out, "I do believe, but help me overcome my unbelief!" (Mark 9:24)

We live in a time when many Christians have a similar problem. They have been taught the Scriptures, but they have not been thoroughly discipled in how to trust and walk with Jesus. They often have good, sound doctrinal understanding. Still, they have no practical frame of reference for stepping out in genuine faith when it comes to trusting Jesus for answers to prayer, miracles, or comfort in times of grief and desperation. These believers truly do *believe* with their heads, but they struggle to believe with their whole lives. They have given mental assent to what the Bible teaches, but they have not fully put their trust in its reality.

Among the folks of the congregation I am blessed to pastor, we have occasionally called this deep, living faith "wheelbarrow faith." That phrase comes from one of our favorite stories.

WHEELBARROW FAITH

This story is a rather famous one – it's known worldwide. It's been reported by countless people over the last 150 years. And it's true.

Charles Blondin was a French tightrope artist, world renowned for his incredible theatrics. Massive crowds would always gather to watch his literally death-defying feats. His favorite place to walk the tightrope was across the Canadian gorge of Niagara Falls. His chosen spot was 2,200 feet across and nearly 200 feet above the water. And that water was flowing at a pace of 6 million cubic feet every minute!

Blondin would thrill audiences who, filled with morbid terror, could not believe what he would do. He once walked all the way across the gorge blindfolded. Another time he walked across the gorge carrying a grown man piggyback. He walked across the gorge on stilts. He hopped across the gorge in a burlap bag! One time he sat down in the middle of the gorge – on the rope – setting up a camping stove where he fried and then ate an egg.

One time, Blondin walked across the gorge and then back again, pushing a wheelbarrow. When he returned, he asked his massive audience, "Do you think I can do it again?" They shouted, "Yes!" He then asked, "Do you think I can do it with a man in the wheelbarrow?" They shouted all the more wildly, "Yes!" Then Blondin asked for a volunteer. The crowd fell silent. After an excruciatingly long pause, a single man stepped forward and sat down into the wheelbarrow.

That is what we mean by "wheelbarrow faith." In today's church, there are masses of people who will shout, "I believe!" But few will actually get into the wheelbarrow. We must understand that our Lord Jesus does not ask us for mental assent. His goal is not that we would simply agree with him theologically. Jesus asks us for complete trust. And to this we may be very much like that desperate father, "Jesus, I do believe. But please help me overcome my unbelief."

3

A BIT OF GREEK

When you and I say, "I believe," we effectively invoke the Greek word *pisteúo*. This word does include mental assent. It covers the believing that occurs when we conclude that something is true or real. We say, "Yeah, I believe in that." But it goes deeper. This word also means "to have confidence in." This speaks of the faithfulness something possesses. It sees steadfastness. It means we have identified reliability. When we use this word, we say we are ready to put our trust in that item or person. This is what our church calls "wheelbarrow faith." It means we are willing to act upon it, to live it out – we will demonstrate what we say we believe with action because of our confidence in it.

The Greek word *pisteúo* is what we want to experience and live out regarding our personal faith in Jesus. We do not just want to give Jesus mental assent – theological agreement. But we want to live out our full trust in Christ every single day. And building that kind of faith on a simple but solid framework – like the Apostles' Creed – helps us ensure that all of our faith "bases" are covered. We'll talk more about that in a minute.

REAL BELIEF

When it comes to really believing – faith with action – the Apostle Paul gives us a great lesson in his letter to the Christians in Rome:

> *In fact, it says,*
> *"The message is very close at hand; it is on your lips and in your heart." And that message is the very message about faith that we preach: If you openly declare that Jesus is Lord and believe in your heart that God raised him from the dead, you will be saved. For it is by believing in your heart that you are made right with God, and it is by openly declaring your faith that you are saved. As the Scriptures tell us, "Anyone who trusts in him will never be disgraced." Jew and Gentile are the same in this respect. They have the same Lord, who gives generously to all who call on him. For "Everyone who calls on the name of the Lord will be saved." But how can they call on him to save them unless they believe in him? And how can they believe in him if they have never heard about him? And how can they hear about*

4

him unless someone tells them? And how will anyone go and tell them without being sent? That is why the Scriptures say, "How beautiful are the feet of messengers who bring good news!"
But not everyone welcomes the Good News, for Isaiah the prophet said, "Lord, who has believed our message?" So faith comes from hearing, that is, hearing the Good News about Christ. (Romans 10:8-17)

Real belief requires both verbal confession and full confidence. It is not enough to espouse our faith; we must also have it indelibly rooted in our hearts. Paul begins by quoting from Moses in Deuteronomy 30:13-14 about how Israel's heart turns to the LORD. What people need to experience this real faith is not far away or hard to get. God has drawn us to his heart, and now we must respond in kind! When the mouth and the heart are in sync on this matter, there will always be a faith response – real belief.

We must note that this real belief begins with two foundational things. First, we must confess with our mouths that Jesus is indeed Lord. The outward expression here is essential, but please know that Paul here is telling us one cannot be saved by the outward alone! Just confessing Jesus as Savior with your lips is not enough. There is a corresponding response in the heart that is required as well. So there's the public declaration of surrender to Christ, and also the conviction in the heart that God did indeed raise Jesus from the dead. There is "wheelbarrow faith" that the resurrection is real – it really happened! The crucifixion of Jesus is the pivotal component of all biblical theology – all belief. However, the resurrection is also non-negotiable. We must *pisteúo* this! We must give it mental assent, yes, but we must also see it as a reliable truth and then base our whole faith life upon it. Real faith – real belief – begins with the combination of confession with the mouth and conviction in the heart.

Real belief offers justification. In our believing – in our "wheelbarrow faith" – we are justified. Many Christians do not fully grasp the importance of this fact. Justification has to do with our righteousness. We can never be righteous enough before God on our own. Earlier in Paul's Roman letter, he writes,

For I am not ashamed of this Good News about Christ. It is the power of God at work, saving everyone who believes—the Jew first and also the Gentile. This Good News tells us how God makes us right in his sight. This is accomplished from start to finish by faith. As the Scriptures say, "It is through faith that a righteous person has life." (Romans 1:16-17)

Interestingly, the word order of that last sentence in Greek is slightly different. It says, "The person who through faith is righteous shall live." It is the faith that makes us righteous. Paul speaks of a righteousness from God that is revealed not only to us but *in us* through the power of the gospel. Because Jesus reigns, we are given *his* righteousness when we have "wheelbarrow faith" in him. Justification is, quite literally, the declaration by God as the ultimate Judge that we are, in fact, fully righteous because of Jesus' shed blood. When God looks at believers in Jesus through the curtain of Christ's blood, that blood "blots out" all of our sin. Make no mistake: there is a record (Revelation 20:12). But for those who have placed their full trust in Jesus, that record is expunged.

You were dead because of your sins and because your sinful nature was not yet cut away. Then God made you alive with Christ, for he forgave all our sins. He canceled the record of the charges against us and took it away by nailing it to the cross. (Colossians 2:13-14)

With the sin addressed, the Judge declares us righteous – that is, justified – and our names are recorded in the Lamb's glorious Book of Life for all eternity (Revelation 20:15).

Real belief leads to salvation. In our confessing, we are saved. The combination of heart and mouth in this faith declaration produces both Christ's righteousness and Christ's salvation in us. Paul writes,

For it is by believing in your heart that you are made right with God, and it is by openly declaring your faith that you are saved. (Romans 10:10)

Notice that, aside from our trusting in (*pisteúo*) Jesus, we have no part in our own salvation. It's critical to understand this. It is all by the love, grace, and mercy of God. Part of having the "wheelbarrow faith" we've been discussing is also giving up any notion that we can earn all or part of our salvation. We cannot. Paul makes this abundantly clear in his letter to the Christians in Ephesus.

> *Once you were dead because of your disobedience and your many sins. You used to live in sin, just like the rest of the world, obeying the devil—the commander of the powers in the unseen world. He is the spirit at work in the hearts of those who refuse to obey God. All of us used to live that way, following the passionate desires and inclinations of our sinful nature. By our very nature we were subject to God's anger, just like everyone else.*
>
> *But God is so rich in mercy, and he loved us so much, that even though we were dead because of our sins, he gave us life when he raised Christ from the dead. (It is only by God's grace that you have been saved!) For he raised us from the dead along with Christ and seated us with him in the heavenly realms because we are united with Christ Jesus. So God can point to us in all future ages as examples of the incredible wealth of his grace and kindness toward us, as shown in all he has done for us who are united with Christ Jesus.*
>
> *God saved you by his grace when you believed.* ***And you can't take credit for this; it is a gift from God. Salvation is not a reward for the good things we have done, so none of us can boast about it.*** (Ephesians 2:1-9, **emphasis mine**)

Salvation is a gift.

Real belief deals with our shame. Shame is part and parcel with sin. Shame was among the first fruits of sin (Genesis 3:7). Shame layers on top of our sin, causing us to run further and faster from our holy Heavenly Father. But Paul quotes from Isaiah 28:16, informing the Roman Christians,

> *As the Scriptures tell us, "Anyone who trusts in him will never be disgraced."* (Romans 10:11)

"Trusts in" here is the Greek word *pisteúo*. "Wheelbarrow faith" gets rid of our disgrace, our shame.

Real belief is for everyone. I love this! God makes his offer to everyone. While some will self-select out, rejecting this incredible gift, the offer is broad in scope. Listen to these promises:

> For *"Everyone who calls on the name of the Lord will be saved."* (Romans 10:13)

> *"For this is how God loved the world: He gave his one and only Son, so that everyone who believes in him will not perish but have eternal life.* (John 3:16)

> *I urge you, first of all, to pray for all people. Ask God to help them; intercede on their behalf, and give thanks for them. Pray this way for kings and all who are in authority so that we can live peaceful and quiet lives marked by godliness and dignity. This is good and pleases God our Savior, who wants everyone to be saved and to understand the truth.* (1 Timothy 2:1-4)

Real belief is for everyone!

Real belief has a recipe. Paul is so practical in his letters. Here in Romans, he shows us that there is a God-designed progression to which we should all pay attention:

> *But how can they call on him to save them unless they believe in him? And how can they believe in him if they have never heard about him? And how can they hear about him unless someone tells them? And how will anyone go and tell them without being sent? That is why the Scriptures say, "How beautiful are the feet of messengers who bring good news!"* (Romans 10:14-15)

1. Those needing saving faith – saving *pisteúo* – must call on Jesus. This is the confession with one's lips.

2. Those needing saving faith – saving *pisteúo* – must believe in Jesus. This is the deep conviction within one's heart.

3. Those needing saving faith must have someone – or multiple people over time – to preach the good news (gospel) to them. This describes one's need to understand that there is a wonderful message that redemption and salvation are available.

4. Those preaching the good news to people who need saving faith must be sent by the church. The gospel ministry is not accidental but intentional, and local churches must raise up and send out people to engage their world with it – and this certainly includes their immediate communities!

5. The "good news" – the gospel – is first and foremost the beautiful declaration that Jesus reigns! He is Lord. And this is key. You see, we are saved because Jesus reigns. We are declared righteous because Jesus reigns. We have a restored eternal relationship with our Heavenly Father because Jesus reigns. In fact, Paul here quotes from the prophet Isaiah,

> *How beautiful on the mountains are the feet of the mes-senger who brings good news, the good news of peace and salvation,* **the news that the God of Israel reigns!** (Isaiah 52:7, **emphasis mine**)

There is a progression God uses to draw men, women, and children to saving faith. This is not simply Christian activity but fostering genuine "wheelbarrow faith"! Their mouths don't just confess it, but their very lives demonstrate full reliance upon it. As a friend of mine puts it, "It is lived out loud."

Real belief is rooted in the Word of Christ. The word of God is the foundation of all of this. It provides the very bedrock of our faith, our belief, our *pisteúo.* Paul concludes his thought:

> *So faith comes from hearing, that is, hearing the Good News about Christ.*(Romans 10:17)

It is not enough for us to believe in our heads only. The call of Jesus is for full-on faith. We believe – yes. We have confidence – yes. But we also trust *completely* and walk it out. And we build that kind of belief from knowing and living out the non-negotiables of apostolic teaching in the scriptures. This journey is not just to know, but to fully embody the belief expressed in the Apostles' Creed.

THIS IS PERSONAL

My passion for this book is very personal. It's not just a concern for the condition of many local churches today – although that is bad enough. It's related to my own story. I am the grandson of a pastor. I was raised in a Christian home. In fact, I am the twenty-fourth ordained minister in the last five generations on my mom's side of the family – and there are more in ministry in the generations that follow me! But I was not discipled. And that's the source of my passion.

I had graduated from college and was in trade school before I was confronted with the gospel of Jesus. And it didn't happen in the church of my upbringing. I knew the message of the gospel, but I had never been challenged to apply it to my own sinful nature. I have many friends and family members still in that congregation, including some former Sunday School teachers. I'm not faulting them. They did what they were taught to do. They were taught to *teach*, not to *disciple*. By the time I went through confirmation at age 13, I knew all the major stories of the Bible and had a basic understanding of church life. But no one had actually taken me by the hand (or, more correctly, by the heart) and walked with me in life to apply all that biblical knowledge for personal transformation and kingdom fruit. I was a student of Jesus, not a disciple. And while I had my act together for Sunday morning, I was pretty much spiritually and morally bankrupt the rest of the week.

It was not until I was in seminary that I had people begin to make this investment into my life. After my salvation in 1986, my older brother connected me with a home bible study that started the process, but it would be another two years before I had true "disciplers" investing in me. And it would not be until the new millennium that I would have a mentor who finally taught me a framework for making authentic disciples for Jesus.

Disciple making is not rocket science. It's not really about how much you know, but about *who* you know. You have a relationship with Jesus, so build redemptive relationships with those you disciple.

Having a simple pathway (like the Apostles' Creed) to use can help virtually any believer in Jesus to do a thorough job in the task of spiritual formation through disciple making. As we spoke of in the "How to Use This Book" section, start by being discipled yourself. When you begin to disciple others, don't just seek to learn information, but pursue personal transformation together. Starting young with people on this journey can help them avoid a lot of unnecessary heartache in their adolescent and teen years, but new believers of all ages should be discipled. The church needs to train people to make disciples again, which brings me to the purpose of this book.

WHAT NOW?

This book has a two-fold purpose. First, I want you to understand and apply the basics of genuine "wheelbarrow" belief in your own life. But it cannot end there because our Savior commissioned every single one of us to make disciples. So the second purpose is to equip you to impart this belief very intentionally into the lives of others. I'm not asking you to simply teach them doctrinal information – although that is a necessity. I'm asking you to actually walk with them on their faith journey to help them grow in their own life-demonstrated *pisteúo*. I'm asking you to invite them to join you in the wheelbarrow.

I have designed *Compelled by Love* to be a very basic tool you can use. There is a whole lot of "theology" I do not cover in this book. That is by design. I wanted to give you a resource that truly focuses on the essentials of the Christian Faith. This book is "Christianity 101."

In the chapters that follow, I will use the simplicity of the Apostles' Creed to walk with you through those basics. Learn them. Camp on them. Ponder them. Pray through them. Wrestle with them. Ask the Holy Spirit to invest them deeply into your soul. Plead for them to become fully assimilated into your head, heart, and life as genuine *pisteúo* – "wheelbarrow faith." And as you do this, prayerfully bring others along for the ride.

As an additional tool to this journey we'll be on together, my dear friend and colleague Gayle Buford has employed her many years of experience as a teacher and curriculum designer to add a brief study guide at the end of each chapter (including this Introduction). In this study guide, she will always address the same four questions:

1. *How do I live out what I have just learned in my own life?*
2. *How do I impart what I have just learned to children?*
3. *How do I impart what I have just learned to teens?*
4. *How do I impart what I have just learned to adults?*

Our goal is to make this book as practical a tool as possible for you to make mature disciples for Jesus.

Depending on your own style and personality, you might do this one-on-one. Others might invest in small clusters of people. You might meet with your "disciples" over a cup of coffee. You might do it together in your family room. In my case, my favorite venue is over lunch. But make it your own. Building on the apostolic essentials outlined in the Creed, grow in your belief together and watch what happens.

Don't just read this book and then set it aside. Step out in faith and engage in it. And know this: I have been praying for you in this adventure since before this text went to print. I know this adventure personally – and I cannot wait for you to experience it for yourself. If you ever get the chance, let me know how it went. You can contact me at *www.beaumeadow.com* or by using the QR code below.

John Kimball,
Oviedo, Florida, January 2024

STUDY GUIDE

IT MAKES A DIFFERENCE

Many Christians today do not exemplify what we have called "wheel-barrow" faith. Faith for them has come to mean a cognitive acceptance of something they deem true. And while this is certainly a part of our Christian Faith, it is merely the beginning. It is possible to have changed one's mind with biblical truth without changing their lifestyle.

People who truly walk by *pisteúo* faith live and act differently. They trust God regardless of their current circumstances. They work hard to live a life that exemplifies Jesus – both by his words and by his works. They pray with discernment and authority. They readily accept their unique part in Christ's mission to redeem the world through disciple making. They wrestle – personally and with others – to understand and apply more difficult truths of Scripture to their lives because they genuinely want to be faithful to carry out "everything Jesus has commanded" (Matthew 28:18-20).

People with only an academic faith tend to align more with the lifestyles of their friends. They are influenced more by people than by God and his Word. They talk about loving and trusting God but show little or no fruit of trust in the way they live. They look more to worldly solutions for problems and to more ordinary sources of relief and resources. They also often will read the Scriptures and may even argue about favorite doctrines, but their knowledge is more theoretical, and their debates are more about winning people to their particular position than finding ways to faithfully live out God's instructions. Ultimately, cognitive Christians trust more in themselves than in God. This is usually their downfall.

HOW DO I LIVE OUT WHAT I HAVE JUST LEARNED IN MY OWN LIFE?

1. Take a moment to stop and pray. Go to the Father about this adventure on which you're about to embark. See if you can spend at least 30 minutes alone with God, balancing your

talking and your listening. You can't hear God's responses to your prayers when you're talking, so portions of silence are critical. Ask the Lord to help you in the following ways:

a.　For understanding – you'll likely be learning many new things.

b.　For clarity – if it's not clear to you, you can't make it clear to others.

c.　For the Holy Spirit – God's Spirit is our Helper, Guide, and Teacher. You can't do this without Him.

d.　For guidance in inviting disciples into your journey – Remember, God wants this more than you do! And don't be surprised if people come to mind you would never have considered on your own. Pay attention to such surprises!

e.　For fruit – that both you and your disciples would learn the information, apply it to your lives as you grow toward maturity, and that the result would be a huge impact on the world around you for Jesus' kingdom and glory.

2.　Take several days to consider what "wheelbarrow faith" looks like in your life. How is it different than just an academic understanding of a doctrinal topic? Who can help you apply what you learn to put it into an ongoing life's practice?

HOW DO I IMPART WHAT I HAVE JUST LEARNED TO CHILDREN?

1.　Begin by praying with the children. Ask God, through the Holy Spirit, to help the children understand more about the Christian faith. Ask God to help them clearly understand the new things they are about to learn.

2.　Using the illustration of Blondin and the wheelbarrow, ask the children why the man who climbed into the wheelbarrow was different than everyone else. Guide them to understand the difference between "knowing" and "acting" on what we believe.

3.　Ask the children what it looks like to act like Jesus.

4. Begin helping the children memorize the Apostles' Creed – it will bless them for the rest of their lives.

5. If you have children in your group who have not yet surrendered to Jesus, begin praying now for the Holy Spirit to open that conversational door so you can explain the gospel. Once they receive Christ, the indwelling presence of the Holy Spirit will make the lessons in this book much more accessible to them.

HOW DO I IMPART WHAT I HAVE JUST LEARNED TO TEENS?

1. Begin by praying with the teens. Ask God, through the Holy Spirit, to increase understanding. You can do this or ask a volunteer.

2. Using the illustration of Blondin and the wheelbarrow, ask the teens why the man who climbed into the wheelbarrow was different than everyone else. Ask them for other examples of the difference between "knowing" and "acting" on what we believe.

3. Spend some time talking about the Greek word *pisteúo*. Ask the teens what makes this particular term so essential to understanding biblical belief?

4. Review the Apostles' Creed together. Look at each stanza. Ask them to begin thinking about why each of those points is essential to their Faith.

5. Challenge the teens to memorize the Apostles' Creed if they have not yet done so in Church or Sunday School.

6. If you have teens in your group who have not yet surrendered to Jesus, begin praying now for the Holy Spirit to open that conversational door so you can explain the gospel. Once they receive Christ, the indwelling presence of the Holy Spirit will make the lessons in this book much more accessible to them.

HOW DO I IMPART WHAT I HAVE JUST LEARNED TO ADULTS?

1. Encourage your adult students to take a moment to stop and pray. Encourage them to go to the Father about this adventure on which they are about to embark, asking the Lord to help them in the following ways:

    a. For understanding – they'll likely be learning many new things.

    b. For clarity – if it's not clear to them, they can't make it clear to others.

    c. For the Holy Spirit – God's Spirit is our Helper, Guide, and Teacher. We can't do this without Him.

    d. For guidance in inviting disciples into their journey – Remind them that God wants this more than they do! Tell them not to be surprised if people come to mind they would never have considered.

    e. For fruit – that they would learn the information, apply it to their lives as they grow toward maturity, and that the result would be a huge impact on the world around them for Jesus' kingdom and glory.

2. Using the illustration of Blondin and the wheelbarrow, ask the adults why the man who climbed into the wheelbarrow was different than everyone else. Ask them for other examples of the difference between "knowing" and "acting" on what we believe. Do they have any illustrations from their own lives?

3. Spend some time talking about the Greek word *pisteúo*. What makes this particular term so essential to understanding biblical belief?

4. Review the Apostles' Creed together. Look at each stanza. Ask them why each of those points is essential to their Faith. What heresies may have been circulating that required clarity on each topic? Are any similar heresies around today?

5. If you have people in your group who have not yet surrendered to Jesus, begin praying now for the Holy Spirit to open that conversational door so you can explain the gospel. Once they receive Christ, the indwelling presence of the Holy Spirit will make the lessons in this book much more accessible to them.

THE APOSTLES' CREED

I believe in God, the Father almighty,

creator of heaven and earth.

I believe in Jesus Christ, his only Son, our Lord,

who was conceived by the Holy Spirit

and born of the virgin Mary.

He suffered under Pontius Pilate,

was crucified, died, and was buried;

he descended to hell.

The third day he rose again from the dead.

He ascended to heaven

and is seated at the right hand of God the Father almighty.

From there he will come to judge the living and the dead.

I believe in the Holy Spirit,

the holy catholic (meaning universal) church,

the communion of saints,

the forgiveness of sins,

the resurrection of the body,

and the life everlasting.

Amen.

CHAPTER 1
The Apostles' Creed

KNOW WHAT YOU SAY YOU BELIEVE

Those who know me have likely heard me express my concern over three great lacks in today's Church: 1) people do not read the Bible as they should, remaining critically unfamiliar with what God has already spoken on faith, ministry, and life in general; 2) people do not pray as they should, living their lives vitally disconnected from God in conversation, devotion, and intercession; and 3) people do not make disciples as they should, having abdicated their primary kingdom responsibility to intentionally pass on their faith to the next spiritual generations, leading folks to maturity in Christ. I believe that all of these things are the fruit of not understanding the basics of their Christian Faith.

From the beginning, the Church has rooted itself in the teaching of Jesus and his apostles – those men who walked with him during his earthly ministry and then were sent out (the word apostle means "sent one") to establish Christ's Church and expand his rule and reign throughout humanity. We see evidence of this apostolic foundation right away in the life of the newly birthed church in Acts:

All the believers devoted themselves to the apostles' teaching, and to fellowship[7], and to sharing in meals (including the Lord's Supper), and to prayer.

A deep sense of awe came over them all, and the apostles performed many miraculous signs and wonders. And all the believers met together in one place and shared everything they had. They sold their property and possessions and shared the money with those in need. They worshiped together at the Temple each day, met in homes for the Lord's Supper, and shared their meals with great joy and generosity— all the while praising God and enjoying the goodwill of all the people. And each day the Lord added to their fellowship those who were being saved. (Acts 2:42-47)

Notice that the believers were devoted to four key components of life together: apostolic teaching, the fellowship of believers, sharing in meals together, and prayer. The first of these was the teaching of the apostles. Having a sure, biblical foundation for our faith changes everything. This is why I love the Apostles' Creed. It is one of the most widely-accepted, authoritative, and historic statements of our Christian Faith.

THE HISTORY OF THE APOSTLES' CREED

A creed is a formal statement or confession of faith. There have been many Christian creeds down through the ages, but there are three early creeds that helped to define and establish what we would call historic, Christian orthodoxy.[8] Each of these creeds has played an important role in helping Jesus' Church to live in a right relationship with him.

The first of these creeds was the Apostles' Creed, originally called the Roman Creed (c. 100 AD). Developed as a clear response to Gnosticism,

---

7   Most English Bibles simply say 'to fellowship,' but in the Greek, there is a definite article in front of that term. This is not devotion to enjoying each other's company, but a devotion to *the* fellowship, the body of Christ. This is a devotion to the family of God on its common redemptive mission.

8   The word orthodoxy has come to mean "conforming to sound doctrine." But there is a nuance that this definition misses. The compound word orthodoxy comes from two Greek words, simply put, *ortho* meaning "correct" and *doxy* meaning "praise/honor." Orthodoxy is not "correct belief," but "correct praise." It speaks of the condition of our lives when we are in full alignment with our God – everything about us is an expression of praise and worship to God.

the Apostles' Creed addressed the false belief that the material world was evil and only the spiritual world was good – leading to the blatant disregard for one's lifestyle as long as he or she had obtained the right "knowledge" (or in Greek, *gnosis*). The Gnostics believed God did not create the world because it was evil. They also believed it impossible that Jesus could have taken on human flesh because that too is evil. They rejected the idea that Jesus actually died, and they held that their special redeeming knowledge was only made available to a select few – not the Church universal. The Apostles' Creed was carefully crafted to address all of these misaligned ideas so the Church could remain on its mission and flourish.

The second creed we should mention is the Nicene Creed (325 AD). This creed came out of the Council of Nicea and was a response to heresy taught by a man named Arius. Arius denied the divinity of Jesus, rejecting the notion that the three Persons of the Trinity (Father, Son and Holy Spirit) were of the same essence. He believed that Jesus was "subordinate" to God the Father, and therefore could not be divine. The creed was crafted to respond to this notion, making it especially clear that Jesus is of "one substance" with the Father. Jesus, the Savior, is fully divine and fully human at the same time.

The third creed to consider is the Definition of Chalcedon (451 AD). A little over 100 years after the Nicene Creed's introduction, the Definition of Chalcedon reaffirmed Nicea's conclusions and partic-ularly targeted heretical teaching about the incarnation of Christ. A man named Eutichus taught that when Jesus took on human flesh, he ceased being fully divine and was also not fully human – he was something other – which went against the foundational teaching about Jesus' nature from the Gospel of John:

In the beginning the Word already existed. The Word was with God, and the Word was God. He existed in the beginning with God. God created everything through him, and nothing was cre-ated except through him. The Word gave life to everything that was created, and his life brought light to everyone. The light shines in the darkness, and the darkness can never extinguish it... So the Word became human and made his home among us. He was full of unfailing love and faithfulness. And we have seen his glory, the glory of the Father's one and only Son. (John 1:1-5, 14)

Creeds like these are important to our Christian Faith because they bring essential clarity on matters of belief, salvation, and life. It is also important that creeds like these were established very early – helping us understand the convictions of the early church as taught by the apostles.

Because it was one of the earliest and most thorough expressions of the Christian Faith, the Apostles' Creed is an excellent framework on which to build our study in this book. What was basic and essential for the early church is still basic and essential for us today. It's also a well-known and widely-accepted statement. So we can see from its use and history that it has remained consistent and biblical from the beginning.

The Apostles' Creed has clear roots in the original teaching of the apostles. If you are unfamiliar with the Apostles' Creed, take a moment to page back to the beginning of this chapter and read it. Read it slowly and thoughtfully. Each of the affirmations given in the creed is directly from the teaching of the apostles or from Jesus himself. Each stanza is foundational to a vibrant and historic Christian Faith. These statements are non-negotiable when it comes to historic, biblical Christianity. Each is an expression of the Scriptures. These stanzas make up what we call the "essentials" of the Faith.

The Apostles' Creed was originally developed in Rome. While components of the creed were already being recited as the church grew during the first century, by the end of the second century, they were collected in the Church at Rome pretty much in the same form we have today. The creed is first quoted, as such, as The Interrogatory Creed of Hippolytus' Apostolic Tradition in 215 AD. And while it had many regional variants over its first 600 years, these were most likely because the church in different regions needed to emphasize other aspects of the Creed to deal with local errors.

The Textus Receptus of 700 AD gives us the form that has been held with conviction by Western Christianity for over 1300 years. As a unique bit of trivia, the Creed, as we know it today, appears to have been published in Southwest France between 710-724 AD. The Creed became the primary framework of the Faith for biblical Christianity from that time forward. And those who follow such a framework are often called "creedal" Christians.

Historically, when someone identifies as a creedal Christian, they are saying they hold to these clear, biblical and historical tenets of the Christian Faith. Such a framework is a standard. It can also be a type of "litmus test" at times. It does not matter what denominational distinctives a person may have; if we are in creedal agreement, we can have beautiful fellowship and ministry fruit together. Nowhere is this more evident to me personally than in the friendship and prayer partnership I have with two other pastors in my city. Father Jon Davis is an Episcopal Priest who loves the Word of God and is passionate about the mission of Christ. Bishop Jayson Quiñones is a Pentecostal pastor and leader who shares those same passions and oversees our local ministerial association. I am a Congregational pastor with the same convictions. Our local church expressions are quite different. Our preferred church polity is very divergent, as are the denominational/associational circles we frequent. However, we are dear brothers in Christ who all share the same creedal convictions. These men are among the deepest friendships I have had in my adult life, and our prayer partnership is nothing short of powerful. Our love for Christ and our creedal commonality bind us so beautifully together despite our vast differences in other areas.

I hope this bit of history has been helpful in understanding the importance and theological consistency of the Apostles' Creed. Are you also beginning to see that a creedal approach to life empowers us to live a more vibrant and fruitful life in Christ, and sets us up to have a greater impact as we impart that life to those around us?

For the remainder of this chapter, I want to investigate one particular passage of Scripture from Paul's first letter to the Christians at Corinth and show you how one lives out a creedal life.

THE CREEDAL LIFE

There are many "creeds" expressed in the New Testament. Most of these are very simple statements, while others are more in-depth. Take some time and prayerfully work through the sample list below, stopping to ponder each passage and how it relates to living a successful creedal lifestyle – maintaining a belief foundation and putting it on display:

1. John 1:1-5, 10-14, 16-18
2. Acts 8:37[9]
3. Romans 1:3-4 and 10:9
4. 1 Corinthians 8:6
5. Philippians 2:5-11
6. Colossians 1:13-20 and some suggest 2:9-15
7. 1 Timothy 2:5-6 and 3:16
8. 2 Timothy 2:8-14
9. 1 Peter 3:18-22

Each of these is helpful. But one of the most powerful creedal teachings in the New Testament is Paul's treatise about the risen Christ, given to the sisters and brothers in Corinth. This passage is used during times of grief and sorrow for a reason. Its beauty and comfort are inarguable:

Let me now remind you, dear brothers and sisters, of the Good News I preached to you before. You welcomed it then, and you still stand firm in it. It is this Good News that saves you if you continue to believe the message I told you—unless, of course, you believed something that was never true in the first place.

I passed on to you what was most important and what had also been passed on to me. Christ died for our sins, just as the Scriptures said. He was buried, and he was raised from the dead on the third day, just as the Scriptures said. He was seen by Peter and then by the Twelve. After that, he was seen by more than 500 of his followers at one time, most of whom are still alive, though some have died. Then he was seen by James and later by all the apostles. Last of all, as though I had been born

---

9   In many Bibles you will have to look in the footnotes for this verse.

at the wrong time, I also saw him. For I am the least of all the apostles. In fact, I'm not even worthy to be called an apostle after the way I persecuted God's church.

But whatever I am now, it is all because God poured out his special favor on me—and not without results. For I have worked harder than any of the other apostles; yet it was not I but God who was working through me by his grace. So it makes no difference whether I preach or they preach, for we all preach the same message you have already believed. (1 Corinthians 15:1-11)

It is so important to know what we believe! So many modern Christians give a form of mental assent to a religious idea, a set of rituals, or a community they love. But when pressed, they have no biblical understanding of what the Christian Faith stands for, what their part is in Jesus' mission, or any ability to defend these things from the Scriptures. Creeds like the Apostles' Creed help us understand and practice "Christianity 101." Let's look at how Paul breaks things down for his readers.

Paul begins with a reminder of their gospel foundation. The gospel of Jesus Christ is the foundation of all our Christian theology. It's the backbone of everything we believe and espouse. All of Old Testament theology looks forward to the cross of Christ. After the four gospels, all New Testament theology looks back to the cross. Christ's crucifixion is the pivotal point of all our doctrine. So Paul begins with that.

Paul emphasizes the importance of what he has taught them. It is essential to know – not just with the head, but with the heart – the foundational truths about Christ and his gospel. Jesus' gospel is indeed a message of salvation, but it's much more than that. The single most important thing we can know from the Scripture is that Jesus Christ reigns supreme! Paul explains this to the Christians in Colossae:

Christ is the visible image of the invisible God. He existed before anything was created and is supreme over all creation, for through him God created everything in the heavenly realms and on earth. He made the things we can see and the things we can't see— such as thrones, kingdoms, rulers, and authorities in the unseen world. Everything was created through him and for him. He existed before anything else, and he holds all creation together. Christ is also the head of the church, which is his body. He is the beginning, supreme over all who rise from the dead. So he is first in everything. For God in all his fullness was pleased to live in Christ, and through him God reconciled everything to himself. He made peace with everything in heaven and on earth by means of Christ's blood on the cross. (Colossians 1:15-20)

Paul pleads with his readers to hold firmly to the teaching they have received from him.

Notice also that Paul roots his teaching to the Scriptures themselves. The Scriptures are God's revelation of himself to us. They are the foundation of everything we understand about our faith and our life. They are also the foundation for the creeds. When we remember that the creeds are generally crafted to combat heresy – bad and unbiblical teaching – down through the ages, it becomes clear that we need that foundation. The truth of Scripture is the key to understanding the real Christian life. When people deny the authority of God's Word, they are setting themselves up for a fall. But for Paul, the Bible's authority was a non-question. It's Paul who writes to Timothy,

But you must remain faithful to the things you have been taught. You know they are true, for you know you can trust those who taught you. You have been taught the holy Scriptures from child-hood, and they have given you the wisdom to receive the salvation that comes by trusting in Christ Jesus. All Scripture is inspired by God and is useful to teach us what is true and to make us realize what is wrong in our lives. It corrects us when we are wrong and teaches us to do what is right. God uses it to prepare and equip his people to do every good work. (2 Timothy 3:14-17)

Paul distills things down to a few non-negotiable truths about the Savior. Again, he roots everything in the Scriptures. Christ died for our sins according to the Scriptures. Christ was buried and rose from the dead on the third day, according to the Scriptures. Paul then lists all those who saw him alive: Peter, the twelve disciples, five hundred others at the same time, James (Jesus' half-brother and the lead apostle in the Jerusalem Church), all of the apostles, and lastly, to Paul himself. Most of these people were still alive as Paul wrote this letter so they could attest to the facts he lists. Paul seems to be inviting his readers to check his sources!

Paul ends with his own testimony. This is important. Our belief and our witness are tied together. We find our Christian story in what we believe. So if our belief is not built on a strong, biblical foundation, neither are our story or our witness!

Paul clearly finds his identity in Christ. We find our identity in what we believe. Christians today often find their identity in almost anything *but* Jesus – their career, their family, their ethnicity, their hobbies, their sexual orientation, their pain. This is what the world does – giving a whole menu of options for the source of one's identity. The church follows suit because we often lack a clear understanding of what we really believe.

Adhering to a creedal statement helps us anchor ourselves to the truth. When we have a solid foundation, our self-importance is tempered, and a visible and victorious life in Christ emerges. We grow into a more unshakable confidence in our Christian Faith. We get to know the Scriptures better. Our personal testimony is clarified and empowered. Our witness becomes more intentional and fruitful. Our identity is immovably planted in Christ alone. And we have the right perspective on who we are and what Christ has done for us. Paul, the great apostle to the Gentiles, has no pride in his pedigree or credentials – although they are pretty impressive. He finds his greatness in being a servant. So did Jesus (Matthew 20:28).

In the chapters that follow, we'll be slowly and methodically walking through the Apostles' Creed together. Don't rush this. You may find some of the stanzas make immediate sense, while others bid you to camp on them for a while. Follow the lead of the Holy Spirit. Solidify these essentials in your own heart, and then follow the suggestions provided to begin imparting these essentials into the lives of others. Keep it simple. Take it slow. Allow this process to bear its fruit.

I'm praying for you as you join the adventure!

STUDY GUIDE

IT MAKES A DIFFERENCE

Creedal Christians have a strong moral and spiritual compass. There are those who recite the creeds, and then there are those who employ them as a rule of life. Creedal Christians are far less likely to be duped by forms of heresy. They tend to have a good, working understanding of the Scriptures and can clearly explain the importance of the gospel. They can likely tell you most, if not all, of the "non-negotiables" in Christian doctrine, even if on an elementary level. And Creedal Christians have a much easier time fellowshipping and ministering with Christians of diverse backgrounds because they can quickly discern critical commonalities upon which such relationships can be based.

Those who are not truly creedal will not have such benefits. They struggle to know if certain perspectives or philosophies are actually biblical. They have no standard by which to recognize heresy, and they fall prey to social movements that are contrary to the heart of God. What's worse, some will even defend such movements and philosophies, thinking they are doing it in Christian love. Non-creedal Christians tend to focus on a few favorite scripture passages, but they rarely have a good command of the Bible as a whole. They also often misunderstand both the content and intent of Christ's gospel. And they enter into ministry partnerships based more on how those relationships make them feel than on any firm biblical foundation.

Creeds, like the Apostles' Creed we are studying, serve a very important and practical purpose.

HOW DO I LIVE OUT WHAT I HAVE JUST LEARNED IN MY OWN LIFE?

1. Take a moment to stop and pray. Ask God, through the Holy Spirit, to increase your understanding of the Christian Faith. Ask Him to reveal and clarify any points that have been confusing or unclear.

2. Over the next few days, read through the list of scriptures given under the heading *The Creedal Life (page 25)*. (Remember

that you may have to check the footnotes in the Acts passage.) Consider how each relates to the truths outlined in the Apostles' Creed. Consider why it matters that the propositions of the Apostles' Creed are rooted in scripture.

3. Consider Paul's teachings in 1 Corinthians 15:1-11, Colossians 1:15-20, and 2 Timothy 3:14-17. Ask yourself the same questions proposed in #2 above: How do they relate to the truths outlined in the Apostles' Creed? Why does it matter?

4. Take several days to consider: Who can help you apply what you learn and put it into an ongoing life practice?

5. How are you living this out right now? How is your life reflective of your understanding of this truth?

HOW DO I IMPART WHAT I HAVE JUST LEARNED TO CHILDREN?

1. Begin by praying with the children. Ask God, through the Holy Spirit, to help the children understand more about the Christian faith. Ask God to help them clearly understand the new things they are about to learn.

2. Spend some time talking with the children about why it is important to know what we believe.

3. Read the Apostles' Creed together, briefly explaining any unfamiliar words. Assure them that their understanding will increase as they continue with the study.

4. Continue to help the children memorize the Apostle's Creed. Remind them of the discussion you just had about the importance of knowing what we believe and tell them that this is a summary of the essential beliefs of our faith.

5. If you have children in your group who have not yet surrendered to Jesus, continue to pray for the Holy Spirit to open that conversational door so you can explain the gospel. Once they receive Christ, the indwelling presence of the Holy Spirit will make the lessons in this book much more accessible to them.

HOW DO I IMPART WHAT I HAVE JUST LEARNED TO TEENS?

1. Begin by praying with the teens. Ask God, through the Holy Spirit, to increase understanding. You can do this or ask a volunteer.

2. Spend some time talking with the teens about why they need to know what they believe.

3. Read the Apostles' Creed out loud. Either read it yourself or ask for a volunteer.

4. Now look at the Creed section by section. Encourage the teens to make notes in a Question Journal (either in a digital or physical form) of anything they find confusing or have heard others question as truth. Assure them that you will discuss each section in detail as the study proceeds. They will be allowed to ask any questions they have as that happens. Encourage them to come back and record the answers they find alongside the questions in their journal.

5. Encourage the teens to memorize the Apostle's Creed. Remind them of the discussion in your last session/meeting about the importance of knowing what they believe and remind them that this is a summary of the essential beliefs of our faith.

6. Consider listening to musical adaptations of the Creed like *This I Believe (The Creed)* by Hillsong (available on YouTube). Have them compare the song's lyrics with the original Creed on which it is based.

7. If you have teens in your group who have not yet surrendered to Jesus, continue to pray for the Holy Spirit to open that conversational door so you can explain the gospel. Once they receive Christ, the indwelling presence of the Holy Spirit will make the lessons in this book much more accessible to them.

HOW DO I IMPART WHAT I HAVE JUST LEARNED TO ADULTS?

1. Take a moment to stop and pray. Encourage the adults to ask God, through the Holy Spirit, to increase their understanding of the Christian Faith. Ask Him to reveal and clarify any points that have been confusing or unclear.

2. Review the Apostles' Creed together. Look at each stanza and encourage them to make note of anything they find confusing, have found difficult to understand or believe in the past, or have heard others question as truth.

3. If they still need to do so, encourage them to memorize the Creed, reminding them that it summarizes the essentials of the faith.

4. Point them to musical versions of the Creed like *This I Believe (The Creed)* by Hillsong (available on YouTube). Encourage them to compare the lyrics with the original Creed.

5. Encourage them to read the scriptures listed in the chapter, including the excerpts from Paul's letters, and discuss why it matters that the Creed expresses essential biblical truths.

6. If you have people in your group who have not yet surrendered to Jesus, continue to pray for the Holy Spirit to open that conversational door so you can explain the gospel. Once they receive Christ, the indwelling presence of the Holy Spirit will make the lessons in this book much more accessible to them.

CHAPTER 2
God: Father Almighty,
Maker of Heaven and Earth

"I believe in God the Father Almighty, Maker of heaven and earth…"

So Paul, standing before the council, addressed them as follows: "Men of Athens, I notice that you are very religious in every way, for as I was walking along I saw your many shrines. And one of your altars had this inscription on it: 'To an Unknown God.' This God, whom you worship without knowing, is the one I'm telling you about.

"He is the God who made the world and everything in it. Since he is Lord of heaven and earth, he doesn't live in man-made temples, and human hands can't serve his needs—for he has no needs. He himself gives life and breath to everything, and he satisfies every need. From one man he created all the nations throughout the whole earth. He decided beforehand when they should rise and fall, and he determined their boundaries.

"His purpose was for the nations to seek after God and perhaps feel their way toward him and find him—though he is not far from any one of us. For in him we live and move and exist. As

some of your own poets have said, 'We are his offspring.' And since this is true, we shouldn't think of God as an idol designed by craftsmen from gold or silver or stone.

"God overlooked people's ignorance about these things in earlier times, but now he commands everyone everywhere to repent of their sins and turn to him. (Acts 17:22-30)

REMEMBERING *PISTEÚO*

One of the most significant challenges Western Christians face today is the temptation to take a purely academic approach to our discipleship. In our modern times, technology is everywhere – cell phones are operational even in some of the remotest spots on Earth. We are driven by information. And while this has obvious benefits, it can also be a detriment. For followers of Jesus, information can substitute for belief. (Read that last sentence again.) We can unwittingly conclude that we are strong believers because we know a lot of information about Jesus, the Bible, or theology. But this is not the case.

We began our adventure together with the Greek word *pisteúo* – translated into English, "believe." It is more than just amassing information. It is more than just giving mental assent. It means that we are persuaded and hold a strong conviction that something is true. It is confidence. It is a trust that is compelled from within the soul. It is our own conclusion that something is reliable, faithful, and trustworthy. We called it "wheelbarrow faith" because it is a belief that leads us to unapologetic action. We don't just accept something in our minds, but it literally governs every aspect of our behavior.

You'll notice that the Apostles' Creed is organized around the three Persons of our Triune God: the Father, the Son, and the Holy Spirit. As we unpack each stanza of the Creed, we will have the opportunity to *pisteúo* each particular truth, growing in our spiritual life and witness as a result. We will come to know our triune God more intimately, and that should change us. And while the Apostles' Creed is very basic in nature, the depth of the change it can bring in us may be profound. But this can only happen if we get beyond knowing more *about* God and actually come to *know* God more personally. Make this your quest.

THE FATHER

As we begin our adventure with the Father, we can take our lead from Jesus. Jesus tells us to know and pray to God as our *Father* – our loving, heavenly Father.

> *"When you pray, don't be like the hypocrites who love to pray publicly on street corners and in the synagogues where everyone can see them. I tell you the truth, that is all the reward they will ever get. But when you pray, go away by yourself, shut the door behind you, **and pray to your Father** in private. Then **your Father**, who sees everything, will reward you.*
>
> *"When you pray, don't babble on and on as the Gentiles do. They think their prayers are answered merely by repeating their words again and again. Don't be like them, **for your Father knows exactly what you need** even before you ask him! Pray like this: **Our Father in heaven**, may your name be kept holy..."*
> (Matthew 6:5-9, **emphasis mine**)

I am blessed that I had a great relationship with my own dad. But I know people for whom that is not true. In fact, one time, when I was preaching on the fatherhood of God in a former church, I had a lady tell me that she could not trust God because of the abuse she had endured for years at the hand of her own dad. This is a real issue. And it's more widespread than we'd like to admit. Satan has deeply wounded way too many people by wrecking their relationships with earthly fathers. He knows that this is one of the surest ways to taint any relationship we may try to have with our Heavenly Father. But I assure you, that can be repaired. In fact, God is really good at it.

As we begin looking at what the Creed says about our Heavenly Father, take a moment and prayerfully give God any baggage you may have in your life from other fatherly relationships. Ask the Lord for real healing. Most of you will experience some relief because God is even more interested in your healing than you are. Some of you may need some extra help. Do not be afraid to ask for it. Pastoral and professional Christian counseling can make a huge difference in such a struggle. Do what you must to be open enough for God to show you what genuine Fatherly love looks like.

UNDERSTANDING GOD'S FATHERHOOD

Seeing God as our Heavenly Father meant something very important to first-century Jews. The Jewish culture saw fathers as both the authoritative leader of the family and also the blessed provider of all their needs. Both of these are ascribed to God when we call him "Father." And while the New Testament writers affirm the fatherhood of God – Paul and John both write about it extensively – the foundation of our understanding comes from Jesus himself in the gospels.

The Father shows mercy to sinners. In its most basic form, mercy is when God does not give us what we deserve. Jesus teaches,

> *"But to you who are willing to listen, I say, love your enemies! Do good to those who hate you. Bless those who curse you. Pray for those who hurt you. If someone slaps you on one cheek, offer the other cheek also. If someone demands your coat, offer your shirt also. Give to anyone who asks; and when things are taken away from you, don't try to get them back. Do to others as you would like them to do to you.*

> *"If you love only those who love you, why should you get credit for that? Even sinners love those who love them! And if you do good only to those who do good to you, why should you get credit? Even sinners do that much! And if you lend money only to those who can repay you, why should you get credit? Even sinners will lend to other sinners for a full return.*

> *"Love your enemies! Do good to them. Lend to them without expecting to be repaid. Then your reward from heaven will be very great, and you will truly be acting as children of the Most High, for he is kind to those who are unthankful and wicked. You must be compassionate, just as your Father is compassionate.*
> (Luke 6:27-36)

It's a hard truth, but anyone who has not surrendered to Christ, receiving God's wonderful gift of salvation in Jesus, is still an enemy to God (Colossians 1:21; Romans 5:10). This is our natural condition because of sin. But Jesus teaches us not to treat our enemies as they deserve because God has not treated us as we deserve. We deserve separation from God. We deserve his wrathful punishment. We deserve what the Bible calls eternal damnation – a forever existence in hell with the devil and his angels (Matthew 25:41). But our loving Heavenly Father offers us Christ so we can escape all of this. That is mercy – and it is the love of our Heavenly Father that extends it to us.

The Father shows grace to the unrighteous. Grace is when God gives us something we do not deserve. Grace and mercy are two inseparable sides of the same "coin." Jesus teaches,

> *"You have heard the law that says, 'Love your neighbor' and hate your enemy. But I say, love your enemies! Pray for those who per-secute you! In that way, you will be acting as true children of your Father in heaven. For he gives his sunlight to both the evil and the good, and he sends rain on the just and the unjust alike. If you love only those who love you, what reward is there for that? Even corrupt tax collectors do that much. If you are kind only to your friends, how are you different from anyone else? Even pagans do that. But you are to be perfect, even as your Father in heaven is perfect.* (Matthew 5:43-48)

Extending genuine love to an enemy is the very definition of grace. Mercy is God *not* giving us what we *do* deserve. Grace is God *giving* us what we *do not* deserve. It's God's grace that offers complete forgiveness in Jesus Christ. It's God's grace that offers us a restored relationship with him – a new covenant relationship (think marriage covenant[10]) rooted in love and intimacy with God. It's God's grace that allows us to partner with him in Christ's mission. We do not deserve any of it, but it is the lavishing love of our Heavenly Father that extends it to us. The apostle John writes,

> *See how very much our Father loves us, for he calls us his chil-dren, and that is what we are! But the people who belong to this world don't recognize that we are God's children because they don't know him.* (1 John 3:1)

---

10   A Christian husband and wife enter into a similar covenantal relationship with each other as they make their vows to each other in their wedding ceremony. It is not a contract that can be dissolved by the mutual consent of the two parties, but is intended to be "until death do us part." Contracts are used to limit liability. Covenants express and affirm mutual responsibility. The marriage covenant is modeled after our relationship with God in Jesus Christ. See Ephe-sians 5:21-33.

God's love for us is overflowing. That is grace.

The Father forgives sins. This truth always moves me. Please understand: God is under absolutely no obligation to forgive any human being. None. God is the Creator. We have only ever been his creation. It is solely the love of our Heavenly Father that precipitates the miracle of forgiveness. In a secret nighttime meeting with the Jewish Ruler and Pharisee, Nicodemus, Jesus shares this truth:

> *"For this is how God loved the world: He gave his one and only Son, so that everyone who believes in him will not perish but have eternal life. God sent his Son into the world not to judge the world, but to save the world through him.*
>
> *"There is no judgment against anyone who believes in him. But anyone who does not believe in him has already been judged for not believing in God's one and only Son.* (John 3:16-18)

In his love, our Heavenly Father intervenes. In his love, he forgives.

The Father knows and meets our needs. I have loved watching my son and daughter-in-law as they became first-time parents. We all remember the fear of bringing that fragile little baby home from the hospital for the first time. More than one dad has asked, "But what if I break it?" But as my son grew into his new fatherly role, it was amazing to witness his fear give way to confidence, and his understanding increase to encompass parental problem-solving, and then actually anticipate the needs of my grandson. I think God gives parents this experience to teach us something critical about himself.

There is an aspect of God as Creator in this as well, but it stands to reason that if God made us, then he knows what we need even better than we do ourselves. In fact, Jesus says so:

> *...for your Father knows exactly what you need even before you ask him!* (Matthew 6:8)
>
> *"That is why I tell you not to worry about everyday life—whether you have enough food and drink, or enough clothes to wear. Isn't life more than food, and your body more than clothing? Look at the birds. They don't plant or harvest or store food in*

barns, for your heavenly Father feeds them. And aren't you far more valuable to him than they are? Can all your worries add a single moment to your life?

"And why worry about your clothing? Look at the lilies of the field and how they grow. They don't work or make their clothing, yet Solomon in all his glory was not dressed as beautifully as they are. And if God cares so wonderfully for wildflowers that are here today and thrown into the fire tomorrow, he will certainly care for you. Why do you have so little faith?

*"So don't worry about these things, saying, 'What will we eat? What will we drink? What will we wear?' These things dominate the thoughts of unbelievers, but **your heavenly Father already knows all your needs**.* (Matthew 6:25-32, **emphasis mine**)

The Father blesses with good gifts. As a loving Father, God does not just give us what we need; he also blesses us beyond what we need as well.

*"You parents—if your children ask for a loaf of bread, do you give them a stone instead? Or if they ask for a fish, do you give them a snake? Of course not! So if you sinful people know how to give good gifts to your children, **how much more will your heavenly Father give good gifts to those who ask him**.* (Matthew 7:9-11, **emphasis mine**)

God desires to bless his children. In fact, the apostle James reminds us,

So don't be misled, my dear brothers and sisters. Whatever is good and perfect is a gift coming down to us from God our Father, who created all the lights in the heavens. He never changes or casts a shifting shadow. He chose to give birth to us by giving us his true word. And we, out of all creation, became his prized possession. (James 1:16-18)

God has shown humanity his heart for blessing from the beginning – and it is a prominent theme in his covenant calling upon the life of Abraham.

The Lord had said to Abram, "Leave your native country, your relatives, and your father's family, and go to the land that I will show you. I will make you into a great nation. I will bless you and make you famous, and you will be a blessing to others. I will bless those who bless you and curse those who treat you with contempt. All the families on earth will be blessed through you." (Genesis 12:1-3)

God desires to bless us.

The Father gives us his kingdom. He gives it to us! This may be most surprising of all. Jesus tells us to

Seek the Kingdom of God above all else, and he will give you everything you need. So don't be afraid, little flock. For it gives your Father great happiness to give you the Kingdom. (Luke 12:31-32)

Jesus tells us that it *pleases* our Heavenly Father to give us his kingdom. We are again reminded not to worry about what we need; the Father already knows all about it. We are to seek his kingdom – that is, God's rule and reign – our Father's dominion and all that comes with it – and he will give us all that we need. It gives our Heavenly Father great happiness to cover us with his rule and reign. More than anything else, this shows us the dimensions of his heart.

We need to stop and ponder what it means to say, "We believe in God the Father." Beyond theological agreement with this statement, what does it really mean for us? It is essential to come to actually know God as our Heavenly Father so that we can know his heart, his nature, and the depths of his love and provision for us.

THE ALMIGHTY

God is not just loving; he is also all-powerful. Both the Old Testament and the New Testament declare the omnipotence of God. When we say God is omnipotent, we are saying he can do anything and everything within his holy will. The psalmist sings,

Not to us, O Lord, not to us, but to your name goes all the glory for your unfailing love and faithfulness.

42

Why let the nations say, "Where is their God?"

Our God is in the heavens, and he does as he wishes. (Psalm 115:1-3)

As the apostle Paul warns the Corinthian Christians to be careful about their various partnerships, he appeals to God's omnipotent nature.

Don't team up with those who are unbelievers. How can righteousness be a partner with wickedness? How can light live with darkness? What harmony can there be between Christ and the devil? How can a believer be a partner with an unbeliever? And what union can there be between God's temple and idols? For we are the temple of the living God. As God said:

"I will live in them and walk among them. I will be their God, and they will be my people. Therefore, come out from among unbelievers, and separate yourselves from them, says the Lord.

Don't touch their filthy things, and I will welcome you.

And I will be your Father, and you will be my sons and daughters, says the Lord Almighty." (2 Corinthians 6:14-18)

And as the apostle John glimpses into heaven during his apocalyptic vision, he hears God speak,

*"I am the Alpha and the Omega—the beginning and the end,"
says the Lord God. "I am the one who is, who always was, and
who is still to come—the Almighty One."* (Revelation 1:8)

God is all-powerful.

Our God calls himself "The Almighty." When God makes his covenant with Abram, changing his name to Abraham – a childless old man whose new name means "Father of a Multitude" – God shows Abraham his nature.

*When Abram was ninety-nine years old, the Lord appeared to
him and said, "I am El-Shaddai—'God Almighty.' Serve me*

faithfully and live a blameless life. I will make a covenant with you, by which I will guarantee to give you countless descendants." (Genesis 17:1-2)

God the Almighty commands Abraham to walk before him. God the Almighty commands Abraham to be blameless. But it is also God the Almighty who can keep such a colossal promise – to make this old man, one as good as dead (Hebrews 11:11-12), the father of a multitude that would outnumber the stars of the sky (Genesis 15:5)!

Nothing is too difficult for our Almighty God. God made good on his promise to Abraham and Sarah, and at the age of 90, she bore Isaac, the covenant son.

"Where is Sarah, your wife?" the visitors asked. "She's inside the tent," Abraham replied. Then one of them said, "I will return to you about this time next year, and your wife, Sarah, will have a son!" Sarah was listening to this conversation from the tent. Abraham and Sarah were both very old by this time, and Sarah was long past the age of having children. So she laughed silently to herself and said, "How could a worn-out woman like me enjoy such pleasure, especially when my master—my husband—is also so old?" Then the Lord said to Abraham, "Why did Sarah laugh? Why did she say, 'Can an old woman like me have a baby?' Is anything too hard for the Lord? I will return about this time next year, and Sarah will have a son." (Genesis 18:9-14)

And the baby was indeed born!

The Lord kept his word and did for Sarah exactly what he had promised. She became pregnant, and she gave birth to a son for Abraham in his old age. This happened at just the time God had said it would. And Abraham named their son Isaac. Eight days after Isaac was born, Abraham circumcised him as God had commanded. Abraham was 100 years old when Isaac was born.

And Sarah declared, "God has brought me laughter. All who hear about this will laugh with me. Who would have said to Abraham that Sarah would nurse a baby? Yet I have given Abraham a son in his old age!" (Genesis 21:1-7)

Among others, the prophet Jeremiah declares the all-powerful nature of God. Here we learn another name for God Almighty, LORD Sabaoth or the Lord of Heaven's Armies.[11]

"O Sovereign Lord! You made the heavens and earth by your strong hand and powerful arm. Nothing is too hard for you! You show unfailing love to thousands, but you also bring the consequences of one generation's sin upon the next. You are the great and powerful God, the Lord of Heaven's Armies. You have all wisdom and do great and mighty miracles. You see the conduct of all people, and you give them what they deserve. You performed miraculous signs and wonders in the land of Egypt— things still remembered to this day! And you have continued to do great miracles in Israel and all around the world. You have made your name famous to this day. (Jeremiah 32:17-20)

Nothing is impossible for our Almighty God. As God's angel visits Mary to inform her of his plans for her to bear the Savior of humanity,

Mary asked the angel, "But how can this happen? I am a virgin."

The angel replied, "The Holy Spirit will come upon you, and the power of the Most High will overshadow you. So the baby to be born will be holy, and he will be called the Son of God. What's more, your relative Elizabeth has become pregnant in her old age! People used to say she was barren, but she has conceived a son and is now in her sixth month. For the word of God will never fail."[12] (Luke 1:34-37.)

---

11   Or Lord of Hosts.

12   The Greek text here literally says, "Nothing is impossible for the word of God." See the New International Version and the New American Standard Bible.

And after Jesus' encounter with a wealthy man who could not give up his riches to become a disciple, Jesus explained,

> *"I tell you the truth, it is very hard for a rich person to enter the Kingdom of Heaven. I'll say it again—it is easier for a camel to go through the eye of a needle than for a rich person to enter the Kingdom of God!"*
>
> *The disciples were astounded. "Then who in the world can be saved?" they asked. Jesus looked at them intently and said, "Humanly speaking, it is impossible. But with God everything is possible."* (Matthew 19:23-26)

God is fully capable of doing anything he wills to do. The gods of the other peoples around Israel in the Old Testament are mute. The gods and goddesses of other cultures are fickle at best and completely useless at worst. The pagans worship gods that do not answer their prayers. These silent gods are made of stone, wood, and metal. But our God – the God of Abraham, the God of the faithful prophets, the God and Father of our Lord Jesus Christ – our God speaks. Our God involves himself in the lives of those he loves. Our God cares. Our God answers prayer. Our God works miracles. Our God is the Almighty!

The apostle Paul tells us that our Almighty God can do things that are beyond our imagination.

> *Now all glory to God, who is able, through his mighty power at work within us, to accomplish infinitely more than we might ask or think. Glory to him in the church and in Christ Jesus through all generations forever and ever! Amen.* (Ephesians 3:20-21)

Our Almighty God is both holy and eternal. When we call him "holy," we mean that he is special, set apart, unique, different – infinitely *other*. This is what the mighty angels in the temple were declaring at the call of the prophet Isaiah.

> *They were calling out to each other, "Holy, holy, holy is the Lord of Heaven's Armies! The whole earth is filled with his glory!"* (Isaiah 6:2-3)

And it is the theme of worship around God's throne in heaven,

> *In front of the throne was a shiny sea of glass, sparkling like crystal. In the center and around the throne were four living beings, each covered with eyes, front and back. The first of these living beings was like a lion; the second was like an ox; the third had a human face; and the fourth was like an eagle in flight. Each of these living beings had six wings, and their wings were covered all over with eyes, inside and out. Day after day and night after night they keep on saying, "Holy, holy, holy is the Lord God, the Almighty— the one who always was, who is, and who is still to come."* (Revelation 4:6-8)

When we call our Almighty God "eternal," we mean that he has always existed and will always exist. He was before the beginning, and he will be after the end. When Christians typically think about eternity, it only runs in one direction – forward. That's because we have a beginning. Our eternity is only in a forward direction. But God was eternal before creation. When the psalmist sings,

> *Praise the Lord, the God of Israel, who lives from everlasting to everlasting. Amen and amen!* (Psalm 41:13)

he is recognizing that God is outside of time (for he invented it!) and exists eternally in *both* directions – eternally past and eternally future. The Levites, under the leadership of Nehemiah, called the people to worship God for this very reason:

> *Then the leaders of the Levites—Jeshua, Kadmiel, Bani, Hashabneiah, Sherebiah, Hodiah, Shebaniah, and Pethahiah— called out to the people: "Stand up and praise the Lord your God, for he lives from everlasting to everlasting!" Then they prayed: "May your glorious name be praised! May it be exalted above all blessing and praise!*

47

"You alone are the Lord. You made the skies and the heavens and all the stars. You made the earth and the seas and every-thing in them. You preserve them all, and the angels of heaven worship you. (Nehemiah 9:5-6)

And this is also the proclamation of the elders in heaven:

And they said, "We give thanks to you, Lord God, the Almighty, **the one who is and who always was,** *for now you have assumed your great power and have begun to reign.*

The nations were filled with wrath, but now the time of your wrath has come. It is time to judge the dead and reward your servants the prophets, as well as your holy people, and all who fear your name, from the least to the greatest. It is time to de-stroy all who have caused destruction on the earth." (Revelation 11:16-18, **emphasis mine**)

Our Almighty God is just and true in all he does. When we say God is "just," we mean that he always does the right thing, at the right time for the right reasons. When we say that he is "true," we are speaking of his utter faithfulness and dependability. People don't always realize this, but God's holiness and his justice go hand in hand. They cannot be separated. God is not influenced by any evil. He is outside of all that is fallen and broken in this world. He has the perfect perspective.

Those who are victorious over the onslaught of the Beast in Revelation sing what is called The Song of Moses and the Lamb. Among other things, they praise God for his true and faithful nature:

"Great and marvelous are your works, O Lord God, the Almighty. Just and true are your ways, O King of the nations. Who will not fear you, Lord, and glorify your name?

For you alone are holy. All nations will come and worship before you, for your righteous deeds have been revealed." (Revelation 15:3-4)

And as God's mighty angels are preparing to pour out God's wrath upon the Earth, one of them shouts,

"You are just, O Holy One, who is and who always was, because you have sent these judgments. Since they shed the blood of your holy people and your prophets, you have given them blood to drink. It is their just reward." And I heard a voice from the altar, saying, "Yes, O Lord God, the Almighty, your judgments are true and just." (Revelation 16:5-7)

Our Almighty God is holy, eternal, just and true in everything!

Our Almighty God is the master over all creation. He is creation's designer, architect, and builder. The psalmist sings,

Let all that I am praise the Lord. O Lord my God, how great you are! You are robed with honor and majesty. You are dressed in a robe of light. You stretch out the starry curtain of the heavens; you lay out the rafters of your home in the rain clouds. You make the clouds your chariot; you ride upon the wings of the wind. The winds are your messengers; flames of fire are your servants. You placed the world on its foundation so it would never be moved. You clothed the earth with floods of water, water that covered even the mountains. (Psalm 104:1-6)

In fact, the psalmist goes on to talk about God's ongoing care of all that he has made. The prophets also concur. Amos prophesies,

For the Lord is the one who shaped the mountains, stirs up the winds, and reveals his thoughts to mankind. He turns the light of dawn into darkness and treads on the heights of the earth. The Lord God of Heaven's Armies is his name! (Amos 4:13)

The Creed beckons us to proclaim, "I believe in God, the Father Almighty..." God is our loving Father. God is the Almighty. God is the lord of heaven's armies. It's essential to understand God is almighty – omnipotent – that he finds nothing impossible. We serve a God that is infinitely able. And all this flows into the final point, he is the Creator of all things.

THE CREATOR

God is creation's designer, architect, and builder, and as such, he is the Source of everything. He is the Creator of heaven and earth. Not only does Genesis give us the creation account, but the rest of the Old and New Testaments proclaim him as creator as well.

> *In the beginning God created the heavens and the earth. The earth was formless and empty, and darkness covered the deep waters. And the Spirit of God was hovering over the surface of the waters. Then God said, "Let there be light," and there was light.* (Genesis 1:1-3)

In his gospel account, the apostle John gives us even more depth on this creative work.

> *In the beginning the Word already existed. The Word was with God, and the Word was God. He existed in the beginning with God. God created everything through him, and nothing was created except through him. The Word gave life to everything that was created, and his life brought light to everyone. The light shines in the darkness, and the darkness can never extinguish it... So the Word became human and made his home among us. He was full of unfailing love and faithfulness. And we have seen his glory, the glory of the Father's one and only Son.* (John 1:1-5, 14 New Living Translation)

Our triune God was fully engaged in creation. God the Father as the "planner," God the Spirit as the "container," and God the Son as the creative "agent." Jesus is the Word of God. When God *said*, "Let there be light," it was Jesus, the Word of God, who did the creating (John 1:3).

God is the creator of heaven and earth. The importance of this fact cannot be overstated. There is a sense in that all the other doctrines we will study on this adventure rest on that one point. In fact, Dr. Ken Ham of the Creation Science Museum notes that all Christian doctrine ultimately finds its foundation in a literal interpretation of Genesis – especially the first eleven chapters. Ham writes,

Suppose that we are being questioned concerning the doctrines Christians believe. Think carefully how you would answer in detail.

- Why do we believe in marriage?
- Why do we promote the wearing of clothes?
- Why are there rules—right and wrong?
- Why are we sinners—what does that mean?
- Why is there death and suffering in the world?
- Why is there to be a new heaven and a new earth?[13]

He goes on to show that all of these questions and many more have their roots in Genesis, the creation account, and in God being the Creator. It's important!

As Creator, God is to be revered. There are three primary components to the proper worship of God: reverence (healthy fear/awe), adoration (love), and glory (faithful obedience). When we begin to understand the depths of what it means for God to be the Creator, it should drive us to worship. We should revere God. The psalmist beckons us,

> *Let the godly sing for joy to the Lord; it is fitting for the pure to praise him. Praise the Lord with melodies on the lyre; make music for him on the ten-stringed harp.*
>
> *Sing a new song of praise to him; play skillfully on the harp, and sing with joy. For the word of the Lord holds true, and we can trust everything he does.*
>
> *He loves whatever is just and good; the unfailing love of the Lord fills the earth. The Lord merely spoke, and the heavens were created.*
>
> *He breathed the word, and all the stars were born. He assigned the sea its boundaries and locked the oceans in vast reservoirs.*
>
> ***Let the whole world fear the Lord, and let everyone stand in awe of him. For when he spoke, the world began! It appeared at his command.*** (Psalm 33:1-9, **emphasis mine**)

---

13 Ken Ham, *Does Genesis Matter?*, online. Answers In Genesis, 1 July 1987, https://answersingenesis.org/genesis/genesis-does-matter/.

We must have a healthy respect for God because he spoke everything into being!

Creation puts God's wisdom, understanding, and knowledge on display. God is the designer. God is the builder. All of creation is his idea. When we see creation, we see the infinite innovation and understanding of God. Who else could have thought up the atom? Who else could produce a creation where there is incredible detail on the subatomic and atomic levels while, at the same time, spreading out something as beautiful and vast as the universe? And who else could have simply spoken all this into being?

Solomon writes,

> *By wisdom the Lord founded the earth; by understanding he created the heavens. By his knowledge the deep fountains of the earth burst forth, and the dew settles beneath the night sky.* (Proverbs 3:19-20)

Creation shows us how very wise our God is. The depths of his knowledge and understanding are beyond our ability to comprehend.

Creation reveals God's sovereignty. As Creator, we see that God is supreme over everything. Nothing existed before him. Nothing can exist without him. King David reminds us,

> *The earth is the Lord's, and everything in it. The world and all its people belong to him. For he laid the earth's foundation on the seas and built it on the ocean depths.* (Psalm 24:1-2)

And while we don't know the composer, it may also be David who later proclaims,

> *The Lord merely spoke, and the heavens were created. He breathed the word, and all the stars were born. He assigned the sea its boundaries and locked the oceans in vast reservoirs. Let the whole world fear the Lord, and let everyone stand in awe of him. For when he spoke, the world began! It appeared at his command.* (Psalm 33:6-9)

Creation shows us that God is the greatest – he is in charge.

Creation reveals God's glory and majesty. We read and sing a lot about God's glory, but many people have difficulty understanding what it is. My preferred way to describe God's glory is his unimaginable beauty. God's majesty describes his ultimate Kingly greatness and dignity. It makes sense, then, that God's glory and majesty are often taken together. Psalm 19, often a favorite among the Psalms of David, professes God's greatness:

> *The heavens proclaim the glory of God. The skies display his craftsmanship. Day after day they continue to speak; night after night they make him known. They speak without a sound or word; their voice is never heard. Yet their message has gone throughout the earth, and their words to all the world. God has made a home in the heavens for the sun. It bursts forth like a radiant bridegroom after his wedding. It rejoices like a great athlete eager to run the race. The sun rises at one end of the heavens and follows its course to the other end. Nothing can hide from its heat.* (Psalm 19:1-6)

And David again proclaims to the whole assembly gathered around him as they give great gifts to build God's temple:

> *"O Lord, the God of our ancestor Israel, may you be praised forever and ever! Yours, O Lord, is the greatness, the power, the glory, the victory, and the majesty. Everything in the heavens and on earth is yours, O Lord, and this is your kingdom. We adore you as the one who is over all things. Wealth and honor come from you alone, for you rule over everything. Power and might are in your hand, and at your discretion people are made great and given strength.*

> *"O our God, we thank you and praise your glorious name!* (1 Chronicles 29:10-13)

As Creator, God sustains everything. Nothing in all creation could continue without God's continuous sustaining power. He sustains us with love. He sustains us with justice. He sustains us with food. Life itself finds its source in him. David sings,

> *Your unfailing love, O Lord, is as vast as the heavens; your faithfulness reaches beyond the clouds. Your righteousness is like the mighty mountains, your justice like the ocean depths.*
>
> *You care for people and animals alike, O Lord. How precious is your unfailing love, O God! All humanity finds shelter in the shadow of your wings. You feed them from the abundance of your own house, letting them drink from your river of delights.*
>
> *For you are the fountain of life, the light by which we see.* (Psalm 36:5-9)

And Paul tells us that God, through Christ, holds all creation together.

> *Christ is the visible image of the invisible God. He existed before anything was created and is supreme over all creation, for through him God created everything in the heavenly realms and on earth. He made the things we can see and the things we can't see— such as thrones, kingdoms, rulers, and authorities in the unseen world. Everything was created through him and for him. He existed before anything else, and he holds all creation together.* (Colossians 1:15-17)

As Creator, God is the Source of everything. In creation, we see his wisdom, his understanding, his knowledge, his glory and his majesty on vibrant display. Creation shows us over and over that God is in charge and that he sustains everything. It's essential to come to know God as Creator because this helps us worship him rightly.

"I believe in God, the Father Almighty, maker of heaven and earth..." As we grow in our relationship with God as Father, we grow in our understanding and experience of his love. As we grow in our relationship with God as Almighty, we grow in our understanding of his ability and power. As we grow in our relationship with God as Creator, we grow in our reverence, adoration, and glory toward him as we see him as our Source and our Sustainer.

STUDY GUIDE

IT MAKES A DIFFERENCE

A healthy understanding of the fatherhood of God is essential for virtually every other aspect of our Christian Faith. Those with a strong foundation in God's fatherhood tend to approach God relationally—those who don't have that foundation approach him theologically, if they consider him at all. God's fatherhood informs our beliefs about how he leads us, provides for us, blesses us, protects us, and much more. Christians who relate to God as their loving heavenly Father tend to trust him far more than those who don't.

Christians with a healthy understanding of God's fatherhood are more accepting of his omnipotence. They progress through their lives knowing that nothing is impossible for One who watches over them. This perspective also significantly impacts how they pray. Finally, because they know he is all-powerful, they also accept that he is the Creator of everything. He knows what is best for everything in creation because he made it all in the first place.

Christians who do not have a solid grasp of the fatherhood of God tend to struggle to give themselves wholly over to him. They often see God as uninvolved in daily life – "out there, somewhere." They may know much about God from various teachings and resources but are bound more to their theological framework than a vibrant relationship with him. They question many of God's attributes, including his omnipotence. They struggle to believe that God really answers prayer. And they may also default to a more secular, scientific explanation for creation.

Our beliefs about the fatherhood of God impact our whole Christian life.

HOW DO I LIVE OUT WHAT I HAVE JUST LEARNED IN MY OWN LIFE?

1. Take a moment to stop and pray. Ask God, through the Holy Spirit, to increase your understanding of the essentials of the Christian Faith. Ask Him to reveal and clarify any points which have been confusing or unclear.

2. Consider your relationship with your earthly father. How does that relationship affect your view of God? Are there parallels? Contrasts? Are there serious rifts in your relationship with your earthly father that would be wise to address with a pastor or other Christian counselor to help you be more comfortable with the concept of God the Father?

3. Reread and consider each of the truths about God in this chapter. Which of these considerations can you capitalize on to understand God more fully? Choose one or two that were more challenging and use a good concordance to research keywords. Meditate on these scriptures this week.[14]

4. Take several days to consider: Who can help you apply what you learn to put into an ongoing life's practice?

5. How are you living this out right now? How is your life reflective of your understanding of this truth?

HOW DO I IMPART WHAT I HAVE JUST LEARNED TO CHILDREN?

Preparing to teach this lesson to children: Gather the following materials before the lesson – blank drawing paper and pencils, markers, colored pencils, or crayons.

1. Begin by praying with the children. Ask God, through the Holy Spirit, to help the children understand more about the Christian faith. Ask God to help them clearly understand the new things they are about to learn.

---

14   A bible concordance is an alphabetical listing of terms found in the bible, usually developed for a specific bible version (e.g., KJV, NIV, etc.), providing verse references for where such terms are found.

2. Continue to work with the children on memorizing the Apostle's Creed. Concentrate especially on the first stanza: *I believe in God, the Father almighty, creator of heaven and earth.*

3. Ask the children what they admire or find good about their own father, or in the absence of a father, ask them to think about a father figure in their lives they admire. Draw parallels between the characteristics they name and our Father God.

4. Ask the children what they believe it means to be "almighty." Guide them to think about why having a Father who is almighty would be desirable. Point out that while earthly fathers are good, they aren't always perfect, but God is.

5. Provide the children with paper and pencils, crayons, or markers. Ask the children to draw a machine of their choice that they wish could be real. (As an illustration, you may want to pick a chore you dislike doing and explain that you would like to see a robot that would move wet clothing from the washer to the dryer automatically, adjust the settings perfectly to dry the clothes, fold them, and put them in the correct drawers; or a personal sized air-conditioned lawn mower that would keep you cool while you mow the lawn.) When they finish, encourage them to share the details of their invention and ask them why they know more about their invention than you do. Obviously, it is because they are the creator. Explain that this is true of God. He knows more about the world and how it should work than anyone else. Why? Because he created it!

6. If you have children in your group who have not yet surrendered to Jesus, continue to pray for the Holy Spirit to open that conversational door so you can explain the gospel. Once they receive Christ, the indwelling presence of the Holy Spirit will make the lessons in this book much more accessible to them.

HOW DO I IMPART WHAT I HAVE JUST LEARNED TO TEENS?

1. Begin by praying with the teens. Ask God, through the Holy Spirit, to increase understanding. You can do this or ask a volunteer.

2. Read the Apostles' Creed out loud. Read it yourself, ask for a volunteer, or read it in unison.

3. Repeat the first stanza, *I believe in God, the Father almighty, creator of heaven and earth,* with emphasis. Encourage the teens to commit this to memory.

4. Have the teens pull out their Question Journals. Ask them to jot down the answers to any questions about the first stanza that are answered in this session. Have them share those discoveries, giving them sufficient time to record any thoughts they wish to capture. Assure them that they can ask any remaining questions about this section at the end of the session.

5. Ask the teens to consider what characteristics of a father are regarded as "good." Ask them why they believe it is essential to understand that God is a good father. Ask them to consider how a faulty understanding might affect a person's relationship with God.

6. Read through the six propositions about God the Father in the subsection titled *Fathers in First Century Judea,* reminding them that these are true of God today. Ask which of these they most identify with and why. Are there any with which they struggle or have heard others question as true?

7. Read through the six propositions about God in the subsection titled *The Almighty.* Ask which of these they most identify with and why. Are there any with which they struggle or have heard others question as true?

8. Read through the six propositions about God in the subsection titled *The Creator.* Ask which of these they most identify with and why. Are there any with which they struggle or have heard others question as true?

9. *Alternative option for 5-8 above: Ask teens to consider why it is important that we believe that God is Almighty and that he is the Creator of Heaven and Earth.*

10. Allow the teens to ask any questions about God the Father, God the Almighty, or God the Creator they had noted in their journals that were not addressed in this discussion.

11. If you have teens in your group who have not yet surrendered to Jesus, continue praying for the Holy Spirit to open that conversational door so you can explain the gospel. Once they receive Christ, the indwelling presence of the Holy Spirit will make the lessons in this book much more accessible to them.

HOW DO I IMPART WHAT I HAVE JUST LEARNED TO ADULTS?

1. Challenge your adults to take a moment to stop and pray, asking God, through the Holy Spirit, to increase their understanding of the essentials of the Christian Faith. Ask Him to reveal and clarify any points which have been confusing or unclear.

2. Review the Apostles' Creed, emphasizing the first stanza: *I believe in God, the Father almighty, creator of heaven and earth.* If they have not done so, encourage them to memorize the Creed in its entirety, reminding them that it summarizes the essentials of the Christian faith.

3. Have participants pull out the notes they made during the last session. Ask them to jot down the answers to any questions about the Creed that were answered during this session and to share those discoveries as they happen. Provide sufficient time to record any thoughts they may wish to capture. Assure them that they will have the opportunity to ask any remaining questions about this section at the end of the session.

4. Ask participants to reflect on their relationship with their earthly fathers. Invite them to share how that relationship may have shaped their perception of God the Father.

5. Read through the six propositions about God the Father in the subsection titled *Fathers in First Century Judea,* reminding them that these are true of God today. Ask which of these they most identify with and why. Are there any with which they struggle or have heard others question as true?

6. Read through the six propositions about God in the subsection titled *The Almighty*. Ask which of these they most identify with and why. Are there any with which they struggle or have heard others question as true?

7. Read through the six propositions about God in the subsection titled *The Creator*. Ask which of these they most identify with and why. Are there any with which they struggle or have heard others question as true?

8. Allow participants to ask any questions about God the Father, God the Almighty, or God the Creator they had noted previously that were not addressed in this discussion.

9. If you have people in your group who have not yet surrendered to Jesus, continue to pray for the Holy Spirit to open that conversational door so you can explain the gospel. Once they receive Christ, the indwelling presence of the Holy Spirit will make the lessons in this book much more accessible to them.

CHAPTER 3
Jesus: God's Son, Our Lord

"I believe in Jesus Christ... God's only Son, our Lord..."

When Jesus arrived at Bethany, he was told that Lazarus had already been in his grave for four days. Bethany was only a few miles down the road from Jerusalem, and many of the people had come to console Martha and Mary in their loss. When Martha got word that Jesus was coming, she went to meet him. But Mary stayed in the house. Martha said to Jesus, "Lord, if only you had been here, my brother would not have died. But even now I know that God will give you whatever you ask."

Jesus told her, "Your brother will rise again."

"Yes," Martha said, "he will rise when everyone else rises, at the last day."

Jesus told her, "I am the resurrection and the life. Anyone who believes in me will live, even after dying. Everyone who lives in me and believes in me will never ever die. Do you believe this, Martha?"

"Yes, Lord," she told him. "I have always believed you are the Messiah, the Son of God, the one who has come into the world from God." (John 11:17-27)

JESUS: HE MIGHT NOT BE WHO YOU THINK HE IS

Everyone in my immediate family is a movie nerd. We can recount the lines from several movies: *The Lord of the Rings* trilogy, *The Hobbit* trilogy, and of course, *The Princess Bride*. For those who know and love this cult classic, there is a villain named Vizzini, played by Wallace Shawn (who is also the voice of Rex in the Toy Story movies... see, I told you I was a movie nerd!). Vizzini is an all-out criminal who is passionate about starting a war between the countries of Florin and Gilder. But every time something doesn't work out according to his detailed plans (which is often), he decries the issue as "Inconceivable!" After yelling the word multiple times in the first 30 minutes of the movie, one of his henchmen, Inigo Montoya, replies, "You keep using that word. I do not think it means what you think it means."

I fear that many in the Church today have a similar problem regarding Jesus. The Jesus they have envisioned bears little resemblance to the real Lord of Glory. They see him as a gentle shepherd, but neglect to realize that he is also capable of wiping out the kings and armies of the earth with the sword of his mouth (Revelation 19:21). People love to see him as Savior, but many resist his lordship (1 Corinthians 8:6) and still others have a hard time accepting him as the ultimate Judge (John 5:22-23; Revelation 20:11-15). I've met way too many well-meaning Christians over the years who believe in a Jesus of their own making: one that does not really resemble the King of kings and Lord of lords.

Understanding who the real Jesus is has deep ramifications on our personal theology and is often also a determining factor in our salvation. It's a big deal to get this right. And so we turn to the Creed for guidance.

THE CHRIST

This will blow some folks' minds (I've seen it happen many times before), but Christ is not Jesus' last name. Christ is Jesus' royal, heavenly title! As the apostle Paul writes about Jesus, he rarely uses Jesus' name without his title – calling him "Jesus Christ" or "Christ Jesus."

> *For everyone has sinned; we all fall short of God's glorious standard. Yet God, in his grace, freely makes us right in his sight. He did this through **Christ Jesus** when he freed us from the penalty for our sins.* (Romans 3:23-24, **emphasis mine**)

> *God has united you with **Christ Jesus**. For our benefit God made him to be wisdom itself. Christ made us right with God; he made us pure and holy, and he freed us from sin.* (1 Corinthians 1:30, **emphasis mine**)

The idea that Jesus is *the* Christ is critical to Paul and should also be critical to us.

Christ is the Greek equivalent of the Hebrew term "Messiah." Theologian George Eldon Ladd remarks, "The title and concept of Messiah is the most important of all the Christological concepts historically if not theologically, because it became the central way of designating the Christian understanding of Jesus."[15] "Christ" is an essential concept to comprehend and correctly apply! For clarity, it may be helpful to refer to the Savior as "Jesus THE Christ."

> *...for the Holy One has given you his Spirit, and all of you know the truth. So I am writing to you not because you don't know the truth but because you know the difference between truth and lies. And who is a liar? Anyone who says that Jesus is not the Christ. Anyone who denies the Father and the Son is an antichrist.* (1 John 2:20-22)

> *Everyone who believes that Jesus is the Christ has become a child of God. And everyone who loves the Father loves his children, too.* (1 John 5:1)

Like "Messiah," "Christ" literally means "Anointed One." While the Jewish understanding of the personal Messiah would develop more during the time between the Old and New Testaments, there is still a clear Old Testament foundation for the Messiah and his task. He would be the ultimate King, conquering all earthly kings. As Samuel's mother, Hannah, praises God, she proclaims,

---

15   George Eldon Ladd, *A Theology of the New Testament*, (Grand Rapids MI: Eerdmans, 1993), p. 135.

"He will protect his faithful ones, but the wicked will disappear in darkness. No one will succeed by strength alone. Those who fight against the Lord will be shattered. He thunders against them from heaven; the Lord judges throughout the earth. He gives power to his king; he increases the strength of his anointed one." (1 Samuel 2:9-10)

And there is a Messianic authority to Psalm 2:

Why are the nations so angry? Why do they waste their time with futile plans? The kings of the earth prepare for battle; the rulers plot together against the Lord and against his anointed one. "Let us break their chains," they cry, "and free ourselves from slavery to God." But the one who rules in heaven laughs. The Lord scoffs at them. Then in anger he rebukes them, terrifying them with his fierce fury. For the Lord declares, "I have placed my chosen king on the throne in Jerusalem, on my holy mountain." The king proclaims the Lord's decree:"The Lord said to me, 'You are my son. Today I have become your Father. Only ask, and I will give you the nations as your inheritance, the whole earth as your possession. You will break them with an iron rod and smash them like clay pots.'" Now then, you kings, act wisely! Be warned, you rulers of the earth! Serve the Lord with reverent fear, and rejoice with trembling. Submit to God's royal son, or he will become angry, and you will be destroyed in the midst of all your activities— for his anger flares up in an instant. But what joy for all who take refuge in him! (Psalm 2:1-12)

The Messiah would be the greatest descendant of King David's line. As Nathan reports to David all the Lord has shown him, he recounts,

"'Furthermore, the Lord declares that he will make a house for you—a dynasty of kings! For when you die and are buried with your ancestors, I will raise up one of your descendants, your own offspring, and I will make his kingdom strong. He is the one who will build a house—a temple—for my name. And I will secure his royal throne forever. I will be his father, and he will be my son. If he sins, I will correct and discipline him with the rod, like

any father would do. But my favor will not be taken from him as I took it from Saul, whom I removed from your sight. Your house and your kingdom will continue before me for all time, and your throne will be secure forever.' " (2 Samuel 7:11-16)

And later, Jeremiah prophesies,

For in that day," says the Lord of Heaven's Armies, "I will break the yoke from their necks and snap their chains. Foreigners will no longer be their masters. For my people will serve the Lord their God and their king descended from David— the king I will raise up for them. "So do not be afraid, Jacob, my servant; do not be dismayed, Israel," says the Lord. (Jeremiah 30:8-10a)

The Messiah would be supernaturally endowed to rid the earth of sin and evil, freeing all peoples once and for all. The prophet Isaiah proclaims,

Nevertheless, that time of darkness and despair will not go on forever. The land of Zebulun and Naphtali will be humbled, but there will be a time in the future when Galilee of the Gentiles, which lies along the road that runs between the Jordan and the sea, will be filled with glory. The people who walk in darkness will see a great light. For those who live in a land of deep darkness, a light will shine. You will enlarge the nation of Israel, and its people will rejoice. They will rejoice before you as people rejoice at the harvest and like warriors dividing the plunder. For you will break the yoke of their slavery and lift the heavy burden from their shoulders. You will break the oppressor's rod, just as you did when you destroyed the army of Midian. The boots of the warrior and the uniforms bloodstained by war will all be burned. They will be fuel for the fire. For a child is born to us, a son is given to us. The government will rest on his shoulders. And he will be called: Wonderful Counselor, Mighty God, Everlasting Father, Prince of Peace. His government and its peace will never end. He will rule with fairness and justice from the throne of his ancestor David for all eternity. The passionate commitment of the Lord of Heaven's Armies will make this happen! (Isaiah 9:1-7)

And again,

> *Out of the stump of David's family will grow a shoot— yes, a new Branch bearing fruit from the old root. And the Spirit of the Lord will rest on him— the Spirit of wisdom and understanding, the Spirit of counsel and might, the Spirit of knowledge and the fear of the Lord. He will delight in obeying the Lord. He will not judge by appearance nor make a decision based on hearsay. He will give justice to the poor and make fair decisions for the exploited. The earth will shake at the force of his word, and one breath from his mouth will destroy the wicked. He will wear righteousness like a belt and truth like an undergarment. In that day the wolf and the lamb will live together; the leopard will lie down with the baby goat. The calf and the yearling will be safe with the lion, and a little child will lead them all. The cow will graze near the bear. The cub and the calf will lie down together. The lion will eat hay like a cow. The baby will play safely near the hole of a cobra. Yes, a little child will put its hand in a nest of deadly snakes without harm. Nothing will hurt or destroy in all my holy mountain, for as the waters fill the sea, so the earth will be filled with people who know the Lord. In that day the heir to David's throne will be a banner of salvation to all the world. The nations will rally to him, and the land where he lives will be a glorious place.* (Isaiah 11:1-10)

Finally, though he would be globally victorious, the Messiah would be recognized throughout Jerusalem by his complete gentleness and humility. And Jesus fulfilled the prophet Zechariah's words about this during his triumphal entry into Jerusalem, which we now celebrate as Palm Sunday.

> *Rejoice, O people of Zion! Shout in triumph, O people of Jerusalem! Look, your king is coming to you. He is righteous and victorious, yet he is humble, riding on a donkey— riding on a donkey's colt. I will remove the battle chariots from Israel and the warhorses from Jerusalem. I will destroy all the weapons used in battle, and your king will bring peace to the nations. His realm will stretch from sea to sea and from the Euphrates River to the ends of the earth.* (Zechariah 9:9-10)

The writer of Hebrews understands Jesus to be that anointed one, the Messiah.

> *And when he brought his supreme Son into the world, God said, "Let all of God's angels worship him." Regarding the angels, he says, "He sends his angels like the winds, his servants like flames of fire." But to the Son he says, "Your throne, O God, endures forever and ever. You rule with a scepter of justice. You love justice and hate evil. Therefore, O God, your God has anointed you, pouring out the oil of joy on you more than on anyone else."* (Hebrews 1:6-9)

So the Christ is God's deliverer, foretold by the prophets (see Isaiah 61:1 and Daniel 9:26). Jesus *is* the Messiah, the Christ! It is essential that we come to know Jesus as the Anointed One so that we may understand the fullness of his mission, the vast prophetic foundation (Jesus' life and ministry fulfilled over 300 prophecies), and the utter victory that he ultimately brings to all those who have trusted in him.

THE SON OF GOD

We don't just believe that Jesus is the Christ, but also that he is God's Son. In fact, Jesus is God's only *begotten* Son. Our God has many children (us!), but only one of these is not adopted. The apostle John tells us that Jesus is God's one and only Son.

> *So the Word became human and made his home among us. He was full of unfailing love and faithfulness. And we have seen his glory, the glory of the Father's one and only Son.* (John 1:14)

> *"For this is how God loved the world: He gave his one and only Son, so that everyone who believes in him will not perish but have eternal life. God sent his Son into the world not to judge the world, but to save the world through him.* (John 3:16-17)

> *God showed how much he loved us by sending his one and only Son into the world so that we might have eternal life through him. This is real love—not that we loved God, but that he loved us and sent his Son as a sacrifice to take away our sins.* (1 John 4:9-10)

While anyone who trusts in the Christ for salvation becomes a child of God (John 1:12), Jesus alone shares God's own nature. People who are redeemed by Jesus' blood share certain things in common with our Heavenly Father; however, there are specific attributes that only Jesus shares with the Father as God's one and only Son:

Jesus shares God's divine nature – It can be argued that the apostle John's primary purpose in writing his version of the gospel is to make this very point. Speaking of Jesus, he writes,

> *In the beginning the Word already existed. The Word was with God, and the Word was God. He existed in the beginning with God. God created everything through him, and nothing was created except through him. The Word gave life to everything that was created, and his life brought light to everyone. The light shines in the darkness, and the darkness can never extinguish it.* (John 1:1-5)

1. Jesus is eternal – see John 1:1

2. Jesus is unchanging – see Hebrews 13:8

3. Jesus is omnipotent (all powerful), omniscient (all knowing), and omnipresent (everywhere at once) – see Philippians 2:6-8; Revelation 1:9-18; 19:11-16

Jesus shares God's sinless nature – as Jesus took on human flesh with all its limitations, he did so without sin. This truth is vitally important as he could not complete his saving work on our behalf if he was a sinner like us.

> *For God made Christ, who never sinned, to be the offering for our sin, so that we could be made right with God through Christ.* (2 Corinthians 5:21)

> *So then, since we have a great High Priest who has entered heaven, Jesus the Son of God, let us hold firmly to what we believe. This High Priest of ours understands our weaknesses, for he faced all of the same testings we do, yet he did not sin.* (Hebrews 4:14-15)

For God called you to do good, even if it means suffering, just as Christ suffered for you. He is your example, and you must follow in his steps. He never sinned, nor ever deceived anyone. He did not retaliate when he was insulted, nor threaten revenge when he suffered. He left his case in the hands of God, who always judges fairly. He personally carried our sins in his body on the cross so that we can be dead to sin and live for what is right. By his wounds you are healed. Once you were like sheep who wandered away. But now you have turned to your Shepherd, the Guardian of your souls. (1 Peter 2:21-25)

And you know that Jesus came to take away our sins, and there is no sin in him. (1 John 3:5)

Because he shares these attributes with our Heavenly Father, Jesus alone could pay the penalty for our sin. The 53rd chapter of Isaiah's prophecy is amazing in that it wraps all these truths together over 700 years before Jesus was even born! God showed Isaiah his plan:

Who has believed our message? To whom has the Lord revealed his powerful arm? My servant grew up in the Lord's presence like a tender green shoot, like a root in dry ground. There was nothing beautiful or majestic about his appearance, nothing to attract us to him. He was despised and rejected— a man of sorrows, acquainted with deepest grief. We turned our backs on him and looked the other way. He was despised, and we did not care. Yet it was our weaknesses he carried; it was our sorrows that weighed him down. And we thought his troubles were a punishment from God, a punishment for his own sins! But he was pierced for our rebellion, crushed for our sins. He was beaten so we could be whole. He was whipped so we could be healed. All of us, like sheep, have strayed away. We have left God's paths to follow our own. Yet the Lord laid on him the sins of us all. He was oppressed and treated harshly, yet he never said a word. He was led like a lamb to the slaughter. And as a sheep is silent before the shearers, he did not open his mouth. Unjustly condemned, he was led away. No one cared that he died without descendants, that his life was cut short in midstream. But he was struck down for the rebellion of my people. He had done no

69

wrong and had never deceived anyone. But he was buried like a criminal; he was put in a rich man's grave. But it was the Lord's good plan to crush him and cause him grief. Yet when his life is made an offering for sin, he will have many descendants. He will enjoy a long life, and the Lord's good plan will prosper in his hands. When he sees all that is accomplished by his anguish, he will be satisfied. And because of his experience, my righteous servant will make it possible for many to be counted righteous, for he will bear all their sins. I will give him the honors of a victorious soldier, because he exposed himself to death. He was counted among the rebels. He bore the sins of many and inter-ceded for rebels. (Isaiah 53:1-12)

We are those rebels! It is so important to come to know Jesus as the Son of God so that we understand he has both a divine and a human nature at the same time, making him the perfect substitute for us in taking God's punishment for our sin.[16]

THE LORD

If Jesus is indeed the long-awaited Messiah (the Christ), and if he is indeed the Son of God who shares God's nature, then it makes sense that our first response must be to *surrender* to him.

Here I must address what I believe to be a dangerous misconception among many modern Christians today – the definition of lordship. I don't know if it is the language of "accepting Jesus into our hearts" or something else, but many Christians today appear to have lost the whole idea of surrendering to the Christ. It's as if we think we can "accept" him as our Savior and get all the benefits he offers without giving up mastery of our own lives – giving him complete control.

The "Lord" is the one who owns and rules you. Let that thought steep in your mind for a moment. To become a Christian – a true follower of Jesus the Christ – is to totally give up our rights and our ownership

---

16 I'm intentionally trying not to get too theological, but this point is critical to understand. The scripture shows us that Jesus was simultaneously 100% God (John 1:1) and 100% human (John 1:14). This dual nature is seen in God's promise to King David (2 Samuel 7:11b-16). It's is also mentioned by the prophet Isaiah (Isaiah 9:6), where *child* is understood to denote Jesus' human nature, and *son* is understood to denote Jesus' divine nature. And it is because of this dual nature (called the "hypostatic union" by theologians) that Jesus was able to pay the penalty for our sins (Philippians 2:5-11).

of our own lives and destinies. To become a Christian is to accept that we are now owned by another. This is the whole concept of being "redeemed." A price was paid for us. The apostle Paul says it this way,

> *Don't you realize that your body is the temple of the Holy Spirit, who lives in you and was given to you by God? You do not belong to yourself, for God bought you with a high price. So you must honor God with your body.* (1 Corinthians 6:19-20)

And Peter tells us what that "high price" was.

> *For you know that God paid a ransom to save you from the empty life you inherited from your ancestors. And it was not paid with mere gold or silver, which lose their value. It was the precious blood of Christ, the sinless, spotless Lamb of God.* (1 Peter 1:18-19)

When we become Christians, we surrender everything to Jesus as Lord. In effect, we become bondservants. When we call Jesus "Lord," it means we fully intend to do what he tells us to do. Jesus, himself, asks a pressing question:

> *"So why do you keep calling me 'Lord, Lord!' when you don't do what I say?* (Luke 6:46)

Jesus had many titles during his earthly ministry – and all of them are titles of lordship. He was called "Rabbi," a teacher who has great experience, knowledge, understanding, wisdom, and authority. He was called "Master," the one who has control over a person or group, particularly servants or slaves. He was called "Lord," the person with the highest rank – often a king.

As Lord, Jesus has all supremacy.

> *Christ is the visible image of the invisible God. He existed before anything was created **and is supreme over all creation**, for through him God created everything in the heavenly realms and on earth. He made the things we can see and the things we can't see— such as thrones, kingdoms, rulers, and authorities in*

the unseen world. Everything was created through him and for him. He existed before anything else, and he holds all creation together. Christ is also the head of the church, which is his body. He is the beginning, supreme over all who rise from the dead. So he is first in everything. For God in all his fullness was pleased to live in Christ, and through him God reconciled everything to himself. He made peace with everything in heaven and on earth by means of Christ's blood on the cross. (Colossians 1:15-20, **emphasis mine**)

As Lord, Jesus reigns over all the earth.

Then the seventh angel blew his trumpet, and there were loud voices shouting in heaven: "The world has now become the Kingdom of our Lord and of his Christ, and he will reign forever and ever." The twenty-four elders sitting on their thrones before God fell with their faces to the ground and worshiped him. (Revelation 11:15-16)

But to the Son he says, "Your throne, O God, endures forever and ever. You rule with a scepter of justice. You love justice and hate evil. Therefore, O God, your God has anointed you, pouring out the oil of joy on you more than on anyone else." He also says to the Son, "In the beginning, Lord, you laid the foundation of the earth and made the heavens with your hands. They will perish, but you remain forever. They will wear out like old clothing. You will fold them up like a cloak and discard them like old clothing. But you are always the same; you will live forever." And God never said to any of the angels, "Sit in the place of honor at my right hand until I humble your enemies, making them a footstool under your feet." (Hebrews 1:8-13)

As Lord, Jesus is the One with all the authority.

Jesus came and told his disciples, "I have been given all authority in heaven and on earth. Therefore, go and make disciples of all the nations, baptizing them in the name of the Father and the

Son and the Holy Spirit. Teach these new disciples to obey all the commands I have given you. And be sure of this: I am with you always, even to the end of the age." (Matthew 28:18-20)

As Lord, Jesus is the One who puts down all opposition to God.

After that the end will come, when he will turn the Kingdom over to God the Father, having destroyed every ruler and authority and power. For Christ must reign until he humbles all his enemies beneath his feet. And the last enemy to be destroyed is death. For the Scriptures say, "God has put all things under his authority." (Of course, when it says "all things are under his authority," that does not include God himself, who gave Christ his authority.) Then, when all things are under his authority, the Son will put himself under God's authority, so that God, who gave his Son authority over all things, will be utterly supreme over everything everywhere. (1 Corinthians 15:24-28)

Jesus is Lord! Jesus is Master! Jesus is King! It is essential to come to know Jesus as Lord so that we fully understand and embrace his supreme authority and power, and that he has the ability to make literally *everything* right in the end.

"I believe in Jesus Christ, God's only Son, our Lord..." Powerful words that remind us of Jesus' Messiahship, that he was the perfect substitute to pay for our sins, and that he is the one to whom we must surrender everything.

STUDY GUIDE

IT MAKES A DIFFERENCE

It's sad that many Christians today do not fully grasp who our Jesus really is. Those who understand that he is the long-awaited Christ (Messiah), knowing what the Bible says about the supernatural power, authority, and gentleness of this anointed one, embrace Jesus as their personal deliverer. They also embrace Jesus as God's Son, sharing God's divine nature in his complete humanity so that he can overcome sin and death. Finally, they are learning to truly live under Jesus' lord-ship – not simply calling him "Lord," but living under his example and direction daily.

People who do not understand who Jesus is often try to fill in the gaps in their belief system by themselves. They don't comprehend Jesus' complete and utter deliverance, so they try to earn their own salva-tion, hoping and praying that they will be "good enough" to get into heaven at the end of their lives. Either that or they unwittingly adopt a more Universalist view that Jesus died, so everyone is safe. They also rarely accept the dual nature of Jesus – that he was both God and man simultaneously – falling prey to some of the historic heresies that incited the need for the creeds in the first place. Finally, they may call him "Lord Jesus," but there is nothing about their lifestyles that demonstrate Jesus is actually in charge. They are like those to whom Jesus said, "Why do you call me Lord, Lord, and then not do what I say?" (Luke 6:46).

The old saying is true: "If Jesus is not Lord of all, he is not Lord at all." The Creed helps us know why personal surrender to the Christ is non-negotiable.

HOW DO I LIVE OUT WHAT I HAVE JUST LEARNED IN MY OWN LIFE?

1. Take a moment to stop and pray. Ask God, through the Holy Spirit, to increase your understanding of the essentials of the Christian Faith. Ask Him to reveal and clarify any points which have been confusing or unclear.

2. Consider your own view of Jesus you had before reading this chapter. How balanced was it? How have you added to your understanding of Jesus as Messiah (Christ), Begotten Son of God, and Lord?

3. Is Jesus Lord of your life? Should he be? If not, what needs to happen to make it so?

4. Take several days to consider: Who can help you apply what you learn to put it into an ongoing life's practice?

5. How are you living this out right now? How is your life
    reflective of your understanding of this truth?

HOW DO I IMPART WHAT I HAVE JUST LEARNED TO CHILDREN?

Preparing to teach this lesson to children: *Run off enough copies
of the pyramid pattern (link provided below) for each child to have
one, plus extras so that you have one to use for an example and you
have a few in case someone accidentally cuts where they shouldn't.
Make your example pyramid. Gather the following materials before
the lesson – patterns referred to above, crayons or markers, glue or
tape, and scissors.*

1. Begin by praying with the children. Ask God, through the Holy
    Spirit, to help the children understand more about the Christian
    faith. Ask God to help them clearly understand the new things
    they are about to learn.

2. Continue to work with the children on memorizing the Apostle's
    Creed. Be sure they have memorized the first two statements:
    *I believe in God, the Father almighty, creator of heaven and
    earth. I believe in Jesus Christ, his only Son, our Lord,*

3. Discuss with the children the fact that Jesus *Christ* actually
    means the same as Jesus the *Messiah. T*he people of Jesus'
    day expected the *Messiah* to deliver them from the cruel rule
    of Rome. That is why they lined up on Palm Sunday to shout,
    "Hosannah!" (Save us!) as Jesus rode into Jerusalem. However,
    Jesus turned out to be different. Explain that Jesus actually
    delivered people from sin. (Depending on age and level of
    exposure to Christian concepts, you may need to explain the
    concept of *sin*.) Discuss why this is an important truth for us
    today.

4. Talk with the children about how Jesus is God's son that God
    sent to earth to deliver us from sin, but first he had to be born,
    grow up, and live a perfect life. He could only save us because

he was also God. Only someone perfect could be stronger than sin and death and prepare us for eternal life in heaven. We celebrate his birth at Christmas.

5. Discuss with the children what it means that Jesus wants to be the Lord of our lives. Lord is a royal title. Most children will realize that a king or queen is in charge and expects to be obeyed. Emphasize that this is God's design for our own good. Earthly kings sometimes do things that are bad for their subjects, but because King Jesus, our Lord, is perfect, he knows what is best for us, and we benefit from obeying what he tells us.

6. Create a visual: Ahead of your time with the children, run off a pyramid pattern such as the one you will find at the link listed below – one per child. Make a couple of extras in case someone makes a mistake. Have scissors, glue sticks, and crayons or markers available. Have the children cut out the pattern, taking care that they do not cut off the tabs. After the pattern is cut, have the children write one of these words/phrases on each face of the pyramid: Jesus, Messiah, Son of God, and Lord. If time allows, they could draw something that reminds them of each of the titles above the printed words (perhaps palm branch, manger, and crown). After doing so, they should fold on the lines along the base, then glue or tape the tabs to create the pyramid. Remind them that Jesus is all of these things and review what each means. You are strongly encouraged to create your own pyramid ahead of time so that the children have a model and can copy the spelling of the words. *https://www. firstpalette.com/printable/square-pyramid.html*

7. If you have children in your group who have not yet surrendered to Jesus, continue to pray for the Holy Spirit to open that conversational door so you can explain the gospel. Once they receive Christ, the indwelling presence of the Holy Spirit will make the lessons in this book much more accessible to them.

HOW DO I IMPART WHAT I HAVE JUST LEARNED TO TEENS?

1. Begin by praying with the teens. Ask God, through the Holy Spirit, to increase understanding. You can do this or ask a volunteer.

2. Read the Apostles' Creed out loud. Read it yourself, ask for a volunteer, or read it in unison.

3. Repeat the first few lines: *I believe in God, the Father almighty, creator of heaven and earth. I believe in Jesus Christ, his only Son, our Lord,* with emphasis. Encourage the teens to commit this to memory.

4. Have the teens pull out their Question Journals. Ask them to jot down the answers to any questions about the Creed that are answered in this session. Have them share those discoveries, giving them sufficient time to record any thoughts they wish to capture. Assure them that they can ask any remaining questions about this section at the end of the session.

5. Have teens make a 3-column chart by folding notebook paper into thirds lengthwise. Title the columns: Jesus Christ, Son of God, and Lord. Have them record characteristics of Jesus as Messiah, Jesus as the Son of God, and Jesus as Lord. Share and discuss their findings.

6. Read through the scripture references in *The Christ* section of the chapter. How does each support the idea that Jesus is the anointed Messiah, the Christ? Add to the information in the first column if new understanding is gained.

7. What difference does it make that each of these is true about Jesus – that he is the Christ (Messiah), the Son of God, and Lord? (Note that Jesus as the only begotten Son of God will be explored more fully in the next chapter.)

8. Allow the teens to ask any questions about Jesus Messiah, Jesus the Son of God, or Jesus as Lord that they had noted in their

journals that were not already addressed. Ask them if/how their understanding of Jesus changed through what they learned in this session.

9. If you have teens in your group who have not yet surrendered to Jesus, continue praying for the Holy Spirit to open that conversational door so you can explain the gospel. Once they receive Christ, the indwelling presence of the Holy Spirit will make the lessons in this book much more accessible to them.

HOW DO I IMPART WHAT I HAVE JUST LEARNED TO ADULTS?

1. Challenge your adults to take a moment to stop and pray, asking God, through the Holy Spirit, to increase their understanding of the essentials of the Christian Faith. Encourage them to ask Him to reveal and clarify any points which have been confusing or unclear.

2. Review the Apostles' Creed, emphasizing the first few lines: *I believe in God, the Father almighty, creator of heaven and earth. I believe in Jesus Christ, his only Son, our Lord.* If they have not done so, encourage them to memorize the Creed in its entirety, reminding them that it is a summary of the essentials of the faith.

3. Have participants pull out the notes they made during the last session. Ask them to jot down the answers to any questions about the Creed that were answered during this session and to share those discoveries as they happen. Provide sufficient time to record any thoughts they may wish to capture. Assure them that they will have the opportunity to ask any remaining questions about this section at the end of the session.

4. Ask participants if they realized that *Christ* was Jesus' title, not his last name, and that *Christ* was another name for Messiah. Why is it important to understand that truth?

5. Read through the scripture references in *The Christ* section of the chapter. How does each support the idea that Jesus is the anointed Messiah, the Christ?

6. Discuss the reasons why it is important that Jesus is God's *only begotten* Son, not just *one of* his created/adopted children. (Note that Jesus as only begotten Son of God will be explored more fully in the next chapter.)

7. Discuss how we can know whether Jesus is Lord. Ask participants whether they can say that Jesus is Lord over their lives. Why does this matter? Does believing in Jesus automatically make him Lord? If not, what steps should we take to make this a reality in our lives?

8. Allow participants to ask any questions about Jesus as Messiah, Son of God, or Lord they had noted previously that were not addressed in this discussion.

9. If you have people in your group who have not yet surrendered to Jesus, continue praying for the Holy Spirit to open that conversational door so you can explain the gospel. Once they receive Christ, the indwelling presence of the Holy Spirit will make the lessons in this book much more accessible to them.

CHAPTER 4
Jesus: Conception and Virgin Birth

"I believe in Jesus Christ... who was conceived by the Holy Spirit, born of the virgin Mary..."

In the sixth month of Elizabeth's pregnancy, God sent the angel Gabriel to Nazareth, a village in Galilee, to a virgin named Mary. She was engaged to be married to a man named Joseph, a descendant of King David. Gabriel appeared to her and said, "Greetings, favored woman! The Lord is with you!"

Confused and disturbed, Mary tried to think what the angel could mean. "Don't be afraid, Mary," the angel told her, "for you have found favor with God! You will conceive and give birth to a son, and you will name him Jesus. He will be very great and will be called the Son of the Most High. The Lord God will give him the throne of his ancestor David. And he will reign over Israel forever; his Kingdom will never end!"

Mary asked the angel, "But how can this happen? I am a virgin."

The angel replied, "The Holy Spirit will come upon you, and the power of the Most High will overshadow you. So the baby to be born will be holy, and he will be called the Son of God. (Luke 1:26-35)

THE BIG DEAL

Years ago, I was discussing the Virgin Birth with a friend who was fairly active in his church but was admittedly not "sold out" to the whole Jesus thing. He had been raised in the church and still went with amazing regularity, but he struggled with many of the core doctrines of the Christian Faith. The doctrine of the Virgin Birth was one he had a hard time accepting. We talked for well over an hour when he finally retorted, "I just don't get why this is such a big deal!" The problem is, if Jesus was not born of a virgin, we have no salvation. Period. It really is a big deal.

What the Bible teaches about Jesus' conception by the Holy Spirit and his Virgin Birth are two sides of the same coin. It is impossible to have one without the other, which is why they are joined in the Apostles' Creed. I would say they are two parts of the same statement.

When told by the angel that she was chosen, Mary asks, "How can this be, since I am a virgin?" Listen carefully once again to his response:

> *The angel replied, "The Holy Spirit will come upon you, and the power of the Most High will overshadow you. So the baby to be born will be holy, and he will be called the Son of God.* (Luke 1:35)

She is a virgin. The Holy Spirit will come upon her, and the power of the Most High God (the Father) will overshadow her. Her child will be *holy* (this is critical), the very Son of God.

PRACTICAL IMPLICATIONS

In some ways, this may be the heart of the Apostles' Creed. These two doctrines are probably the most challenged by those who have moved into heretical directions down through history. Therefore, it's imperative for every believer to have a good grasp on them and to know why they are foundational to the Christian Faith.

Some people think the Virgin Birth is a kind of peripheral doctrine – really not that important – and certainly not worth fighting over. But nothing could be further from the truth! The Virgin Birth is absolutely central to the Christian Faith and to your salvation.

If Jesus was not conceived by the Holy Spirit and born of a virgin, then the Bible is wholly unreliable. You might think that's an odd place to start – and even a bit of a reach on my part – but hear me out. We've already talked about how the Scriptures are God's revelation of himself to humanity and how they provide the only reliable rule for our faith and practice. But what if we concluded that the very rule from which all that comes is fallible? We're sunk. That's why we must start here.

Most modern Christians, if they consider the Virgin Birth at all, think that it is a "gospel" thing. While it certainly is foundational to the good news of Jesus the Christ, would you be surprised to learn that it is really a whole Bible thing?

1. *Moses taught it (Genesis 3:15)*

    The *protoevangelium* or "the first proclamation of the gospel" is found in Genesis 3:15, where, on the heels of humanity's sinful rejection of God's lordship, God pronounces the impact of their decision:

    Then the Lord God said to the serpent, "Because you have done this, you are cursed more than all animals, domestic and wild. You will crawl on your belly, groveling in the dust as long as you live. And I will cause hostility between you and the woman, and between your offspring and her offspring. He will strike your head, and you will strike his heel." (Genesis 3:14-15)

    The word "offspring" there is the word for seed (think male seed). A dear friend and Old Testament theologian who also happens to be a Messianic Rabbi once told me that this is the only place in all of ancient Hebrew literature where the word for "seed" is attributed to a woman instead of a man. All the way back in Genesis 3, God is giving us a glimpse of his plans for the Virgin Birth! The woman's offspring (Jesus) will crush the serpent's head (Satan)!

2. *Isaiah taught it (Isaiah 7:14)*

    This passage is more familiar to many people because it is a regular part of our Christmas celebration each year:

All right then, the Lord himself will give you the sign. Look!
The virgin will conceive a child! She will give birth to a son
and will call him Immanuel (which means 'God is with us').
(Isaiah 7:14)

Over 700 years before Jesus was born, the Lord gave
Isaiah this prophecy. Isaiah proclaimed that a virgin would
give birth to a child, and he would have a special name:
Immanuel, which is Hebrew for "God with us." Matthew
later quotes this prophecy when recounting the angel's visit
to Jesus' earthly father, Joseph.

3. *Jeremiah taught it (Jeremiah 31:22)*

This one is a little more cryptic, but most scholars agree that
Jeremiah sees the Virgin Birth here:

"Is not Israel still my son, my darling child?" says the Lord.
"I often have to punish him, but I still love him. That's
why I long for him and surely will have mercy on him. Set
up road signs; put up guideposts. Mark well the path by
which you came. Come back again, my virgin Israel; return
to your towns here. How long will you wander, my way-
ward daughter? For the Lord will cause something new to
happen— Israel will embrace her God." (Jeremiah 31:20-22)

It is likely that verse 22 is a word from God to the prophet
about the Virgin Birth, when God himself will invade humanity to redeem them and bring them back to himself.

4. *Matthew taught it (Matthew 1:18-25)*

Matthew's gospel account teaches the Virgin Birth blatantly:

This is how Jesus the Messiah was born. His mother, Mary,
was engaged to be married to Joseph. But before the mar-
riage took place, while she was still a virgin, she became
pregnant through the power of the Holy Spirit. Joseph, to
whom she was engaged, was a righteous man and did not
want to disgrace her publicly, so he decided to break the
engagement quietly. As he considered this, an angel of the
Lord appeared to him in a dream. "Joseph, son of David,"
the angel said, "do not be afraid to take Mary as your wife.

*For the child within her was conceived by the Holy Spirit.
And she will have a son, and you are to name him Jesus, for
he will save his people from their sins." All of this occurred
to fulfill the Lord's message through his prophet: "Look!
The virgin will conceive a child! She will give birth to a son,
and they will call him Immanuel, which means 'God is with
us.' " When Joseph woke up, he did as the angel of the Lord
commanded and took Mary as his wife. But he did not have
sexual relations with her until her son was born. And Joseph
named him Jesus.* (Matthew 1:18-25)

And as Matthew quotes from the prophet, he is quoting
from what Isaiah has already said.

5. *Luke taught it (Luke 1:26-38)*

We've already looked at a portion of this passage:

*In the sixth month of Elizabeth's pregnancy, God sent the
angel Gabriel to Nazareth, a village in Galilee, to a virgin
named Mary. She was engaged to be married to a man
named Joseph, a descendant of King David. Gabriel appeared to her and said, "Greetings, favored woman! The
Lord is with you!"*

*Confused and disturbed, Mary tried to think what the angel
could mean. "Don't be afraid, Mary," the angel told her,
"for you have found favor with God! You will conceive and
give birth to a son, and you will name him Jesus. He will be
very great and will be called the Son of the Most High. The
Lord God will give him the throne of his ancestor David.
And he will reign over Israel forever; his Kingdom will
never end!"*

*Mary asked the angel, "But how can this happen? I am a
virgin." The angel replied, "The Holy Spirit will come upon
you, and the power of the Most High will overshadow you.
So the baby to be born will be holy, and he will be called
the Son of God. What's more, your relative Elizabeth has
become pregnant in her old age! People used to say she was
barren, but she has conceived a son and is now in her sixth
month. For the word of God will never fail."*

Mary responded, "I am the Lord's servant. May everything you have said about me come true." And then the angel left her. (Luke 1:26-38)

Again, Luke the Physician recounts every detail from his gospel research, and he makes the Virgin Birth very plain to his readers.

6. *John taught it (John 1:14)*

The context of John's first chapter is clear – it's all about all the things that God has caused to happen – creation, the arrival of light in the darkness, our adoption as God's children, and the Word becoming flesh. John's is the last gospel to be written. He knew of the work of Mark, Matthew, and Luke, and so he would clearly have Jesus' conception by the Holy Spirit (God-caused) and the Virgin Birth in mind as he wrote about Jesus' incarnation:

So the Word became human and made his home among us. He was full of unfailing love and faithfulness. And we have seen his glory, the glory of the Father's one and only Son. (John 1:14)

7. *Paul taught it (Galatians 4:4-5)*

Some say that Paul never taught on the Virgin Birth, but just because we don't have a direct statement about it in his letters does not mean he never taught on it. In fact, Galatians 4 is likely a reference to it by Paul:

But when the right time came, God sent his Son, born of a woman, subject to the law. God sent him to buy freedom for us who were slaves to the law, so that he could adopt us as his very own children. And because we are his children, God has sent the Spirit of his Son into our hearts, prompting us to call out, "Abba, Father." Now you are no longer a slave but God's own child. And since you are his child, God has made you his heir. (Galatians 4:4-7)

We know that Luke was a traveling companion of Paul's and was likely working on both his gospel account and Acts while he was with him. Luke clearly understood and wrote about both Jesus' conception by the Holy Spirit and the Virgin Birth. Paul also was a Pharisee, and as such, would have been required to know the prophecies from the Old Testament era by heart. Paul knew about the Virgin Birth.

Here's the point: If all these authors over a nearly 2000-year period all believed it and taught it, then it's either true, they are deceived, or they are outright liars. In any case, we could not trust anything they teach or write if the Virgin Birth is a lie. That means you have to distrust and ignore Genesis, Exodus, Leviticus, Numbers, Deuteronomy, Isaiah, Jeremiah, Lamentations, Matthew, Luke and Acts, John, 1, 2 & 3 John, Revelation, Romans, 1 & 2 Corinthians, Galatians, Ephesians, Philippians, Colossians, 1 & 2 Thessalonians, 1 & 2 Timothy, Titus, Philemon and possibly Hebrews (because some think Paul may be its author). Nearly half of the Bible and virtually all of the New Testament would be untrustworthy if the Virgin Birth is not true! Percolate on that for a moment.

THEOLOGICAL IMPLICATIONS

I don't want to get too deep, but this next part is vital to understand.

If Jesus was not conceived by the Holy Spirit and born of a virgin, he was not the Son of God. You read that right. Everything we learned in the previous chapter is moot. If Jesus had a human father, he was not the only begotten Son of God. Period. This means that Jesus could not be the Christ. This means that Jesus has no rightful claim of lordship over our lives. If Jesus had a human father, then he did not share God's nature – Jesus would only be human.

But Jesus *was* conceived by the Holy Spirit and born of a virgin, so he was the Son of God and could accomplish God's purposes.

> *After his baptism, as Jesus came up out of the water, the heavens were opened and he saw the Spirit of God descending like a dove and settling on him. And a voice from heaven said, "This is my dearly loved Son, who brings me great joy."* (Matthew 3:16-17)

> *Six days later Jesus took Peter and the two brothers, James and John, and led them up a high mountain to be alone. As the men watched, Jesus' appearance was transformed so that his face*

shone like the sun, and his clothes became as white as light. Suddenly, Moses and Elijah appeared and began talking with Jesus. Peter exclaimed, "Lord, it's wonderful for us to be here! If you want, I'll make three shelters as memorials—one for you, one for Moses, and one for Elijah." But even as he spoke, a bright cloud overshadowed them, and a voice from the cloud said, "This is my dearly loved Son, who brings me great joy. Listen to him." (Matthew 17:1-5)

So they arrived at the other side of the lake, in the region of the Gerasenes. When Jesus climbed out of the boat, a man possessed by an evil spirit came out from the tombs to meet him. This man lived in the burial caves and could no longer be restrained, even with a chain. Whenever he was put into chains and shackles—as he often was—he snapped the chains from his wrists and smashed the shackles. No one was strong enough to subdue him. Day and night he wandered among the burial caves and in the hills, howling and cutting himself with sharp stones. When Jesus was still some distance away, the man saw him, ran to meet him, and bowed low before him. With a shriek, he screamed, "Why are you interfering with me, Jesus, Son of the Most High God? In the name of God, I beg you, don't torture me!" For Jesus had already said to the spirit, "Come out of the man, you evil spirit." (Mark 5:1-8)

So Jesus explained, "I tell you the truth, the Son can do nothing by himself. He does only what he sees the Father doing. Whatever the Father does, the Son also does. For the Father loves the Son and shows him everything he is doing. In fact, the Father will show him how to do even greater works than healing this man. Then you will truly be astonished. For just as the Father gives life to those he raises from the dead, so the Son gives life to anyone he wants. In addition, the Father judges no one. Instead, he has given the Son absolute authority to judge, so that everyone will honor the Son, just as they honor the Father. Anyone who does not honor the Son is certainly not honoring the Father who sent him. "I tell you the truth, those who listen to my message and believe in God who sent me have eternal life. They will never be condemned for their sins, but they have already passed from death into life. (John 5:19-24)

In your own time, look at Romans 1:4, Hebrews 1:5, 1 John 4:10, and Galatians 4:4-7.

If Jesus was not conceived by the Holy Spirit and born of a virgin, there is no incarnation. This may seem incredibly obvious, but it's important. The incarnation is the point in history when Jesus, as the second person of our Triune God, took on human flesh. God became man. The ultimate revelation of God to humanity is found in the *man*, Jesus the Christ!

> *You must have the same attitude that Christ Jesus had. Though he was God, he did not think of equality with God as something to cling to. Instead, he gave up his divine privileges; he took the humble position of a slave and was born as a human being. When he appeared in human form, he humbled himself in obedience to God and died a criminal's death on a cross. Therefore, God elevated him to the place of highest honor and gave him the name above all other names, that at the name of Jesus every knee should bow, in heaven and on earth and under the earth, and every tongue declare that Jesus Christ is Lord, to the glory of God the Father.* (Philippians 2:5-11)

If Jesus was not conceived by the Holy Spirit and born of a virgin, God has not been revealed to us in Christ, and, frankly, he is a lying imposter. But because Jesus *was* conceived by the Holy Spirit and born of a virgin, he is the perfect union of God and humanity. And keep in mind that this union between God and humanity is one of the primary issues many of the great creeds were written to defend.

In your own time, look at Romans 1:1-4; 9:1-5; Colossians 2:9-10; and 1 John 4:1-3.

If Jesus was not conceived by the Holy Spirit and born of a virgin, he was not free of sin. The apostle Paul writes,

> *When we were utterly helpless, Christ came at just the right time and died for us sinners. Now, most people would not be willing to die for an upright person, though someone might perhaps be willing to die for a person who is especially good. But God showed his great love for us by sending Christ to die for us while*

we were still sinners. And since we have been made right in God's sight by the blood of Christ, he will certainly save us from God's condemnation. For since our friendship with God was restored by the death of his Son while we were still his enemies, we will certainly be saved through the life of his Son. So now we can rejoice in our wonderful new relationship with God because our Lord Jesus Christ has made us friends of God. (Romans 5:6-11)

Part of Jesus having his Heavenly Father's nature is that Jesus was free from all sin. He was conceived by the *Holy* Spirit. If Jesus had a human father and mother, he would necessarily have inherited humanity's sin cycle (Romans 5:12-14). In fact, King David tells us that every single human being is conceived in sin:

Have mercy on me, O God, because of your unfailing love. Because of your great compassion, blot out the stain of my sins. Wash me clean from my guilt. Purify me from my sin. For I recognize my rebellion; it haunts me day and night. Against you, and you alone, have I sinned; I have done what is evil in your sight. You will be proved right in what you say, and your judgment against me is just. **For I was born a sinner— yes, from the moment my mother conceived me.** *But you desire honesty from the womb, teaching me wisdom even there. Purify me from my sins, and I will be clean; wash me, and I will be whiter than snow. Oh, give me back my joy again; you have broken me— now let me rejoice. Don't keep looking at my sins. Remove the stain of my guilt. Create in me a clean heart, O God. Renew a loyal spirit within me. Do not banish me from your presence, and don't take your Holy Spirit from me.* (Psalm 51:1-11, **emphasis mine**)

The only way that this generational sin cycle of humanity could be broken is for Jesus to have a Divine, sin-free Father! Because Jesus was conceived by the *Holy* Spirit and born of a virgin, he was conceived without sin.

For God made Christ, who never sinned, to be the offering for our sin, so that we could be made right with God through Christ. (2 Corinthians 5:21)

In your own time, look at Hebrews 4:15, 1 Peter 2:22, and 1 John 3:5.

If Jesus was not conceived by the Holy Spirit and born of a virgin, we have no hope of salvation. If Jesus had a human father and mother, he could not redeem us.

> *But when the right time came, God sent his Son, born of a woman, subject to the law. God sent him to buy freedom for us who were slaves to the law, so that he could adopt us as his very own children. And because we are his children, God has sent the Spirit of his Son into our hearts, prompting us to call out, "Abba, Father." Now you are no longer a slave but God's own child. And since you are his child, God has made you his heir.* (Galatians 4:4-7)

To redeem humanity, Jesus had to have a divine nature. To redeem humanity, Jesus had to be sin-free. To redeem humanity, Jesus had to be eternal. And none of these facts would be true of Jesus if both his parents were human beings! But because Jesus was indeed conceived by the Holy Spirit and born of a virgin, he could take on all the sins of the world and give us his righteousness!

In your own time, look at John 1:29, 1 John 3:5, and 1 John 4:10.

"I believe in Jesus Christ…who was conceived by the Holy Spirit and born of the Virgin Mary…" It's so important for us to come to know Jesus' unique conception and Virgin Birth so that we can trust the veracity of the Bible, believe that Jesus really is the Son of God, understand the importance of his dual nature as the God-man, trust that he is sin-free and thereby we can be saved.

STUDY GUIDE

IT MAKES A DIFFERENCE

Admittedly, the doctrines of Jesus' conception by the Holy Spirit and his Virgin Birth are challenging to understand. But this makes them no less critical to embrace! Those who accept their essential nature tend to have a much deeper appreciation of their salvation and a more steadfast belief in the unity and authority of the scriptures. They know these are not "peripheral" matters but of central importance to their Faith. They understand that these two doctrines, taken together, are essential to the person and work of Jesus – or he could not have been who he claimed himself to be.

Those who do not believe in, or have not considered the implications of Jesus' Holy Spirit conception and Virgin Birth, miss a pivotal foundation block to their Faith. They have not engaged in dialog regarding the ramifications of minimizing these doctrines, and they likely don't realize how many other components of their belief are impacted by such a view. Those in this position usually have not considered the other critical doctrines of the Christian Faith either. They find it more difficult to explain (let alone defend) their Faith and tend to have a much shallower understanding of their own salvation.

If Christ was not conceived by the Holy Spirit and born of a virgin, Christianity is a false religion.

HOW DO I LIVE OUT WHAT I HAVE JUST LEARNED IN MY OWN LIFE?

1. Take a moment to stop and pray. Ask God, through the Holy Spirit, to increase your understanding of the essentials of the Christian Faith. Ask Him to reveal and clarify any points which have been confusing or unclear.

2. Take time to read the additional scriptures referred to at the end of each of the points in the section *Theological Implications.* Consider how each supports the proposition stated in italics that precedes it.

3. Have you encountered someone who claims to doubt the Virgin Birth of Christ? Have you questioned it yourself? Did you feel prepared to defend this doctrine? How has this chapter helped?

4. Take several days to consider: Who can help you apply what you learn to put it into an ongoing life's practice?

5. How are you living this out right now? How is your life reflective of your understanding of this truth?

HOW DO I IMPART WHAT I HAVE JUST LEARNED TO CHILDREN?

Preparing to teach this lesson to children: *Run off copies of the words to the Christmas carol "Silent Night," plus any other familiar carols you desire to use that are theologically sound. Consider gathering printed pictures, or bookmark some on your computer or cell phone, that show Christmas symbols with religious significance such as the nativity scene, candles, stars, or Christmas gifts.*

1. Begin by praying with the children. Ask God, through the Holy Spirit, to help the children understand more about the Christian faith. Ask God to help them clearly understand the new things they are about to learn.

2. Continue to work with the children on memorizing the Apostle's Creed. Be sure they have memorized through this part: *I believe in God, the Father almighty, creator of heaven and earth. I believe in Jesus Christ, his only Son, our Lord, who was conceived by the Holy Spirit and born of the virgin Mary.*

3. Take time to compare and contrast Jesus' birth with the birth of other babies with which the children might be familiar.

4. Sing the first verse of the Christmas carol *"Silent Night."* Be sure to provide a printed copy of the words. Children have been known to misunderstand some of them. In child-appropriate terms, discuss what the phrases *"Round yon Virgin mother and child"* and *"Holy Infant so tender and mild"* mean. (*Holy* means set apart for a certain divine purpose). Talk about why we sing songs like this at Christmas and why Christmas is such a "big deal" on the Christian calendar.

5. Discuss Christmas customs that remind us of Jesus' birth, such as gift-giving, Christmas pageants, Christmas candles, and Christmas carols that talk about Jesus.

6. If you have children in your group who have not yet surrendered to Jesus, continue praying for the Holy Spirit to open that

conversational door so you can explain the gospel. Once they receive Christ, the indwelling presence of the Holy Spirit will make the lessons in this book much more accessible to them.

HOW DO I IMPART WHAT I HAVE JUST LEARNED TO TEENS?

1. Begin by praying with the teens. Ask God, through the Holy Spirit, to increase understanding. You can do this or ask a volunteer.

2. Read the Apostles' Creed out loud. Read it yourself, ask for a volunteer, or read it in unison.

3. Repeat the first few lines: *I believe in God, the Father almighty, creator of heaven and earth. I believe in Jesus Christ, his only Son, our Lord, who was conceived by the Holy Spirit and born of the virgin Mary,* giving purposeful emphasis to each stanza. Encourage the teens to commit this to memory.

4. Have the teens pull out their Question Journals. Ask them to jot down the answers to any questions about the Creed that are answered in this session. Have them share those discoveries, giving them sufficient time to record any thoughts they wish to capture. Assure them that they can ask any remaining questions about this section at the end of the session.

5. Ask the teens why they believe so many people struggle with the truth of the Virgin Birth as presented in scripture.

6. Ask the teens to review the teachings about Jesus' birth as they are traced through the Old and New Testaments in the *Practical Implications* section, especially focusing on the last paragraph. Discuss why this is compelling evidence for the special circumstance of Jesus' birth.

7. Ask the teens to re-read the four theological implications outlined in the *Theological Implications* section. Why are those truths so essential to the Christian faith?

8. Ask the teens why and how the Virgin Birth matters to them.

9. Ask the teens what they could say to a friend who doubts the truth or importance of the Virgin Birth that might cause them to be willing to reconsider their stance.

10. Allow the teens to ask any questions about the Virgin Birth that they had noted in their journals that were not addressed in this discussion. Ask them if/how their understanding of Jesus changed through what they learned in this session.

11. If you have teens in your group who have not yet surrendered to Jesus, continue to pray for the Holy Spirit to open that conversational door so you can explain the gospel. Once they receive Christ, the indwelling presence of the Holy Spirit will make the lessons in this book much more accessible to them.

HOW DO I IMPART WHAT I HAVE JUST LEARNED TO ADULTS?

1. Challenge your adults to take a moment to stop and pray, asking God, through the Holy Spirit, to increase their understanding of the essentials of the Christian Faith. Encourage them to ask Him to reveal and clarify any points which have been confusing or unclear.

2. Review the Apostles' Creed, emphasizing the first few lines: *I believe in God, the Father almighty, creator of heaven and earth. I believe in Jesus Christ, his only Son, our Lord, who was conceived by the Holy Spirit and born of the virgin Mary.* If they have not done so, encourage them to memorize the Creed in its entirety, reminding them that it summarizes the essentials of the faith.

3. Have participants pull out the notes they made during the last session. Ask them to jot down the answers to any questions about the Creed that may be answered during this session, and to share those discoveries as they happen. Provide sufficient time to record any thoughts they may wish to capture. Assure them that they will have the opportunity to ask any remaining questions about this section at the end of the session.

4. Ask participants to review the teachings about Jesus' birth as traced through the Old and New Testaments in the *Practical Implications* section, especially focusing on the last paragraph. Discuss why this is compelling evidence for the special circumstance of Jesus' birth.

5. Ask participants to re-read the four theological implications set forth in the *Theological Implications* section. How do these truths support the contention that the Holy Spirit conception and Virgin Birth are essential doctrines to the Christian faith?

6. Ask participants what they could say to a friend who doubts the truth or importance of the Virgin Birth that might cause them to be willing to reconsider their stance.

7. Allow participants to ask any questions about Jesus' conception by the Holy Spirit and Virgin Birth they had previously noted that were not addressed in this discussion.

8. If you have people in your group who have not yet surrendered to Jesus, continue to pray for the Holy Spirit to open that conversational door so you can explain the gospel. Once they receive Christ, the indwelling presence of the Holy Spirit will make the lessons in this book much more accessible to them.

CHAPTER 5
Jesus: Suffering, Death and Burial

"I believe in Jesus Christ...who suffered under Pontius Pilate, was crucified, died and was buried..."

After they had nailed him to the cross, the soldiers gambled for his clothes by throwing dice. Then they sat around and kept guard as he hung there. A sign was fastened above Jesus' head, announcing the charge against him. It read: "This is Jesus, the King of the Jews." Two revolutionaries were crucified with him, one on his right and one on his left.

The people passing by shouted abuse, shaking their heads in mockery. "Look at you now!" they yelled at him. "You said you were going to destroy the Temple and rebuild it in three days. Well then, if you are the Son of God, save yourself and come down from the cross!"

The leading priests, the teachers of religious law, and the elders also mocked Jesus. "He saved others," they scoffed, "but he can't save himself! So he is the King of Israel, is he? Let him come down from the cross right now, and we will believe in him! He trusted God, so let God rescue him now if he wants him! For he said, 'I am the Son of God.'" Even the revolutionaries who were crucified with him ridiculed him in the same way.

At noon, darkness fell across the whole land until three o'clock. At about three o'clock, Jesus called out with a loud voice, "Eli, Eli, lema sabachthani?" which means "My God, my God, why have you abandoned me?"

Some of the bystanders misunderstood and thought he was calling for the prophet Elijah. One of them ran and filled a sponge with sour wine, holding it up to him on a reed stick so he could drink. But the rest said, "Wait! Let's see whether Elijah comes to save him."

Then Jesus shouted out again, and he released his spirit. At that moment the curtain in the sanctuary of the Temple was torn in two, from top to bottom. The earth shook, rocks split apart, and tombs opened. The bodies of many godly men and women who had died were raised from the dead. They left the cemetery after Jesus' resurrection, went into the holy city of Jerusalem, and appeared to many people.

The Roman officer and the other soldiers at the crucifixion were terrified by the earthquake and all that had happened. They said, "This man truly was the Son of God!"

And many women who had come from Galilee with Jesus to care for him were watching from a distance. Among them were Mary Magdalene, Mary (the mother of James and Joseph), and the mother of James and John, the sons of Zebedee.

As evening approached, Joseph, a rich man from Arimathea who had become a follower of Jesus, went to Pilate and asked for Jesus' body. And Pilate issued an order to release it to him. Joseph took the body and wrapped it in a long sheet of clean linen cloth. He placed it in his own new tomb, which had been carved out of the rock. Then he rolled a great stone across the entrance and left. (Matthew 27:25-60)

How often do you read the crucifixion account? Years ago, I preached on the crucifixion of Christ as part of a larger series on Matthew, and that message fell in October. After the worship service was concluded, a parishioner told me they didn't remember ever reading that passage at a time other than Holy Week. That's a shame. But I'll bet it's more common than we'd like to think.

Jesus' suffering and death are the heart of our Christian Faith. It is the pivotal point of all history and also of all Christian theology. As I already pointed out, the whole Old Testament looks forward to the cross. And after the gospels, the entire New Testament looks back to the cross. Paul wrote about the importance of the cross in his letters. The cross is truly the most evil thing and the most beautiful thing in history simultaneously.

God is all-powerful. He actually used Satan's ultimate act of revenge against Christ to accomplish our complete redemption! As sinful humanity, driven by a Satanic appetite against God, put Jesus to death on the cross at Calvary, we followed through on the very sacrifice that would set us free! God was never not in control.

DID IT REALLY HAPPEN?

Some question the veracity of the crucifixion of Christ. They believe it's a myth. Still others have relegated the crucifixion story to one Sunday a year and give it very little thought the other 364 days. But the crucifixion of Jesus the Christ is one of the most-reported events in history. And we have multiple non-Christian sources that confirm it.

1. *Jewish historian Flavius Josephus reports about it.* Josephus lived during the time of Christ and was a trusted historian. He is best known for his *Antiquities of the Jews.* Josephus was a priest and eventually joined the Pharisees. As a Jew, he had no vested interest in reporting on the crucifixion. It was just a matter of current events.

2. *Roman historian Tacitus reports about it.* Tacitus was both an historian and a politician. He is widely regarded as one of the great Roman historians of his day. His work, *Annals*, is filled with references to the life and ministry of Jesus, including the crucifixion. Tacitus was a non-Christian Roman who actually did not think highly of the Christian movement. So his report is very helpful in confirming many facts about Jesus' life from a non-Biblical perspective.

3. *Roman historian Suetonius reports about it.* Suetonius is most famous for his histories about the Roman emperors. He reports widely about the Christian movement in his biography of Nero.

4. *Roman Governor Pliny the Younger refers to it.* Pliny the Younger provided many letters of historical significance. And in some of these, he refers to the Christian community and their need to be punished, even referencing executions – including the crucifixion of Christ.

5. *The gospels detail it.* This, of course, goes without saying. Even so, the gospels are important historical works in themselves. Because other sources can corroborate them, their information is essential even in non-Christian circles.

6. *The Letters of Paul explain it.* Paul goes into great detail in explaining the importance of Jesus' death on the cross. Again, this may be expected, but the historicity of his letters is well known.

7. *Hundreds of eyewitnesses confirm it.* The crucifixion took place at a busy crossroads for a reason. The Romans used this method to create a public deterrent to crime and uprisings. Literally hundreds of people would have been witnesses to the crucifixion, and these could verify the reports about it in the days and months (even years) that followed.

8. *Various and sundry other extra-biblical manuscript segments attest to it.*

The life and the death of Jesus are just as well documented as the life and impact of Julius Caesar! Therefore, we can trust the account's veracity and spend our time and energy learning why it is so critically important.

WHAT DID IT ACCOMPLISH?

Now we come to one of the most essential questions we face as believers in Jesus the Christ: What did Jesus' death accomplish? What follows is beautifully instructive and horribly sobering at the same time. And it is all on our behalf.

Jesus' death was about substitution. Jesus' death was substitutionary. Jesus suffered and died *in our place.* Jesus, who had no sin, took on our sin! (2 Corinthians 5:21) Theologian Elmer Towns notes that 21 different passages in Scripture explicitly say Jesus died for us.

Paul writes to the Christians at Rome,

> *Therefore, since we have been made right in God's sight by faith, we have peace with God because of what Jesus Christ our Lord has done for us. Because of our faith, Christ has brought us into this place of undeserved privilege where we now stand, and we confidently and joyfully look forward to sharing God's glory.*
>
> *We can rejoice, too, when we run into problems and trials, for we know that they help us develop endurance. And endurance develops strength of character, and character strengthens our confident hope of salvation. And this hope will not lead to disappointment. For we know how dearly God loves us, because he has given us the Holy Spirit to fill our hearts with his love.*
>
> *When we were utterly helpless, Christ came at just the right time and died for us sinners. Now, most people would not be willing to die for an upright person, though someone might perhaps be willing to die for a person who is especially good. But God showed his great love for us by sending Christ to die for us while we were still sinners.* (Romans 5:1-8)

And Peter tells his readers,

> *For God called you to do good, even if it means suffering, just as Christ suffered for you. He is your example, and you must follow in his steps.*
>
> *He never sinned, nor ever deceived anyone.*
>
> *He did not retaliate when he was insulted, nor threaten revenge when he suffered.*
>
> *He left his case in the hands of God, who always judges fairly.*
>
> *He personally carried our sins in his body on the cross so that we can be dead to sin and live for what is right.*

By his wounds you are healed.

Once you were like sheep who wandered away.

But now you have turned to your Shepherd, the Guardian of your souls. (1 Peter 2:21-25)

Finally, it is the theme of heaven's worship.

And they sang a new song with these words:

"You are worthy to take the scroll and break its seals and open it. For you were slaughtered, and your blood has ransomed people for God from every tribe and language and people and nation. And you have caused them to become a Kingdom of priests for our God. And they will reign on the earth." (Revelation 5:8-10)

Jesus voluntarily stepped into our place, taking our punishment for our sin, fully substituting for us under the wrath of God.

Jesus' death was about redemption. What does it mean to redeem something? Its most basic definition is that someone pays a price to regain possession of something or someone. For those who love the Old Testament story of Ruth, Boaz is called a "Kinsman-redeemer." Boaz literally redeems the whole family line of his distant cousin, Elimelech, by redeeming and marrying Ruth. For us, Jesus' death has paid the *ransom price* for our souls. We are redeemed. And Jesus understood that this was his ultimate mission. He tells his disciples,

But among you it will be different. Whoever wants to be a leader among you must be your servant, and whoever wants to be first among you must become your slave. For even the Son of Man came not to be served but to serve others and to give his life as a ransom for many." (Matthew 20:26-28)

The apostle Paul explains that, in God's grace, the penalty (price) has been paid for our sins by Jesus and that by punishing Jesus, God demonstrates he is still righteous by not ignoring sin.

For everyone has sinned; we all fall short of God's glorious standard. Yet God, in his grace, freely makes us right in his sight. He did this through Christ Jesus when he freed us from the penalty for our sins. For God presented Jesus as the sacrifice for sin. People are made right with God when they believe that Jesus sacrificed his life, shedding his blood. This sacrifice shows that God was being fair when he held back and did not punish those who sinned in times past, for he was looking ahead and including them in what he would do in this present time. God did this to demonstrate his righteousness, for he himself is fair and just, and he makes sinners right in his sight when they believe in Jesus. (Romans 3:23-26)

Paul teaches Timothy that this redemption purchased our freedom.

There is one God and one Mediator who can reconcile God and humanity—the man Christ Jesus. He gave his life to purchase freedom for everyone. This is the message God gave to the world at just the right time. (1 Timothy 2:5-6)

Peter makes it abundantly clear that we were *ransomed* by Jesus.

And remember that the heavenly Father to whom you pray has no favorites. He will judge or reward you according to what you do. So you must live in reverent fear of him during your time here as "temporary residents." For you know that God paid a ransom to save you from the empty life you inherited from your ancestors. And it was not paid with mere gold or silver, which lose their value. It was the precious blood of Christ, the sinless, spotless Lamb of God. God chose him as your ransom long before the world began, but now in these last days he has been revealed for your sake. (1 Peter 1:17-20)

Jesus' death is about atonement. Jesus' death provided full restoration of what had been destroyed by sin and Satan. Atonement is actually a compound word that simply means at-ONE-ment. It is making what is broken, tainted, destroyed whole again.

The writer of Hebrews explains that this atoning work of restoration was personal.

> *Therefore, it was necessary for him to be made in every respect like us, his brothers and sisters, so that he could be our merciful and faithful High Priest before God. Then he could offer a sacrifice that would take away the sins of the people. Since he himself has gone through suffering and testing, he is able to help us when we are being tested.* (Hebrews 2:17-18)

And the apostle John describes this atoning work's value to the whole world.

> *My dear children, I am writing this to you so that you will not sin. But if anyone does sin, we have an advocate who pleads our case before the Father. He is Jesus Christ, the one who is truly righteous. He himself is the sacrifice that atones for our sins— and not only our sins but the sins of all the world.* (1 John 2:1-2)

He goes on to show how this atoning work should ultimately impact all of our relationships as well.

> *Dear friends, let us continue to love one another, for love comes from God. Anyone who loves is a child of God and knows God. But anyone who does not love does not know God, for God is love.*
>
> *God showed how much he loved us by sending his one and only Son into the world so that we might have eternal life through him. This is real love—not that we loved God, but that he loved us and sent his Son as a sacrifice to take away our sins.*
>
> *Dear friends, since God loved us that much, we surely ought to love each other.* (1 John 4:7-11).

Jesus' death was about satisfaction. God is righteous. God's law is righteous. Sin must be punished. The penalty cannot be ignored. God is love – this is true and is the reason Jesus was given (see John 3:16-17), but that does not negate God's utter justice! Jesus' death paid the penalty. Jesus' death *satisfied* the righteousness of God and the requirement of the righteous law. And Jesus understood what he was doing.

> *"Don't misunderstand why I have come. I did not come to abolish the law of Moses or the writings of the prophets. No, I came to accomplish their purpose. I tell you the truth, until heaven and earth disappear, not even the smallest detail of God's law will disappear until its purpose is achieved." (*Matthew 5:17-18)

> *"The Father loves me because I sacrifice my life so I may take it back again. No one can take my life from me. I sacrifice it voluntarily. For I have the authority to lay it down when I want to and also to take it up again. For this is what my Father has commanded."* (John 10:17-18)

Paul explains how Jesus' death brings satisfaction for Jews and Gentiles alike.

> *For Christ himself has brought peace to us. He united Jews and Gentiles into one people when, in his own body on the cross, he broke down the wall of hostility that separated us. He did this by ending the system of law with its commandments and regulations. He made peace between Jews and Gentiles by creating in himself one new people from the two groups. Together as one body, Christ reconciled both groups to God by means of his death on the cross, and our hostility toward each other was put to death.*

> *He brought this Good News of peace to you Gentiles who were far away from him, and peace to the Jews who were near. [18] Now all of us can come to the Father through the same Holy Spirit because of what Christ has done for us.* (Ephesians 2:14-18)

God was satisfied with Jesus' death, canceling the "record of charges" once and for all time.

> *You were dead because of your sins and because your sinful nature was not yet cut away. Then God made you alive with*

Christ, for he forgave all our sins. He canceled the record of the charges against us and took it away by nailing it to the cross. (Colossians 2:13-14)

Jesus' death is about reconciliation. Jesus' death made our forgiveness possible. From the time of Genesis chapter 3, humanity has been at odds with God. Throughout the Old Testament, God repeatedly tries to restore his relationship with the "crown of his creation," humanity. But humanity keeps rejecting those offers. Humanity keeps breaking God's covenant over and over. Our relationship with God, our Father, is *finally* reconciled because of the cross. We're forgiven because of Jesus' death.

Reconciliation is the very heart of our Faith. Jesus left his heavenly throne for the purpose of establishing forgiveness. And so it becomes a primary purpose of every Christ-follower. Paul explains,

> *So we have stopped evaluating others from a human point of view. At one time we thought of Christ merely from a human point of view. How differently we know him now! This means that anyone who belongs to Christ has become a new person. The old life is gone; a new life has begun!*
>
> *And all of this is a gift from God, who brought us back to himself through Christ. And God has given us this task of reconciling people to him. For God was in Christ, reconciling the world to himself, no longer counting people's sins against them. And he gave us this wonderful message of reconciliation. So we are Christ's ambassadors; God is making his appeal through us. We speak for Christ when we plead, "Come back to God!" (2 Corinthians 5:16-20)*

And the reconciliation fostered by Christ's death is thorough.

> *This includes you who were once far away from God. You were his enemies, separated from him by your evil thoughts and actions. Yet now he has reconciled you to himself through the*

death of Christ in his physical body. As a result, he has brought you into his own presence, and you are holy and blameless as you stand before him without a single fault.

But you must continue to believe this truth and stand firmly in it. Don't drift away from the assurance you received when you heard the Good News. The Good News has been preached all over the world, and I, Paul, have been appointed as God's servant to proclaim it. (Colossians 1:21-23)

Jesus' death was about judgment. The death of Jesus ushers in God's ultimate judgment on sin and Satan. Paul beautifully articulates God's judgment on our sin and how it loses its power over us.

Since we have been united with him in his death, we will also be raised to life as he was. We know that our old sinful selves were crucified with Christ so that sin might lose its power in our lives. We are no longer slaves to sin. For when we died with Christ we were set free from the power of sin. And since we died with Christ, we know we will also live with him. We are sure of this because Christ was raised from the dead, and he will never die again. Death no longer has any power over him. When he died, he died once to break the power of sin. But now that he lives, he lives for the glory of God. So you also should consider yourselves to be dead to the power of sin and alive to God through Christ Jesus. (Romans 6:5-11)

Our "old man" or "old nature" that could not *not* sin has been crucified with Christ! We are no longer slaves to sinfulness! We no longer need to fear God's condemnation because it has already been levied on our "old nature."

So now there is no condemnation for those who belong to Christ Jesus. And because you belong to him, the power of the life-giving Spirit has freed you from the power of sin that leads to death. The law of Moses was unable to save us because of the weakness of our sinful nature. So God did what the law could not do. He sent his own Son in a body like the bodies we sinners have. And in that body God declared an end to sin's control over us by giving his Son as a sacrifice for our sins. He did this so that the just requirement of the law would be fully satisfied for us, who no longer follow our sinful nature but instead follow the Spirit. (Romans 8:1-4)

Our old sinful selves have been crucified with Jesus! Jesus accomplished what the Law could not:

My old self has been crucified with Christ. It is no longer I who live, but Christ lives in me. So I live in this earthly body by trusting in the Son of God, who loved me and gave himself for me. I do not treat the grace of God as meaningless. For if keeping the law could make us right with God, then there was no need for Christ to die. (Galatians 2:20-21)

But the death of Christ doesn't just bring God's judgment on our sin; it also brings God's judgment on Satan! The Father's prophecy of judgment on the serpent way back in Genesis 3 is now a reality!

Then the Lord God said to the serpent,

"Because you have done this, you are cursed more than all animals, domestic and wild. You will crawl on your belly, groveling in the dust as long as you live. And I will cause hostility between you and the woman, and between your offspring and her offspring. He will strike your head, and you will strike his heel." (Genesis 3:14-15)

Jesus has crushed Satan's head! Jesus has triumphed! His death is the very tool God has used to disarm the powers and authorities of evil. We are free.

When you came to Christ, you were "circumcised," but not by a physical procedure. Christ performed a spiritual circumcision—the cutting away of your sinful nature. For you were buried with Christ when you were baptized. And with him you were raised to new life because you trusted the mighty power of God, who raised Christ from the dead.

You were dead because of your sins and because your sinful nature was not yet cut away. Then God made you alive with Christ, for he forgave all our sins. He canceled the record of the charges against us and took it away by nailing it to the cross. In this way, he disarmed the spiritual rulers and authorities. He shamed them publicly by his victory over them on the cross. (Colossians 2:11-15)

God's righteous judgment has fallen upon both our sin and our enemy!

Finally, Jesus' death was about cleansing. And it's not just a one-time cleansing, but *daily* cleansing. If all these other things are true, then we can also rest assured that God has made a way for us to *remain* free! The apostle John writes,

But if we confess our sins to him, he is faithful and just to forgive us our sins and to cleanse us from all wickedness. If we claim we have not sinned, we are calling God a liar and showing that his word has no place in our hearts. (1 John 1:9-10)

Jesus' death did not just pay the *backward* penalty for our sin; it paid the penalty *forward* as well! And with the ongoing work of the Holy Spirit transforming us from within, we continuously become more like Jesus every day!

Dear friends, we are already God's children, but he has not yet shown us what we will be like when Christ appears. But we do know that we will be like him, for we will see him as he really is. And all who have this eager expectation will keep themselves pure, just as he is pure. (1 John 3:2-3)

"I believe in Jesus Christ, who suffered under Pontius Pilate, was crucified, died, and was buried..." Jesus was a real person with a real history. The crucifixion really happened, and there is ample historical evidence to confirm it. And because Jesus, the very Son of God, died on the cross of Calvary, we know:

- He substituted for us, standing in our place for the punishment of our sin

- He redeemed us, paying the necessary ransom to buy us back for God

- He atoned for us, restoring all that was destroyed by sin

- He satisfied the righteous requirements of God and the Law, so we are declared righteous

- He reconciled us, making full forgiveness possible and opening the way for us to have an eternal covenant relationship with the Father

- He judged both sin and Satan, the final blow to Satan and disarming all spiritual power arrayed against God and his people

- He provides continuous cleansing for all those who surrender to him as Master and Savior, offering new forgiveness for every wayward thought, word, and deed after our initial salvation so we are never condemned again

It's so important that we come to know the truth about Jesus' suffering and death!

STUDY GUIDE

IT MAKES A DIFFERENCE

Christians who trust the biblical account of Jesus' suffering, death, and burial tend to have a very stable faith. They accept the faithfulness of the Scriptures, knowing that these events, as well as others in Jesus' life, are historically affirmed more widely than many other events in Western civilization. More importantly, they realize what Jesus' death accomplished on their behalf: that he died in their place, redeeming them completely from their sins, restoring their relationship with God, and satisfying his punishing wrath. They understand that, because of Jesus' sacrifice, they can be reconciled to God and other human beings. They celebrate that, despite ongoing missteps in this life, they remain beautifully cleansed and righteous before God.

Those who do not trust or have yet to study the Biblical account of Jesus' crucifixion typically question more about the fullness of their salvation. They do not have the blessing of understanding what the Scripture says about Jesus' efforts on their behalf to set them free from sin and death. They have more fear – of God and of dying. And because they do not have a clear understanding of the foundation of reconciliation they have been lovingly given, they tend to have more unreconciled relationships – even open conflict – than their trusting counterparts. They may even continue to try to earn the salvation that, in reality, they already possess because they do not understand how thoroughly they have been cleansed of sin.

HOW DO I LIVE OUT WHAT I HAVE JUST LEARNED IN MY OWN LIFE?

1. Take a moment to stop and pray. Ask God, through the Holy Spirit, to increase your understanding of the essentials of the Christian Faith. Ask Him to reveal and clarify any points which have been confusing or unclear.

2. Meditate on the thought from the introduction, "*The cross is truly the most evil thing and the most beautiful thing in history simultaneously.*" With which descriptor do you most identify? Why?

3. Have you heard someone question the veracity of Jesus' death by crucifixion? How would this chapter help you answer that question?

4. What has Christ's death on the cross accomplished in your life?

5. Take several days to consider: Who can help you apply what you learn to put it into an ongoing life's practice?

6. How are you living this out right now? How is your life reflective of your understanding of this truth?

HOW DO I IMPART WHAT I HAVE JUST LEARNED TO CHILDREN?

***Preparing to teach this lesson to children:** See suggestion #6 below. Decide how you want to create the visual representation of the cross with the children. Gather the needed supplies ahead of the lesson.*

1. Begin by praying with the children. Ask God, through the Holy Spirit, to help the children understand more about the Christian faith. Ask God to help them clearly understand the new things they are about to learn.

2. Continue to work with the children on memorizing the Apostle's Creed. Be sure they have memorized through this part: *I believe in God, the Father almighty, creator of heaven and earth. I believe in Jesus Christ, his only Son, our Lord, who was conceived by the Holy Spirit and born of the virgin Mary. He suffered under Pontius Pilate, was crucified, died, and was buried...*

3. Ask the children if they have ever been treated unfairly. Most have – at least from their perspective. Tell them that Satan put it in certain people's hearts to treat Jesus unfairly. He never did anything wrong, but these people, because of Satan's prompting, accused him of mocking and dishonoring God. They had Jesus beaten, killed, and buried. Most children have had enough experience with the death of a pet, a family friend, a grandparent, or perhaps someone closer, to know that death is usually final here on earth. Let them know that even though that is the case for regular people, Jesus was stronger than even death! God would fool and defeat Satan's plan to keep Jesus dead. We will talk more about that in another chapter.

4. Tell the children a story about someone who took another person's punishment. Tell one from your experience or use this one: *Virginia was just learning to drive, and by accident, she ran into the neighbor's fence. Her car was not seriously damaged, but the fence was ruined. No one saw who did it, but she went home and tearfully confessed to her dad what happened. Her dad went to the neighbor and let him know that one of his children had hit the fence. Her dad paid the neighbor for a new fence, even though it was Virginia, not he, who caused the damage. The family did not have a lot of money, so it cost him a lot to accept the responsibility for something he did not do.* Ask the children why someone would do such a thing. Perhaps they will recognize it means the person who

took the punishment did it out of love. If they do not, guide their thinking in that direction. Talk to them in child-appropriate language about sin, which always deserves punishment, and tell them that Jesus volunteered to take the punishment for our sin because he loves us.

5. Explain to the children that the penalty for sin is death. In Old Testament times, the punishment for sin was that an animal had to die in place of the person who sinned. This was called animal sacrifice. Jesus was perfect, so he was the perfect sacrifice. We no longer have to kill animals to hide our sin and make our lives right before God. Because of Jesus, God sees our lives as clean if we ask him to forgive our sin. This is the reason perfect Jesus died.

6. Talk to the children about the fact that Jesus' death for our sake is why we see the cross as a symbol of the Christian faith. The cross was the way Jesus was killed, and seeing the symbol of the cross reminds us that Jesus took our punishment for sin so that we don't have to be punished. The cross reminds us to be grateful.

7. Have the children draw a picture of a cross and write a "Thank you Jesus" message over or under it. If you have time, you may choose to have the children make a cross to take home from sticks or other materials. Here is a link to several ideas: *https:// modpodgerocksblog.com/cross-crafts/* Some are very simple, others more complex, so choose one that works for you and the age of children you are working with.

8. If you have children in your group who have not yet surrendered to Jesus, continue to pray for the Holy Spirit to open that conversational door so you can explain the gospel. Once they receive Christ, the indwelling presence of the Holy Spirit will make the lessons in this book much more accessible to them.

HOW DO I IMPART WHAT I HAVE JUST LEARNED TO TEENS?

1. Begin by praying with the teens. Ask God, through the Holy Spirit, to increase understanding. You can do this or ask a volunteer.

2. Read the Apostles' Creed out loud. Read it yourself, ask for a volunteer, or read it in unison.

3. Repeat the first few lines with purposeful emphasis: *I believe in God, the Father almighty, creator of heaven and earth. I believe in Jesus Christ, his only Son, our Lord, who was conceived by the Holy Spirit and born of the virgin Mary. He suffered under Pontius Pilate, was crucified, died, and was buried.* Encourage the teens to commit this to memory.

4. Have the teens pull out their Question Journals. Ask them to jot down the answers to any questions about the Creed that are answered in this session. Have them share those discoveries, giving them sufficient time to record any thoughts they wish to capture. Assure them that they can ask any remaining questions about this section at the end of the session.

5. Re-read this statement near the end of the introduction: *The cross is truly the most evil thing and the most beautiful thing in history simultaneously.* Discuss how that could be true.

6. Ask the teens to review the confirmation statements in the section, *Did it Really Happen?.* Ask if they were aware of the non-biblical records of the event. Discuss how these accounts, taken with scripture, help confirm the truth of the crucifixion.

7. Ask the teens to imagine how grateful they would be to someone who took a punishment they deserved. Point out that this was what Jesus actually did.

8. Read the bullet points near the end of the chapter that detail what Jesus' death accomplished. Point out that in order to apply these truths to our own lives, we simply must accept Jesus' sacrifice for our sins. These truths are immediately applicable to all who will personally accept them.

9. Allow the teens to ask any questions about Jesus' trial, death and/or burial and the importance of these events that they had noted in their journals that were not addressed in this discussion. Ask them if/how their understanding of Jesus changed through what they learned in this session.

10. Ask the teens how they would explain the truth and importance of Christ's suffering and death to someone uncertain about it. If they feel comfortable doing so, they might pair up and role play with someone being the "doubter" and someone explaining how they know the crucifixion happened and the importance it has.

11. If you have teens in your group who have not yet surrendered to Jesus, continue to pray for the Holy Spirit to open that conversational door so you can explain the gospel. Once they receive Christ, the indwelling presence of the Holy Spirit will make the lessons in this book much more accessible to them.

HOW DO I IMPART WHAT I HAVE JUST LEARNED TO ADULTS?

1. Challenge your adults to take a moment to stop and pray, asking God, through the Holy Spirit, to increase their understanding of the essentials of the Christian Faith. Encourage them to ask Him to reveal and clarify any points which have been confusing or unclear.

2. Review the Apostles' Creed, emphasizing the first few lines: *I believe in God, the Father almighty, creator of heaven and earth. I believe in Jesus Christ, his only Son, our Lord, who was conceived by the Holy Spirit and born of the virgin Mary. He suffered under Pontius Pilate, was crucified, died, and was buried.* If they have not done so, encourage them to memorize the Creed in its entirety, reminding them that it is a summary of the essentials of the faith.

3. Have participants pull out the notes they made during the last session. Ask them to jot down the answers to any questions about the Creed answered during this session, and to share those discoveries as they happen. Provide sufficient time to record

any thoughts they may wish to capture. Assure them that they will have the opportunity to ask any remaining questions about this section at the end of the session.

4. This chapter states that the suffering and death of Jesus is the heart of the Christian faith. Why would Dr. Kimball make that assertion? What support does the chapter give?

5. How could the section, *Did it Really Happen?* help support the truth of the crucifixion to someone who had doubts? Ask if they were aware of the abundance of extra-biblical evidence for the event and encourage them to discuss the significance of such evidence.

6. Ask participants to take a moment to meditate on the price Jesus paid on their behalf. Read each of the bullet points at the end of the chapter slowly, allowing time for each person to think about how each truth affects their own life and the lives of those they love. At the end of this time, invite participants to share any feelings, questions, or insights this exercise raised.

7. Allow participants to ask any questions about Jesus' suffering and death they had noted previously that were not addressed in this discussion.

8. If you have people in your group who have not yet surrendered to Jesus, continue to pray for the Holy Spirit to open that conversational door so you can explain the gospel. Once they receive Christ, the indwelling presence of the Holy Spirit will make the lessons in this book much more accessible to them.

CHAPTER 6
Jesus: Descent to Hell

"I believe in Jesus Christ... He descended into hell..."

Instead, you must worship Christ as Lord of your life. And if someone asks about your hope as a believer, always be ready to explain it. But do this in a gentle and respectful way. Keep your conscience clear. Then if people speak against you, they will be ashamed when they see what a good life you live because you belong to Christ. Remember, it is better to suffer for doing good, if that is what God wants, than to suffer for doing wrong!

Christ suffered for our sins once for all time. He never sinned, but he died for sinners to bring you safely home to God. He suffered physical death, but he was raised to life in the Spirit.

So he went and preached to the spirits in prison— those who disobeyed God long ago when God waited patiently while Noah was building his boat. Only eight people were saved from drowning in that terrible flood. And that water is a picture of baptism, which now saves you, not by removing dirt from your body, but as a response to God from a clean conscience. It is effective because of the resurrection of Jesus Christ.

Now Christ has gone to heaven. He is seated in the place of honor next to God, and all the angels and authorities and powers accept his authority. (1 Peter 3:15-22)

If the stanza of the Virgin Birth in the Apostles' Creed is the most challenged by non-believers, the stanza about Jesus descending into hell is the most challenged by Christians. And there are some good reasons for it. The words "He descended into hell" are a later amendment to the Creed. That phrase is not actually in the earliest versions, being added about 200 years later around 390 AD. Many Christians are bothered by this phrase, thinking that it means Jesus went to a place where he suffered for sin. They will quickly tell you that Jesus' suffering was indeed real, but it was on the cross. He did not have to suffer in hell. I agree.

AN ONGOING DEBATE

Before we get into the actual biblical teaching itself, discussing the primary divergent interpretations within the Church on this issue may be helpful. The first view says that *Jesus declared victory to dead saints and led them out of Sheol to Heaven.* This is the view held by the Roman Catholic Church. They would believe that Jesus went to meet all those who were faithful to God and died before his incarnation (i.e., when he took on human flesh). These people were waiting – in Sheol, or the place of the dead – for Jesus to open heaven for them.

A second view says that *Jesus declared complete victory over Satan and pronounced condemnation.* This is the view held by many Lutherans today. They would believe that Jesus' whole purpose in hell was to declare his ultimate victory over Satan, sin, death, and the grave. Jesus' descent into hell was, in essence, a victory lap.

A third view says that *Jesus went to paradise, a specific part of Hades, and declared a "fuller" truth of the gospel to them.* This view is held by many in the Anglican Church. They see beauty in the fact that God had not forgotten the faithful dead. Jesus then leads the oppressed out in victory.

A fourth view says that *Jesus went to hell and proclaimed the gospel so people had a second chance for salvation.* And while I would argue that this view comes directly up against scriptures like Hebrews 9:27, which states it is appointed *once* for a man to die and then he faces judgment, various groups hold this view or something similar to it.

A fifth view says that *Jesus did not go to hell and that passages like 1 Peter 3:18ff speak of something altogether different.* Many in the Reformed side of the Church would take this position.

Unlike the other doctrinal statements in the Apostles' Creed, the challenge we face with this stanza is that no single biblical text clearly teaches any of these views. Staunch, biblically-minded people have been all over the map on this topic. The Scripture is just not as cut-and-dried on this point as it is on the others. And yet, the idea was important enough for some of the historic church fathers to include it in a later revision of the Creed.

There is so much more historic investigation we could do, looking at the views of theologians like Ignatius, Polycarp, Justin Martyr, Irenaeus, and even John Calvin, but what I would like to do for our purposes here is to seek a unifying, biblical truth. There are clearly divergent opinions, but there is also considerable agreement. And this is where we must begin.

In what follows, I will lay out for you my own journey on this topic, being as biblically faithful as possible, and explain what I have concluded about this creedal statement and the passages used to support it. In full disclosure, I will also tell you that some of my dearest friends and colleagues in ministry have a different view than I do on some of these points. I will make it clear when I am expressing my own conclusions.

UNIFYING TRUTH

In the quest to find what unifies us all on the doctrinal statement, "Jesus descended into hell," it's essential to begin by understanding some of the terms used. The first term we must define is the Hebrew word *Sheol*. *Sheol* and the Greek word *Hades* refer to the realm of the dead. This is understood in both languages as a temporary place for souls awaiting their final resurrection, either to eternal life and glory or to everlasting judgment and damnation. This is the word used in the Apostles' Creed. It quite literally could be translated (and some say it *should* be translated), "He descended into Hades."

The second term we must define is the Hebrew word *Gehenna*. This is understood as the Hebrew word for hell. Gehenna was a literal place just outside the gates of Jerusalem, formerly used in ancient times for child sacrifice to the false god Molech. By Jesus' day, it was a place used for burning refuse and incinerating/cremating the bodies of diseased people who had died. Jesus used Gehenna as his illustration for hell – a place of outer darkness, rotting stench, continuous fire, suffering, weeping, wailing, and gnashing of teeth.

Hades is a holding place. Gehenna is a place of judgment and torment. They are not the same. This becomes important for us. The later revision of the Apostles' Creed uses the word *hades*. Understanding this, now I will walk you through my own perspective on this stanza of the Apostles' Creed.

Jesus endured God's punishment on the cross on our behalf. Jesus' suffering was endured at Calvary.

> *At noon, darkness fell across the whole land until three o'clock. At about three o'clock, Jesus called out with a loud voice, "Eli, Eli, lema sabachthani?" which means "My God, my God, why have you abandoned me?"*
>
> *Some of the bystanders misunderstood and thought he was calling for the prophet Elijah. One of them ran and filled a sponge with sour wine, holding it up to him on a reed stick so he could drink. But the rest said, "Wait! Let's see whether Elijah comes to save him."*
>
> *Then Jesus shouted out again, and he released his spirit.* (Matthew 27:45-50)

We get just a glimpse of Jesus' agony right near the end when he cries out a plea to his Father. Recall Paul's words to the Christians at Corinth,

> *For God made Christ, who never sinned, to be the offering for*
> *our sin, so that we could be made right with God through Christ.*
> (2 Corinthians 5:21)

The Greek phrase there indicates that Jesus actually *became* sin itself. Because he took on our sin and its related punishment, Jesus finally experienced broken fellowship with God on the cross. Remember that our Triune God is eternal – both toward the past and toward the future. For the first time in eternity, the Son experienced a broken relationship with the Father and the Spirit! It was the final blow he had to endure to take on the human plight in its entirety. Because of sin, all human beings are in broken fellowship with God. For the first time in eternity, Jesus experienced the forsakenness of sin.

Jesus' experience of God's punishing wrath and resulting broken fellowship was part of his suffering on the cross. Therefore, I believe the descent into hell (really Hades) was not for his suffering and punishment – all of that was endured on the cross. All of the camps I mentioned are in agreement on that point.

Jesus declared, "It is finished!" The phrase in Greek corresponds to the declaration "paid in full."

> *Jesus knew that his mission was now finished, and to fulfill Scripture*
> *he said, "I am thirsty." A jar of sour wine was sitting there, so they*
> *soaked a sponge in it, put it on a hyssop branch, and held it up to*
> *his lips. When Jesus had tasted it, he said, "It is finished!" Then he*
> *bowed his head and gave up his spirit.* (John 19:28-30)

Jesus' mission was finished. The debt was paid. There was nothing more to be suffered – nothing more owed. The ransom was given. The total work of atonement and propitiation (satisfying God's wrath) had been completed. We are all in agreement on that point.

Jesus offered up his spirit and died. Jesus was in control of his very life right to the end. Earlier, he taught his followers,

> *"The Father loves me because I sacrifice my life so I may take*
> *it back again. No one can take my life from me. I sacrifice it*

voluntarily. For I have the authority to lay it down when I want to and also to take it up again. For this is what my Father has commanded." (John 10:17-18)

Jesus *gave* his life. A sinless and wholly voluntary sacrifice, he expressed the Father's love and grace by dying, embodying the required penalty for sin. We are all in agreement on that point.

Jesus was not abandoned by the Father to the grave, not did his body see decay. Under the power of the Holy Spirit after the birth of the Church, Peter preaches,

> *"Dear brothers, think about this! You can be sure that the patriarch David wasn't referring to himself, for he died and was buried, and his tomb is still here among us. But he was a prophet, and he knew God had promised with an oath that one of David's own descendants would sit on his throne. David was looking into the future and speaking of the Messiah's resurrection. He was saying that God would not leave him among the dead or allow his body to rot in the grave.*
>
> *"God raised Jesus from the dead, and we are all witnesses of this."* (Acts 2:29-32)

The resurrection of Jesus interrupted the decay process. Death could not hold Jesus! The grave and its decay had no real power over him. We are all in agreement on that point.

Jesus suffered an actual, physical death but was made alive again by the Spirit. In his first letter, Peter writes to the church,

> *Christ suffered for our sins once for all time. He never sinned, but he died for sinners to bring you safely home to God. He suffered physical death, but he was raised to life in the Spirit.* (1 Peter 3:18)

This is the beginning of the passage of Scripture that leads to the creedal statement in question – that Jesus descended into hell. Jesus clearly died physically and was buried physically. His death was a real, human death. We are all in agreement on that point.

Jesus descended into Hades. There is still substantial agreement here, but it begins to diverge in the details. I want to review two Scripture passages as we move through the next few points to give some Biblical context. For this part, let me quote from the New American Standard Bible, as it is one of the most literal, word-for-word English translations we have. Paul writes to the Ephesians,

> *But to each one of us grace was given according to the measure of Christ's gift. Therefore it says,"When He ascended on high, He led captive a host of captives, And He gave gifts to men." (Now this expression, "He ascended," what does it mean except that He also had descended into the lower parts of the earth? He who descended is Himself also He who ascended far above all the heavens, that He might fill all things.)* (Ephesians 4:7-10, New American Standard Bible)

And again, from Peter's first letter to the Church,

> *For Christ also died for sins once for all, the just for the unjust, in order that He might bring us to God, having been put to death in the flesh, but made alive in the spirit; in which also He went and made proclamation to the spirits now in prison, who once were disobedient, when the patience of God kept waiting in the days of Noah, during the construction of the ark, in which a few, that is, eight persons, were brought safely through the water. And corresponding to that, baptism now saves you—not the removal of dirt from the flesh, but an appeal to God for a good conscience— through the resurrection of Jesus Christ, who is at the right hand of God, having gone into heaven, after angels and authorities and powers had been subjected to Him.* (1 Peter 3:18-22, New American Standard Bible)

Both passages talk about a "descending" and an "ascending." Here is where we begin looking at my own conclusions. Many will agree with me, but other biblically faithful people may not.

Jesus preached – he "made proclamation." The word Peter uses in 1 Peter 3:19 is the Greek word *ekeruzen* – the word for ordinary proclamation. It is not the Greek word *euangelizomai* – the word for evangelizing. I believe that Jesus was announcing his total and complete victory in Hades. This is not evangelizing people who have died in their sin! The word here is for preaching. He's not offering salvation to anyone. Rather, he's trumpeting that *heaven's rule and reign is complete!* Satan is defeated!

Jesus preached to disobedient spirits. In the New Testament, "spirit" is not used anywhere else for a departed human being. That would be the word "soul." Every use like this of "spirit" is of a demon or unclean spirit. Now, exactly who these particular spirits are, I don't know. That understanding is above my pay grade. But some theologians believe these may be the "Sons of God" from Genesis 6 – possibly fallen spirits that participated in the depravity of humanity that caused God to bring the flood of Noah on the earth. Look at the passage from 1 Peter again,

> *For Christ also died for sins once for all, the just for the unjust, in order that He might bring us to God, having been put to death in the flesh, but made alive in the spirit; in which also He went and made proclamation to the spirits now in prison, who once were disobedient, when the patience of God kept waiting in the days of Noah, during the construction of the ark...* (1 Peter 3:18-19, New American Standard Bible)

It certainly fits the context. Then add to this Paul's proclamation in Colossians 2:13-15,

> *And when you were dead in your transgressions and the uncircumcision of your flesh, He made you alive together with Him, having forgiven us all our transgressions, having canceled out the certificate of debt consisting of decrees against us and which was hostile to us; and He has taken it out of the way, having nailed it to the cross.* ***When He had disarmed the rulers and authorities, He made a public display of them, having triumphed over them through Him.*** (Colossians 2:13-15, New American Standard Bible, **emphasis mine**)

124

Jesus disarmed them and made a spectacle of them, triumphing over them! And so, my own perspective is that Jesus descended into *Hades* – the realm of the dead – to preach or proclaim his utter victory to the disobedient spirits imprisoned there. Heaven has won!

Finally, *on the third day, Jesus rose from the dead.* The penalty was paid. Satan and his forces were defeated, disarmed, and vanquished. Sin was atoned for. Death was destroyed. And Jesus made a public spectacle of the forces of evil! We joyfully celebrate and give thanks for the Cross of Jesus, his willing sacrifice, his abundant love for us, and his victory over death – on these things we all agree. While there are many differing opinions on what Jesus did while in Hades, we are all again unified in the result. Jesus is Lord!

"I believe in Jesus Christ, …[who] was crucified, died, and was buried; he descended into *hades*. The third day he rose again from the dead…" Hallelujah! Can you agree with me that this truth – even with its different nuances – is important for our faith? Wrapped up in this stanza of our Creed is the truth that Jesus endured God's punishment for our sin on the cross, that the total work of our atonement was completed, that Jesus did all this voluntarily out of his love for us, that the resurrection interrupted the cycle of death and decay – meaning death's power has been broken, and that Jesus took that proclamation of victory all the way to *hades* so that all the forces of darkness would know that heaven won! We serve a powerful and victorious Savior.

STUDY GUIDE

IT MAKES A DIFFERENCE

Many people today do not like to talk about hell. Some churches avoid the subject altogether. But the reality is that Jesus taught more about hell than he did about heaven. Hell is real whether people like it or not. And Christians who understand what the Bible – and specifically Jesus – teaches about hell have a far deeper appreciation for their redemption and eternal life. They know that Jesus' victory over sin and death is all-encompassing for those who surrender to him as the Christ. They believe that Jesus didn't just wear their sins like a cloak but that he actually *became* their sin so they could become righteous in him. They accept the biblical teaching that Jesus voluntarily took their punishment as he hung on the cross. They proclaim that Jesus' resurrection makes it possible for them to rise from the dead one day as well. They celebrate eternal life and that death for the believer is not an end but, indeed, a new beginning.

Those who avoid the subject of hell typically forfeit all of these assurances. In fact, they may not even realize that God offers them. They often have a superficial grasp on the whole concept of redemption and may fall prey to worldly or universalist notions that Jesus saves everyone. Many may also minimize or repudiate the idea of sin. They are usually okay with the proposition that Jesus makes forgiveness and eternal life possible, but they don't like the violence of the cross. Some reject the notion that a loving Heavenly Father would sentence his Son to die. Because these ideas are opposed to the truth of Scripture, those who hold them reject accountability for their sins and live as if they are in charge of their own lives.

HOW DO I LIVE OUT WHAT I HAVE JUST LEARNED IN MY OWN LIFE?

1. Take a moment to stop and pray. Ask God, through the Holy Spirit, to increase your understanding of the essentials of the Christian Faith. Ask Him to reveal and clarify any points which have been confusing or unclear.

2. After reading the chapter, meditate on the unifying truths presented and consider the reasons the church fathers would have found it advisable to add this phrase to the Creed.

3. Take several days to consider: Who can help you apply what you learn to put the truths of this chapter into an ongoing life's practice?

4. How are you living this out right now? How is your life reflective of your understanding of this truth?

HOW DO I IMPART WHAT I HAVE JUST LEARNED TO CHILDREN?

Preparing to teach this lesson to children: *You will create a "Jesus Won" banner for this lesson. Depending on the number of children in your study, their ages, and any physical restrictions because of the location of your lesson, this may take different forms. See # 4 for various ideas. In any event, you will need some form of large paper and crayons, markers, and possibly scissors, glue sticks, and other decorative materials such as shiny or colorful paper or magazine pictures.*

1. Begin by praying with the children. Ask God, through the Holy Spirit, to help the children understand more about the Christian faith. Ask God to help them clearly understand the new things they are about to learn.

2. Continue to work with the children on memorizing the Apostle's Creed. Be sure they have memorized through this part: *I believe in God, the Father almighty, creator of heaven and earth. I believe in Jesus Christ, his only Son, our Lord, who was conceived by the Holy Spirit and born of the virgin Mary. He suffered under Pontius Pilate, was crucified, died, and was buried; he descended into hell.*

3. Let the children know that when regular people die, they go to live with Jesus in heaven (if they were believers) and normally do not come back to earth. Jesus, on the other hand, was stronger than even death. He fooled Satan and defeated his plan to keep Jesus dead. Jesus showed he was stronger and more powerful than even sin and death by going down to hell and announcing his victory!

4. Discuss the fact that Jesus likely descended into hell to announce that he had defeated evil and death once and for all. This is a cause for celebration! Ask the children how they would celebrate a big, important announcement like this. Use some of their ideas to create a "Jesus Won" banner. Below are some ideas of the form this banner could take. Choose one for your

group and gather the materials. If you have a suitable place to do so, these "Victory" banners or posters could be hung in the room to stay throughout the study.

   a. Children could simply write a title such as "Jesus Tells Hell He's the Strongest!" or "Jesus Announces He Won the Battle!" or even simply, "Jesus Won!" or "Jesus is Bigger than Satan!" Children could use markers or crayons to draw their ideas under the title.
   b. After writing the title, children could cut out various pictures or shapes to represent the concept of a victory announcement and glue them on their paper.
   c. If you are working with children who are old enough to work together successfully to agree on and create a design, you could secure a strip of paper several feet long. A roll of butcher paper works nicely. Children could work together, using various materials such as crayons, markers, magazine pictures, colorful shapes, etc. to create a victory banner that celebrates Jesus' announcement that he won and is Lord over all – even death and sin. Be sure to write a title in large letters at the top, bottom, or even through the middle.

5. If you have children in your group who have not yet surrendered to Jesus, continue to pray for the Holy Spirit to open that conversational door so you can explain the gospel. Once they receive Christ, the indwelling presence of the Holy Spirit will make the lessons in this book much more accessible to them.

HOW DO I IMPART WHAT I HAVE JUST LEARNED TO TEENS?

1. Begin by praying with the teens. Ask God, through the Holy Spirit, to increase understanding. You can do this or ask a volunteer.

2. Read the Apostles' Creed out loud. Read it yourself, ask for a volunteer, or read it in unison.

3. Repeat the first few lines: *I believe in God, the Father almighty, creator of heaven and earth. I believe in Jesus Christ, his only*

*Son, our Lord, who was conceived by the Holy Spirit and born
of the virgin Mary. He suffered under Pontius Pilate, was
crucified, died, and was buried; he descended into hell.* with
emphasis. Encourage the teens to commit this to memory.

4. Have the teens pull out their Question Journals. Ask them to
jot down the answers to any questions about the Creed that are
answered in this session. Have them share those discoveries,
giving them sufficient time to record any thoughts they wish to
capture. Assure them that they can ask any remaining questions
about this section at the end of the session.

5. Ask the teens what they know about hell. Many will simply
state it is a terrible place of punishment for those who have
been "bad" people in this life. Point out that this concept is
most closely aligned with the term *Gehenna.* Discuss the
term *Hades,* which is the one used in this phrase of the Creed.
Why is understanding the difference in terms important? This
might be a good chance to remind teens that Jesus' sacrifice
paid for our sins, and if we belong to him, we need not fear the
punishment of hell.

6. Acknowledge, but don't dwell on, that there are different views
of exactly what happened when Jesus "descended into hell."
Instead, spend the time reading over the "Unifying Truths"
listed in that section. Read each of the italicized statements in
this section. Ask the teens which of these seems most important
to them. Were there any they were unaware of prior to reading
this chapter?

7. Allow the teens to ask any questions about Jesus' descent into
hell that they had noted in their journals that were not addressed
in this discussion. Ask them if/how their understanding of Jesus
changed through what they learned in this session.

8. If you have teens in your group who have not yet surrendered
to Jesus, continue praying for the Holy Spirit to open that
conversational door so you can explain the gospel. Once they
receive Christ, the indwelling presence of the Holy Spirit will
make the lessons in this book much more accessible to them.

HOW DO I IMPART WHAT I HAVE JUST LEARNED TO ADULTS?

1. Challenge your adults to take a moment to stop and pray, asking God, through the Holy Spirit, to increase their understanding of the essentials of the Christian Faith. Encourage them to ask Him to reveal and clarify any points which have been confusing or unclear.

2. Review the Apostles' Creed, emphasizing the first few lines: *I believe in God, the Father almighty, creator of heaven and earth. I believe in Jesus Christ, his only Son, our Lord, who was conceived by the Holy Spirit and born of the virgin Mary. He suffered under Pontius Pilate, was crucified, died, and was buried; he descended into hell.* If they have not done so, encourage them to memorize the Creed in its entirety, reminding them that it is a summary of the essentials of the Christian faith.

3. Have participants pull out the notes they made during previous sessions. Ask them to jot down the answers to any questions about the Creed that may be answered during this session and to share those discoveries as they happen. Provide sufficient time to record any thoughts they may wish to capture. Assure them that they will have the opportunity to ask any questions that were not answered in this session at the end of the session.

4. Briefly review the five divergent views on the interpretation of this phrase listed in the section *"An Ongoing Debate."* Ask participants if they have heard or been taught any of these. Remind them that this is the one phrase most challenged by Christians. Ask why they believe this is so, and if it is, why do they believe the writers of the Creed included it.

5. Ask participants why it is important to properly understand this phrase to distinguish among the various words translated as "hell" (Sheol/Hades vs. Gehenna) in English language Bibles. How does this add to the understanding of the phrase?

6. Read over the *"Unifying Truths"* listed in the section by that title. They are the italicized statements. Do you agree with

Dr. Kimball's choice of these as among the most important, unifying interpretations that can be drawn from the statement, "He descended into hell."? What about the concluding statement in the next to last paragraph, "While there are many differing opinions on what Jesus did while in Hades, we are all again unified in the result. Jesus is Lord!"? Does that ring true to you? Explain.

7. Re-read the final paragraph of this chapter as an affirmation of faith in Jesus Christ and his redemptive work on our behalf.

8. Allow participants to ask any questions about Jesus' descent into hell they had noted previously that were not addressed in this discussion.

9. If you have people in your group who have not yet surrendered to Jesus, continue to pray for the Holy Spirit to open that conversational door so you can explain the gospel. Once they receive Christ, the indwelling presence of the Holy Spirit will make the lessons in this book much more accessible to them.

CHAPTER 7
Jesus: Resurrection

"I believe in Jesus Christ...that on the third day he rose again from the dead..."

Early on Sunday morning, as the new day was dawning, Mary Magdalene and the other Mary went out to visit the tomb.

Suddenly there was a great earthquake! For an angel of the Lord came down from heaven, rolled aside the stone, and sat on it. His face shone like lightning, and his clothing was as white as snow. The guards shook with fear when they saw him, and they fell into a dead faint.

Then the angel spoke to the women. "Don't be afraid!" he said. "I know you are looking for Jesus, who was crucified. He isn't here! He is risen from the dead, just as he said would happen. Come, see where his body was lying. And now, go quickly and tell his disciples that he has risen from the dead, and he is going ahead of you to Galilee. You will see him there. Remember what I have told you."

The women ran quickly from the tomb. They were very frightened but also filled with great joy, and they rushed to give the disciples the angel's message. And as they went, Jesus met them and greeted them. And they ran to him, grasped his feet, and worshiped him. Then Jesus said to them, "Don't be afraid! Go tell my brothers to leave for Galilee, and they will see me there." (Matthew 28:1-10)

Several years ago, when my children were still young, our family spent New Year's Day with my aging mother at Disney's Hollywood Studios in Orlando, Florida. At the time, I was pastoring a church in Virginia, so this was a big vacation for us. We had a great time experiencing the "magic" of Disney. But then we happened upon something that made a memory I will never forget.

This trip took place before Hollywood Studios stopped their backstage tram tour (that area is now Star Wars Galaxy's Edge), and we ended our day on the tram, seeing all the cars, props, and paraphernalia from some of our favorite movies. As we moved through the line to get to the tram, various rooms were created as "sets" for recent Disney movies. One of those sets was the sacrificial Stone Table scene from C.S. Lewis' *The Lion, the Witch, and the Wardrobe.*[17] We knew the movie was featured there at that time, but I was not prepared for the emotional reaction I would have to see a life-sized Stone Table. The line widened to the whole room at that point, so I was able to dwell there for several minutes before moving on.

My memories of reading the book as a kid at Camp Talahi in Howell, Michigan, came flooding back. The vivid picture of Aslan's sacrifice in the movie (which we had watched on the big screen just weeks before) whirled in my mind. And then Aslan's declaration to Lucy and Susan as he meets them at dawn – very much alive – cycled in the room over a speaker system: "If the witch understood the true meaning of sacrifice, she might have interpreted the Deep Magic differently, for when a willing victim who has committed no treachery, dies in a traitor's stead, the stone table will crack and even death itself will turn backwards."

---

17   *The Chronicles of Narnia: The Lion, the Witch and the Wardrobe,* based upon the book by C. S. Lewis, Walt Disney Pictures and Walden Media, directed by Andrew Adamson, 2006.

I have a picture of that table – cleaved in two – in my desk drawer. Every time I see it, I remember the power of that day. In his brilliant way, C.S. Lewis put the resurrection story into a beloved children's book – and ultimately into a Disney film!

GOD'S INCREDIBLE PLAN

The Creed joyfully proclaims, "On the third day, He arose again from the dead…" In C.S. Lewis' words, that's the day that "even death itself [turned] backwards." The resurrection of Jesus Christ is God's incredible plan for our salvation. It has literally been his plan from the beginning.

There are clear indications of the resurrection of the dead in the Old Testament. By the time Jesus is born, there is already a very well-developed theology of resurrection among the Jews. In fact, there was a theological battle between the largest Jewish sects of Jesus' time. The Sadducees rejected the notion of the resurrection. But the Pharisees not only accepted it, they taught about it.

Many Christians have relied upon Isaiah 26 for comfort in times of personal or family upheaval.

> *You will keep in perfect peace all who trust in you, all whose thoughts are fixed on you!*
>
> *Trust in the Lord always, for the Lord God is the eternal Rock.* (Isaiah 26:3-4)

But few people realize that the prophet ends this psalm of praise with a verse about the resurrection!

> *But those who die in the Lord will live; their bodies will rise again! Those who sleep in the earth will rise up and sing for joy!*
>
> *For your life-giving light will fall like dew on your people in the place of the dead!* (Isaiah 26:19)

The prophet Ezekiel's vision of the valley of dry bones is a resurrection story.

The Lord took hold of me, and I was carried away by the Spirit of the Lord to a valley filled with bones. He led me all around among the bones that covered the valley floor. They were scattered everywhere across the ground and were completely dried out. Then he asked me, "Son of man, can these bones become living people again?"

"O Sovereign Lord," I replied, "you alone know the answer to that."

Then he said to me, "Speak a prophetic message to these bones and say, 'Dry bones, listen to the word of the Lord! This is what the Sovereign Lord says: Look! I am going to put breath into you and make you live again! I will put flesh and muscles on you and cover you with skin. I will put breath into you, and you will come to life. Then you will know that I am the Lord.' "

So I spoke this message, just as he told me. Suddenly as I spoke, there was a rattling noise all across the valley. The bones of each body came together and attached themselves as complete skeletons. Then as I watched, muscles and flesh formed over the bones. Then skin formed to cover their bodies, but they still had no breath in them.

Then he said to me, "Speak a prophetic message to the winds, son of man. Speak a prophetic message and say, 'This is what the Sovereign Lord says: Come, O breath, from the four winds! Breathe into these dead bodies so they may live again.' "

So I spoke the message as he commanded me, and breath came into their bodies. They all came to life and stood up on their feet—a great army. (Ezekiel 37:1-10)

Daniel receives a word from God about the end times, and in it, he describes *two* resurrections – some to everlasting life and the rest to shame and everlasting contempt.

"At that time Michael, the archangel who stands guard over your nation, will arise. Then there will be a time of anguish greater than any since nations first came into existence. But at that time every one of your people whose name is written in the book will be rescued. Many of those whose bodies lie dead and buried will

rise up, some to everlasting life and some to shame and ever-lasting disgrace. Those who are wise will shine as bright as the sky, and those who lead many to righteousness will shine like the stars forever. But you, Daniel, keep this prophecy a secret; seal up the book until the time of the end, when many will rush here and there, and knowledge will increase." (Daniel 12:1-4)

Interestingly, God even gives Daniel a vision of the Lamb's book of life, which is part of John's revelation of God's end-time judgment.

I saw the dead, both great and small, standing before God's throne. And the books were opened, including the Book of Life. And the dead were judged according to what they had done, as recorded in the books. The sea gave up its dead, and death and the grave gave up their dead. And all were judged according to their deeds. Then death and the grave were thrown into the lake of fire. This lake of fire is the second death. And anyone whose name was not found recorded in the Book of Life was thrown into the lake of fire. (Revelation 20:11-15)

Job, as he endures his trials, proclaims in faith about his own resurrection.

"Oh, that my words could be recorded.

Oh, that they could be inscribed on a monument, carved with an iron chisel and filled with lead, engraved forever in the rock.

"But as for me, I know that my Redeemer lives, and he will stand upon the earth at last.

And after my body has decayed, yet in my body I will see God!

I will see him for myself. Yes, I will see him with my own eyes. I am overwhelmed at the thought! (Job 19:23-27)

There are many other places in the Old Testament where we get glimpses of the resurrection of the dead. In your own time, check out Isaiah 53:1-12; Psalm 16:8-11; 49:15, and Hosea 6:1-2; 13:14. These became the basis of the Pharisees' theology on the topic – a theology Jesus not only adopted himself but fulfilled!

From the moment humanity sinned, rejecting their relationship with God for the deceiver, God had a plan for complete redemption. We have already referred to the *protoevangelium* found in Genesis 3:15. God finds the first man and woman hiding from him in their shame – their eyes had been opened in a way God never desired for them. They knew they were naked and tried to cover themselves – the covering they had in their glorious relationship with God had been stripped away. God speaks – revealing the consequences of their decision and his judgment upon the serpent:

> *Then the Lord God said to the serpent,*
>
> *"Because you have done this, you are cursed more than all animals, domestic and wild.*
>
> *You will crawl on your belly, groveling in the dust as long as you live.*
>
> *And I will cause hostility between you and the woman, and between your offspring and her offspring.*
>
> ***He will strike your head, and you will strike his heel.***" (Genesis 3:14-15, **emphasis mine**)

The Hebrew term used for "strike" can also mean "crush." It's a brutal blow bringing severe injury. The indication is that the offspring of the woman would deliver a fatal blow to the serpent. The payment for sin is made in Jesus' death. The victory over Satan is firmly and forever established in the resurrection!

Isaiah's prophecy of the suffering servant clearly expresses God's plan in Christ, including the resurrection. One of the most compelling Old Testament proofs for the resurrection of Christ is found in Isaiah 53, especially verses 8-11. This singular chapter foreshadows the work of Jesus some 700 years before he is born.

> *Who has believed our message?*
> *To whom has the Lord revealed his powerful arm?*
> *My servant grew up in the Lord's presence like a tender green shoot, like a root in dry ground.*
> *There was nothing beautiful or majestic about his appearance, nothing to attract us to him.*

He was despised and rejected— a man of sorrows, acquainted with deepest grief.
We turned our backs on him and looked the other way.
He was despised, and we did not care.
Yet it was our weaknesses he carried; it was our sorrows that weighed him down.
And we thought his troubles were a punishment from God, a punishment for his own sins!
But he was pierced for our rebellion, crushed for our sins.
He was beaten so we could be whole.
He was whipped so we could be healed.
All of us, like sheep, have strayed away.
We have left God's paths to follow our own.
Yet the Lord laid on him the sins of us all.
He was oppressed and treated harshly, yet he never said a word.
He was led like a lamb to the slaughter.
And as a sheep is silent before the shearers, he did not open his mouth.
Unjustly condemned, he was led away.
No one cared that he died without descendants, that his life was cut short in midstream.
But he was struck down for the rebellion of my people.
He had done no wrong and had never deceived anyone.
But he was buried like a criminal; he was put in a rich man's grave.

But it was the Lord's good plan to crush him and cause him grief.

Yet when his life is made an offering for sin, he will have many descendants.

He will enjoy a long life, and the Lord's good plan will prosper in his hands.

When he sees all that is accomplished by his anguish, he will be satisfied.

And because of his experience, my righteous servant will make it possible for many to be counted righteous, for he will bear all their sins. (Isaiah 53:1-11)

There is so much in this passage: He carried our sorrows, he was pierced for our rebellion, he was crushed for our sins, he was led like a lamb to the slaughter, he was unjustly condemned and died, and yet, after his life is made an offering for sin, *he will have many descendants and will enjoy a long life!*

A Messianic friend once told me that long ago this passage used to be a regular part of the readings in synagogues, but that today the Jewish prophetic reader (the Haftarah) leads readers through Isaiah 52 and then skips to Isaiah 54. Apparently, many years ago this chapter caused a lot of confusion for Jewish people. Most Jews today are completely unfamiliar with it.[18]

This passage is about the Messiah and his suffering on behalf of God's people. Clearly, it speaks of his resurrection from the dead.

David prophetically writes about the resurrection of his own descendant.

I will bless the Lord who guides me; even at night my heart instructs me.

I know the Lord is always with me.

I will not be shaken, for he is right beside me.

No wonder my heart is glad, and I rejoice.

My body rests in safety.

For you will not leave my soul among the dead or allow your holy one to rot in the grave.

You will show me the way of life, granting me the joy of your presence and the pleasures of living with you forever. (Psalm 16:8-11, **emphasis mine**)

And as Peter preaches to the gathered crowd on the Day of Pentecost, he quotes these very verses and explains that this passage prophetically speaks of Jesus.

"Dear brothers, think about this! You can be sure that the patriarch David wasn't referring to himself, for he died and was buried, and his tomb is still here among us. But he was a prophet,

18   If you're interested, there is a fascinating video produced by Medabrim.org.il that shows several Jews in Jerusalem encountering this "Forbidden Chapter" for the very first time. *The Forbidden Chapter in the Tanakh,* online, https://www.youtube.com/watch?v=IXSBR047MMk.

and he knew God had promised with an oath that one of David's own descendants would sit on his throne. David was looking into the future and speaking of the Messiah's resurrection. He was saying that God would not leave him among the dead or allow his body to rot in the grave. "God raised Jesus from the dead, and we are all witnesses of this. (Acts 2:29-32)

Way before Jesus was born, God's incredible plan was already established. And the great work of Christ would be accomplished as he rises from the dead! So now we'll look at the resurrection itself.

THE RESURRECTION REALITY

Theologian Millard Ericksen writes, "The resurrection is particularly significant, for inflicting death was the worst thing sin and the powers of sin could do to Christ. In the inability of death to hold him is symbolized the totality of his victory. What more can the forces of evil do if someone who they have killed does not stay dead?"[19]

Jesus didn't stay dead! Jesus rose from the grave! And we have testimony that he was not only seen by his apostles after his resurrection but by hundreds of people. In fact, he was seen by over 500 people at the same time (1 Corinthians 15:6).

The resurrection of Jesus Christ was the heart of the early Christian message. As Peter stands before the masses in Jerusalem on the Day of Pentecost, he makes Jesus' resurrection the prominent proof that he is indeed the Messiah.

"People of Israel, listen! God publicly endorsed Jesus the Nazarene by doing powerful miracles, wonders, and signs through him, as you well know. But God knew what would happen, and his prearranged plan was carried out when Jesus was betrayed. With the help of lawless Gentiles, you nailed him to a cross and killed him. But God released him from the horrors of death and raised him back to life, for death could not keep him in its grip. King David said this about him:

'I see that the Lord is always with me.

---

19   Millard Erickson, *Christian Theology,* Grand Rapids, MI: Baker Book House, 1985, p. 776.

I will not be shaken, for he is right beside me.

No wonder my heart is glad, and my tongue shouts his praises!

My body rests in hope.

For you will not leave my soul among the dead or allow your Holy One to rot in the grave.

You have shown me the way of life, and you will fill me with the joy of your presence.'

"Dear brothers, think about this! You can be sure that the patriarch David wasn't referring to himself, for he died and was buried, and his tomb is still here among us. But he was a prophet, and he knew God had promised with an oath that one of David's own descendants would sit on his throne. David was looking into the future and speaking of the Messiah's resurrection. He was saying that God would not leave him among the dead or allow his body to rot in the grave.

"God raised Jesus from the dead, and we are all witnesses of this. Now he is exalted to the place of highest honor in heaven, at God's right hand. And the Father, as he had promised, gave him the Holy Spirit to pour out upon us, just as you see and hear today. For David himself never ascended into heaven, yet he said,

'The Lord said to my Lord, "Sit in the place of honor at my right hand until I humble your enemies, making them a footstool under your feet." '

"So let everyone in Israel know for certain that God has made this Jesus, whom you crucified, to be both Lord and Messiah!" (Acts 2:22-36)

The Apostle Paul consistently wove the resurrection into his teaching. Perhaps his best-known treatise is in his letter to the Christians at Corinth.

I passed on to you what was most important and what had also been passed on to me. Christ died for our sins, just as the Scriptures said. He was buried, and he was raised from the dead on the third day, just as the Scriptures said. He was seen by Peter and then by the Twelve. After that, he was seen by more

*than 500 of his followers at one time, most of whom are still
alive, though some have died. Then he was seen by James and
later by all the apostles. Last of all, as though I had been born
at the wrong time, I also saw him. For I am the least of all the
apostles. In fact, I'm not even worthy to be called an apostle
after the way I persecuted God's church.* (1 Corinthians 15:3-9)

If the resurrection is the heart of the apostolic teaching, it must be the
heart of our message as well.

*The resurrection proves the rule and reign (kingdom) of our triune
God.* There is no more powerful demonstration of our God's ultimate
rule, authority, and ability than the resurrection. God the Son, Jesus,
tells us that nobody took his life from him, he gave it of his own free
will, and he has the authority to take it back up again.

> *"The Father loves me because I sacrifice my life so I may take
> it back again. No one can take my life from me. I sacrifice it
> voluntarily. For I have the authority to lay it down when I want
> to and also to take it up again. For this is what my Father has
> commanded."* (John 10:17-18)

God the Father raised Jesus from the dead – it was impossible for death to
keep him in the grave.

> *But God released him from the horrors of death and raised him
> back to life, for death could not keep him in its grip.* (Acts 2:24)

God the Holy Spirit raised Jesus from the dead and will do the same for all
those who put their full faith in Jesus.

> *The Spirit of God, who raised Jesus from the dead, lives in you.
> And just as God raised Christ Jesus from the dead, he will give
> life to your mortal bodies by this same Spirit living within you.*
> (Romans 8:11)

The Father, the Son, and the Holy Spirit together are involved in the resurrection of Christ, proving our triune God's rule and reign.

This letter is from Paul, a slave of Christ Jesus, chosen by God to be an apostle and sent out to preach his Good News. God promised this Good News long ago through his prophets in the holy Scriptures. **The Good News is about his Son. In his earthly life he was born into King David's family line, and he was shown to be the Son of God when he was raised from the dead by the power of the Holy Spirit. He is Jesus Christ our Lord.** *Through Christ, God has given us the privilege and authority as apostles to tell Gentiles everywhere what God has done for them, so that they will believe and obey him, bringing glory to his name.* (Romans 1:1-5, **emphasis mine**)

In your own time, you might also look at Romans 10:9, 1 Corinthians 6:14, Galatians 1:1, and Ephesians 1:17-20.

The resurrection proves Jesus is the Son of God. We have previously talked about Jesus as the Messiah, Jesus as the Son of God, and Jesus as our Lord. All of these things are confirmed by the resurrection of Christ.

One day the Pharisees and Sadducees came to test Jesus, demanding that he show them a miraculous sign from heaven to prove his authority.

He replied, "You know the saying, 'Red sky at night means fair weather tomorrow; red sky in the morning means foul weather all day.' You know how to interpret the weather signs in the sky, but you don't know how to interpret the signs of the times! Only an evil, adulterous generation would demand a miraculous sign, but the only sign I will give them is the sign of the prophet Jonah." Then Jesus left them and went away. (Matthew 16:1-4)

The "sign of Jonah" is a direct reference to the resurrection. Jonah was in the belly of the fish for three days as good as dead, and then God instructed the fish to spit him onto dry land. Jesus uses this sign to show the Pharisees and Sadducees "proof" that he is the Son of God. Interestingly, we know that Nicodemus and Joseph of Arimathea were Pharisees who became followers of Jesus as the Messiah. There were unnamed others. We're told that a number of priests placed their trust in him as Messiah as well (Acts 6:7).

Peter explains the prophecies about Christ as he preaches to the people of Antioch,

> *"Brothers—you sons of Abraham, and also you God-fearing Gentiles—this message of salvation has been sent to us! The people in Jerusalem and their leaders did not recognize Jesus as the one the prophets had spoken about. Instead, they condemned him, and in doing this they fulfilled the prophets' words that are read every Sabbath. They found no legal reason to execute him, but they asked Pilate to have him killed anyway.*
>
> *"When they had done all that the prophecies said about him, they took him down from the cross and placed him in a tomb.* **But God raised him from the dead!** *And over a period of many days he appeared to those who had gone with him from Galilee to Jerusalem. They are now his witnesses to the people of Israel.*
>
> *"And now we are here to bring you this Good News.* **The promise was made to our ancestors, and God has now fulfilled it for us, their descendants, by raising Jesus.** *This is what the second psalm says about Jesus:*
>
> *'You are my Son. Today I have become your Father.'*
>
> **For God had promised to raise him from the dead, not leaving him to rot in the grave.** *He said, 'I will give you the sacred blessings I promised to David.' Another psalm explains it more fully: 'You will not allow your Holy One to rot in the grave.' This is not a reference to David, for after David had done the will of God in his own generation, he died and was buried with his ancestors, and his body decayed. No, it was a reference to someone else—* **someone whom God raised and whose body did not decay.** (Acts 13:26-37, **emphasis mine**)

The resurrection proves that Jesus is indeed the Son of God.

The resurrection validates all of Jesus' teaching and promises. This is important. The resurrection is like a God-sized exclamation mark at the end of Jesus' earthly teaching ministry because Jesus made the resurrection a key component of his message.

Jesus taught about his own resurrection, telling his disciples about his suffering before it happened.

From then on Jesus began to tell his disciples plainly that it was necessary for him to go to Jerusalem, and that he would suffer many terrible things at the hands of the elders, the leading priests, and the teachers of religious law. He would be killed, but on the third day he would be raised from the dead. (Matthew 16:21)

After they gathered again in Galilee, Jesus told them, "The Son of Man is going to be betrayed into the hands of his enemies. He will be killed, but on the third day he will be raised from the dead." And the disciples were filled with grief. (Matthew 17:23)

As Jesus was going up to Jerusalem, he took the twelve disciples aside privately and told them what was going to happen to him. "Listen," he said, "we're going up to Jerusalem, where the Son of Man will be betrayed to the leading priests and the teachers of religious law. They will sentence him to die. Then they will hand him over to the Romans to be mocked, flogged with a whip, and crucified. But on the third day he will be raised from the dead." (Matthew 20:17-19)

After his transfiguration, Jesus instructed his disciples to tell no one about what they saw until after his resurrection.

Six days later Jesus took Peter and the two brothers, James and John, and led them up a high mountain to be alone. As the men watched, Jesus' appearance was transformed so that his face shone like the sun, and his clothes became as white as light. Suddenly, Moses and Elijah appeared and began talking with Jesus.

Peter exclaimed, "Lord, it's wonderful for us to be here! If you want, I'll make three shelters as memorials—one for you, one for Moses, and one for Elijah."

But even as he spoke, a bright cloud overshadowed them, and a voice from the cloud said, "This is my dearly loved Son, who brings me great joy. Listen to him." The disciples were terrified and fell face down on the ground.

Then Jesus came over and touched them. "Get up," he said. "Don't be afraid." And when they looked up, Moses and Elijah were gone, and they saw only Jesus.

As they went back down the mountain, Jesus commanded them, "Don't tell anyone what you have seen until the Son of Man has been raised from the dead." (Matthew 17:1-9)

After the Last Supper, on the way to the Mount of Olives, Jesus told his disciples what they needed to do after his resurrection.

On the way, Jesus told them, "Tonight all of you will desert me. For the Scriptures say,

'God will strike the Shepherd, and the sheep of the flock will be scattered.'

But after I have been raised from the dead, I will go ahead of you to Galilee and meet you there." (Matthew 26:31-32)

After Jesus cleared the temple of the money changers, he even hinted to the Jewish leaders that he would be raised from the dead.

Then his disciples remembered this prophecy from the Scriptures: "Passion for God's house will consume me."

But the Jewish leaders demanded, "What are you doing? If God gave you authority to do this, show us a miraculous sign to prove it."

"All right," Jesus replied. "Destroy this temple, and in three days I will raise it up."

"What!" they exclaimed. "It has taken forty-six years to build this Temple, and you can rebuild it in three days?" But when Jesus said "this temple," he meant his own body. After he was raised from the dead, his disciples remembered he had said this, and they believed both the Scriptures and what Jesus had said. (John 2:17-22)

The resurrection proves that Jesus is the very source of all life. In fact, one commentator put it this way, "Jesus does more than *give* life. He *is* life, and that's why death has no power over him!"[20]

In the beginning the Word already existed.

The Word was with God, and the Word was God.

He existed in the beginning with God.

God created everything through him, and nothing was created except through him.

The Word gave life to everything that was created, and his life brought light to everyone. (John 1:1-4, ***emphasis mine***)

Jesus told her, "I am the resurrection and the life. Anyone who believes in me will live, even after dying. Everyone who lives in me and believes in me will never ever die. Do you believe this, Martha?" (John 11:25-26)

Jesus told him, "I am the way, the truth, and the life. No one can come to the Father except through me. (John 14:6)

And this is what God has testified: He has given us eternal life, and this life is in his Son. Whoever has the Son has life; whoever does not have God's Son does not have life. (1 John 5:11-12)

Well then, should we keep on sinning so that God can show us more and more of his wonderful grace? Of course not! Since we have died to sin, how can we continue to live in it? Or have you forgotten that when we were joined with Christ Jesus in baptism, we joined him in his death? For we died and were buried with Christ by baptism. And just as Christ was raised from the dead by the glorious power of the Father, now we also may live new lives.

Since we have been united with him in his death, we will also be raised to life as he was. We know that our old sinful selves were crucified with Christ so that sin might lose its power in our lives. We are no longer slaves to sin. For when we died with Christ we were set free from the power of sin. And since we died with

---

20   "Why is the Resurrection of Jesus Important," GotQuestions.Org, https://www.gotquestions.org/resurrection-Christ-important.html

Christ, we know we will also live with him. We are sure of this because Christ was raised from the dead, and he will never die again. Death no longer has any power over him. When he died, he died once to break the power of sin. But now that he lives, he lives for the glory of God. So you also should consider your-selves to be dead to the power of sin and alive to God through Christ Jesus. (Romans 6:1-11)

When I saw him, I fell at his feet as if I were dead. But he laid his right hand on me and said, "Don't be afraid! I am the First and the Last. I am the living one. I died, but look—I am alive forever and ever! And I hold the keys of death and the grave. (Revelation 1:17-18)

The resurrection validates life in the "upside down" kingdom. You might remember the brouhaha that was created by a rent-a-mob when Paul and Silas began their ministry in Thessalonica. Luke recounts in Acts 17,

But some of the Jews were jealous, so they gathered some trou-blemakers from the marketplace to form a mob and start a riot. They attacked the home of Jason, searching for Paul and Silas so they could drag them out to the crowd. Not finding them there, they dragged out Jason and some of the other believers instead and took them before the city council. **"Paul and Silas have caused trouble all over the world,"** *they shouted, "and now they are here disturbing our city, too.* (Acts 17:5-6, **emphasis mine**)

Where the New Living Translation says they have "caused trouble all over the world," the Greek text (and many other English translations) actually says they have "turned the world upside down." To pre-Chris-tian people, it may indeed look like Jesus and his followers live an up-side-down and backward lifestyle. But in reality, it is the kingdom life-style that is right-side up! Jesus demonstrates right-side-up living in his teaching and earthly ministry.

- Whoever finds his life will lose it (Matthew 10:38-39)
- Whoever loses his life for Jesus' sake will find it (Matthew 16:24-28)

- The greatest among you will be your servant (Matthew 20:26-28)
- The first will be last; the last will be first (Matthew 20:16)
- Whoever exalts himself will be humbled and whoever humbles himself will be exalted (Matthew 23:11-12)
- The whole beloved list of beatitudes shows this right-side-up kingdom culture (Matthew 5:1-12)

The resurrection proves the redemption and coming renewal of Christ's followers. Just like in Daniel's prophecy in the Old Testament, Jesus tells us that there are *two* resurrections – those who are good will rise unto life, and those who are evil will rise unto condemnation.

Then Peter said to him, "We've given up everything to follow you. What will we get?"

Jesus replied, "I assure you that when the world is made new and the Son of Man sits upon his glorious throne, you who have been my followers will also sit on twelve thrones, judging the twelve tribes of Israel. And everyone who has given up houses or brothers or sisters or father or mother or children or property, for my sake, will receive a hundred times as much in return and will inherit eternal life. But many who are the greatest now will be least important then, and those who seem least important now will be the greatest then. (Matthew 19:27-30)

Don't be so surprised! Indeed, the time is coming when all the dead in their graves will hear the voice of God's Son, and they will rise again. Those who have done good will rise to experience eternal life, and those who have continued in evil will rise to experience judgment. (John 5:28-29)

Abraham never wavered in believing God's promise. In fact, his faith grew stronger, and in this he brought glory to God. He was fully convinced that God is able to do whatever he promises. And because of Abraham's faith, God counted him as righteous. And when God counted him as righteous, it wasn't just for Abraham's benefit. It was recorded for our benefit, too, assuring us that God will also count us as righteous if we believe in him, the one who raised Jesus our Lord from the dead. He was handed over to die because of our sins, and he was raised to life to make us right with God. (Romans 4:20-25)

The resurrection undergirds everything. Our redemption rests on the foundation of the resurrection. The resurrection launches the renewal of all things. The resurrection gives us real victory over sin and death. The resurrection makes our justification possible – we are so cleansed by Jesus, receiving his righteousness, that God declares us fully righteous in Christ!

"On the third day, he arose again from the dead..." It is critical that we both understand and believe this truth! We must base our whole life upon it. The resurrection of Jesus is not just a nice bedtime story. It is the central truth of the entire Christian Faith.

He is Risen! He is Risen Indeed, Alleluia!

STUDY GUIDE

IT MAKES A DIFFERENCE

Christians who have studied and taken to heart the Creed's teaching on Jesus' resurrection can see God's overarching purpose from the time sin entered the world (Genesis 3). They often also have a special appreciation for passages like Isaiah 53, which clearly foretells God's plan to be completed in the Messiah. They understand that death is the primary result of humanity's sin and that the resurrection overcame death once and for all for those who have surrendered to Jesus. They see the resurrection of Jesus as the heart of the Christian faith and message. They celebrate the fact that the resurrection of Jesus forever proves the rule and reign of God – even over death. And they confidently depend on the resurrection's radical validation of Jesus' life and teaching, not to mention the new way of living he established.

Those who struggle with the biblical teaching on the resurrection of Jesus struggle with their faith. They do not accept the above-mentioned proofs and, when pressed, will often explain the resurrection as a form of resuscitation rather than the complete and utter victory of God over evil. Because the resurrection of Jesus undergirds everything in the Christian faith and way of life, those who have a weak grasp on this truth also question many other foundational aspects of their walk with Christ.

In the words of Paul, if Christ has not been raised from the dead, then Christians are more to be pitied than anyone else in the world. (1 Corinthians 15:19).

HOW DO I LIVE OUT WHAT I HAVE JUST LEARNED IN MY OWN LIFE?

1. Take a moment to stop and pray. Ask God, through the Holy Spirit, to increase your understanding of the essentials of the Christian Faith. Ask Him to reveal and clarify any points which have been confusing or unclear.

2. Take time to read the Old Testament prophecies concerning the resurrection, as Dr. Kimball suggested (Isaiah 53:1-12; Psalm 16:8-11; 49:15, and Hosea 6:1-2; 13:14). Think about why these passages were included in the Old Testament.

3. Read the additional New Testament passages Dr. Kimball suggested (Romans 10:9, 1 Corinthians 6:14, Galatians 1:1, and Ephesians 1:17-20) that support the Triune God's involvement in Jesus' resurrection. Think about the significance of the fact that all three persons of the Trinity were part of the plan.

4. After reading the chapter, meditate on the significance of the resurrection in your own life and the life of those you love, both now and through eternity.

5. Take several days to consider: Who can help you apply what you learn to put it into an ongoing life's practice?

6. How are you living this out right now? How is your life reflective of your understanding of this truth?

HOW DO I IMPART WHAT I HAVE JUST LEARNED TO CHILDREN?

Preparing to teach this lesson to children: *Find a picture of the kind of tomb in which Jesus was likely buried – a cave carved into rock with a large, heavy stone in front. Such pictures are readily available by doing an online search for "Jesus' tomb" in Google Images or another provider. Gather the following for each child: two plain white paper plates (either dessert or regular size), crayons, and one roundhead paper fastener. You will also need a pair of scissors, a thumb tack, a knife, and an ice pick or some other sharp object to get the hole for the paper fastener started for the children. It is advisable to create a sample ahead of time so the children know what their craft is supposed to look like when completed.*

1. Begin by praying with the children. Ask God, through the Holy Spirit, to help the children understand more about the Christian faith. Ask God to help them clearly understand the new things they are about to learn.

2. Continue to work with the children on memorizing the Apostle's Creed. Be sure they have memorized through this part: *I believe in God, the Father almighty, creator of heaven and earth. I believe in Jesus Christ, his only Son, our Lord, who was conceived by the Holy Spirit and born of the virgin Mary. He suffered under Pontius Pilate, was crucified, died, and was buried; he descended into hell. The third day he rose again from the dead.*

3. Remind the children again that even though when regular people die, they go to live with Jesus in heaven (if they were believers) and normally do not come back to earth. Jesus was stronger than even death. He fooled and defeated Satan's plan to keep Jesus dead. Jesus showed he was stronger and more powerful than even sin and death. On the third day after he died he rose to life here on earth again.

4. Show the children the picture of the kind of tomb that was common in that day for important people to be buried in. Explain that the stone in front would be very heavy for women to move by themselves and that Pilate had stationed guards at the tomb to make sure no one tried to remove Jesus' body without permission. They were afraid that the disciples could

try to fool people into believing that Jesus had risen from the dead by stealing his body, so they put armed guards in front of the tomb.

5. Read the story of the resurrection from Matthew 28:1-10 from a modern language version, such as the New Living Translation (the passage is included at the beginning of this chapter). Ask why the guards fainted. Talk about the emotions the women would have felt at seeing the angel and hearing his message. Ask them what command the angel gave and talk about why he would have given this message to the women. Also discuss how the women would have felt about actually seeing Jesus when they expected him to still be dead. Tell them that other versions of the story explain that the women, upon hearing the angel's message, first thought that someone had stolen Jesus' body. Why would they think that? And why was it important that they actually saw the risen Jesus for themselves?

6. Create a "Jesus is alive!" craft. Give each child two paper plates. Explain that the plates are the shape of the round stone in front of the tomb (only much lighter in weight). Have them color one completely gray or brown to represent the stone. On the other plate, they should write, "He is not here. He is risen!". Then have them fill the rest of the space on that plate with bright colors such as yellow and orange. Stack the plates on top of one another and punch a hole near the bottom of the plates so that the children can stick the prongs of the fastener through. Show them how to spread the prongs apart to secure the fastener, then allow them to "roll the stone away" by swinging the "stone" away like the angel did to show that Jesus is no longer in the tomb but alive. When they do so, they could shout, "He is not here. He is risen!"

7. If you have children in your group who have not yet surrendered to Jesus, continue praying for the Holy Spirit to open that conversational door so you can explain the gospel. Once they receive Christ, the indwelling presence of the Holy Spirit will make the lessons in this book much more accessible to them.

HOW DO I IMPART WHAT I HAVE JUST LEARNED TO TEENS?

1. Begin by praying with the teens. Ask God, through the
    Holy Spirit, to increase understanding. You can do this or
    ask a volunteer.

2. Read the Apostles' Creed out loud. Read it yourself, ask for a
    volunteer, or read it in unison.

3. Repeat the first several lines: *I believe in God, the Father
    almighty, creator of heaven and earth. I believe in Jesus Christ,
    his only Son, our Lord, who was conceived by the Holy Spirit
    and born of the virgin Mary. He suffered under Pontius Pilate,
    was crucified, died, and was buried; he descended into hell.
    The third day he rose again from the dead.* Encourage the teens
    to commit this to memory.

4. Have the teens pull out their Question Journals. Ask them to
    jot down the answers to any questions about the Creed that are
    answered in this session. Have them share those discoveries,
    giving them sufficient time to record any thoughts they wish to
    capture. Assure them that they can ask any remaining questions
    about this section at the end of the session.

5. How does the section *God's Incredible Plan* give credence to
    the reality of the resurrection?

6. Dr. Kimball asserts that the resurrection was the heart of the
    apostle's message and should be the heart of ours as well. In
    what sense is the resurrection at the heart of the Christian
    message? Why is it so essential?

7. Why is it important to note that Jesus himself taught about his
    resurrection *before his death?*

8. How does the reality of Jesus' death and resurrection affect your
    life now and for eternity?

9. Allow teens to ask any questions about Jesus' resurrection
    that they had noted in their journals that were not addressed in
    this discussion. Ask them if/how their understanding of Jesus
    changed through what they learned in this session.

10. If you have teens in your group who have not yet surrendered to Jesus, continue praying for the Holy Spirit to open that conversational door so you can explain the gospel. Once they receive Christ, the indwelling presence of the Holy Spirit will make the lessons in this book much more accessible to them.

HOW DO I IMPART WHAT I HAVE JUST LEARNED TO ADULTS?

1. Challenge your adults to take a moment to stop and pray, asking God, through the Holy Spirit, to increase their understanding of the essentials of the Christian Faith. Encourage them to ask Him to reveal and clarify any points which have been confusing or unclear.

2. Review the Apostles' Creed, emphasizing the first several lines: *I believe in God, the Father almighty, creator of heaven and earth. I believe in Jesus Christ, his only Son, our Lord, who was conceived by the Holy Spirit and born of the virgin Mary. He suffered under Pontius Pilate, was crucified, died, and was buried; he descended into hell. The third day he rose again from the dead.* If they have not done so, encourage them to memorize the Creed in its entirety, reminding them that it is a summary of the essentials of the Christian faith.

3. Have participants pull out the notes they made during previous sessions. Ask them to jot down the answers to any questions about the Creed that may be answered during this session and to share those discoveries as they happen. Provide sufficient time to record any thoughts they may wish to capture. Assure them that they will have the opportunity to ask any questions that were not answered in this session at the end of the session.

4. How does the section *God's Incredible Plan* give credence to the reality of the resurrection?

5. Dr. Kimball asserts that the resurrection was the heart of the apostle's message and should be the heart of ours as well. In what sense is the resurrection at the heart of the Christian message? Why is it so essential?

6. Read the other italicized truths about the resurrection in *The Resurrection Reality* section. Discuss the significance of each of these statements regarding the resurrection. Which of these gives a fresh perspective to the resurrection for the participants?

7. Discuss how the reality of Jesus' death and resurrection affects the participants' lives, and the lives of those they know and love, now and for eternity?

8. Allow participants to ask any questions about Jesus' resurrection they had noted previously that were not addressed in this discussion.

9. If you have people in your group who have not yet surrendered to Jesus, continue to pray for the Holy Spirit to open that conversational door so you can explain the gospel. Once they receive Christ, the indwelling presence of the Holy Spirit will make the lessons in this book much more accessible to them.

CHAPTER 8
Jesus: Ascension and Session

"I believe in Jesus Christ...that he ascended into heaven, and sits at the right hand of God, the Father Almighty..."

So when the apostles were with Jesus, they kept asking him, "Lord, has the time come for you to free Israel and restore our kingdom?"

He replied, "The Father alone has the authority to set those dates and times, and they are not for you to know. But you will receive power when the Holy Spirit comes upon you. And you will be my witnesses, telling people about me everywhere—in Jerusalem, throughout Judea, in Samaria, and to the ends of the earth."

After saying this, he was taken up into a cloud while they were watching, and they could no longer see him. As they strained to see him rising into heaven, two white-robed men suddenly stood among them. "Men of Galilee," they said, "why are you standing here staring into heaven? Jesus has been taken from you into heaven, but someday he will return from heaven in the same way you saw him go!" (Acts 1:6-11)

"I believe in Jesus Christ...that he ascended into heaven, and sits at the right hand of God, the Father Almighty..." *Ascension* and *Session*. Church folks have likely heard these terms but may not actually know what we're talking about. The ascension of Jesus is that moment when Jesus was visibly and bodily taken up into heaven before many witnesses. The session of Jesus is the ongoing rule and reign of Jesus from the very right hand of God. In this chapter, I'll show that these two doctrinal points are just as important as the resurrection, but few Christians celebrate them anymore.

THE ASCENSION OF JESUS

Jesus had already alerted his disciples of his ascension. The ascension of Jesus should not have been a surprise to those who were under his teaching for three years. After speaking to his disciples about being the bread of life, and referring to the consumption of his body and blood, they were confused and concerned.

> *Many of his disciples said, "This is very hard to understand. How can anyone accept it?"*
>
> *Jesus was aware that his disciples were complaining, so he said to them, "Does this offend you? Then what will you think if you see the Son of Man ascend to heaven again?* (John 6:60-62)

He told them they would see the ascension. Later, as Jesus was telling them about his departure, he comforts them.

> *"Don't let your hearts be troubled. Trust in God, and trust also in me. There is more than enough room in my Father's home. If this were not so, would I have told you that **I am going to prepare a place for you**? When everything is ready, I will come and get you, so that you will always be with me where I am.* (John 14:1-3 **emphasis mine**)

And as he teaches them about the coming work of the Holy Spirit, Jesus reminds them of his ascension to the Father.

"But now I am going away to the one who sent me, and not one of you is asking where I am going. Instead, you grieve because of what I've told you. But in fact, it is best for you that I go away, because if I don't, the Advocate won't come. If I do go away, then I will send him to you. And when he comes, he will convict the world of its sin, and of God's righteousness, and of the coming judgment. (John 16:5-8)

Yes, I came from the Father into the world, and now I will leave the world and return to the Father." (John 16:28)

And as Mary Magdalene meets and embraces the risen Christ at the garden tomb, Jesus asks her to release him.

Mary was standing outside the tomb crying, and as she wept, she stooped and looked in. She saw two white-robed angels, one sitting at the head and the other at the foot of the place where the body of Jesus had been lying. "Dear woman, why are you crying?" the angels asked her.

"Because they have taken away my Lord," she replied, "and I don't know where they have put him."

She turned to leave and saw someone standing there. It was Jesus, but she didn't recognize him. "Dear woman, why are you crying?" Jesus asked her. "Who are you looking for?"

She thought he was the gardener. "Sir," she said, "if you have taken him away, tell me where you have put him, and I will go and get him."

"Mary!" Jesus said.

She turned to him and cried out, "Rabboni!" (which is Hebrew for "Teacher").

"Don't cling to me," Jesus said, "for I haven't yet ascended to the Father. But go find my brothers and tell them, 'I am ascending to my Father and your Father, to my God and your God.'" (John 20:11-17)

Jesus also warned his accusers that he would take the seat of ultimate authority as God's Son. We will talk more about the "Right Hand of

God" in a few pages but understand that this is the position of power next to the King. Remember that James and John wanted such a position when Jesus came into power (see John 10:37-40). They even got their mother to insert her influence.

After teaching on the most important commandment, Jesus gave the Pharisees a lesson about their own Messiah.

> *Then, surrounded by the Pharisees, Jesus asked them a question: "What do you think about the Messiah? Whose son is he?"*
>
> *They replied, "He is the son of David."*
>
> *Jesus responded, "Then why does David, speaking under the inspiration of the Spirit, call the Messiah 'my Lord'? For David said,*
>
> *'The Lord said to my Lord, Sit in the place of honor at my right hand until I humble your enemies beneath your feet.'*
>
> *Since David called the Messiah 'my Lord,' how can the Messiah be his son?"*
>
> *No one could answer him. And after that, no one dared to ask him any more questions.* (Matthew 22:41-46)

And as Jesus is being tried by the Jewish Ruling Council, he talks about his ultimate authority.

> *Then the people who had arrested Jesus led him to the home of Caiaphas, the high priest, where the teachers of religious law and the elders had gathered. Meanwhile, Peter followed him at a distance and came to the high priest's courtyard. He went in and sat with the guards and waited to see how it would all end.*
>
> *Inside, the leading priests and the entire high council were trying to find witnesses who would lie about Jesus, so they could put him to death. But even though they found many who agreed to give false witness, they could not use anyone's testimony. Finally, two men came forward who declared, "This man said, 'I am able to destroy the Temple of God and rebuild it in three days.' "*

Then the high priest stood up and said to Jesus, "Well, aren't you going to answer these charges? What do you have to say for yourself?" But Jesus remained silent. Then the high priest said to him, "I demand in the name of the living God—tell us if you are the Messiah, the Son of God."

Jesus replied, "You have said it. And in the future you will see the Son of Man seated in the place of power at God's right hand and coming on the clouds of heaven." (Matthew 26:57-64)

The story of the ascension of Jesus is split up between three passages – one in Matthew, one in Mark, and one in Acts. In the pages that follow, I'm going to help you see the whole story by taking those passages together. But first, I want to explain the different parts of the ascension story in sequence to help them make better sense.

1. *Jesus' ascension began with a priestly blessing over his faithful followers (Luke 24:50).* I love that the last thing Jesus did as his earthly ministry came to a close was to bless the folks! I can just see him raising his hands in Aaronic style to pronounce his final benediction over those who had remained faithfully with him.

2. *Jesus commissioned his faithful followers to continue what he had begun by his authority (Matthew 28:18-20; Mark 16:15-18; Acts 1:8).* All of the ascension accounts – Matthew, Mark and Acts – teach us this.

3. *Jesus was surrounded by the cloud of God's glory (Acts 1:9).* I've said this to my congregation many times: this was no "cumulonimbus cloud"! It was the *shekinah* glory of God surrounding him![21] We have seen this "cloud" many times before. In Genesis 15, it is the "flaming torch and smoking firepot" that establishes the covenant with Abraham. In Exodus, it is the "pillar of cloud" that led the people of Israel, covered the tent of meeting, and overwhelmed the entire top of Mount Sinai as God met with Moses. In 2 Chronicles, it is the "great cloud" of God's glory that was so thick the priests could not minister

---

21   *Shekinah* is the Hebrew term for "settling" and is used to describe the very presence of God and his glory "dwelling" in a space.

in the temple. In Jesus' transfiguration, it is the "bright cloud" that overshadowed them all on the top of the mountain. And in Revelation, it is the "cloud" upon which Jesus and his countless entourage return in glory!

4. *Jesus was "taken up" into heaven (Luke 24:51; Acts 1:9-10).* Theologian Elmer Towns says this was both an ascension and an assumption: "The first implies Christ is entering the presence of the Father in a triumphant display of power and majesty. The second emphasizes the Father's act in exalting His Son and putting Heaven's seal of approval on all that Christ did on earth."[22]

5. *Jesus ascended to the* highest *heavens, exalted over and ruling the entire universe.* Jesus is in, and reigns from, the *highest* place. Paul says that Jesus is higher than all the heavens (Ephesians 4:10). The writer of Hebrews says Jesus, as great High Priest, has entered heaven – given the highest place of honor in heaven (Hebrews 4:14; 7:26). And again, Paul reminds us that God elevated Jesus to the place of highest honor, and gave him the name that is above all other names (Philippians 2:9-11).

6. *Jesus indeed is seated at God's right hand (Mark 16:9; Acts 2:33-36; 5:31; 7:55-56; Ephesians 1:20; Hebrews 10:12; 1 Peter 3:22; Revelation 3:21; 22:1).* Jesus is God's "right-hand man" – that one who is most trusted and in a near-equal position. This position on earth is a king's trusted advisor (think about Joseph's relationship to Pharaoh near the end of Genesis). It is said this phrase, "right-hand man," comes from the days of chivalry when a king's most trusted viceroy would be to his right, where if need arose he could draw his sword in protection of his sovereign without any obstruction.

7. *Finally, Jesus' ascension concluded with an angelic announcement (Acts 1:10-11).* How fitting. Do you see the

---

22   Elmer Towns, *Theology for Today,* Mason, Ohio: Cengage Learning, 2008, p. 246.

proverbial bookends? Jesus' birth was announced by an angel. Now his ascension to the right hand of God in glory is punctuated the same way.

SEWING THE PIECES TOGETHER

There is a wonderful literary tool called a "harmony." I have a few in my library. A harmony is a collection of related books or passages provided side-by-side, with the primary storyline highlighted as a thread throughout that "sews" them all together. I have a harmony of the books of Samuel, Kings, and Chronicles that weaves the chronological history of God's people together in one long thread. I also have a harmony of the Four Gospels, which allows one to read the whole gospel narrative from all four evangelists in one chronological thread.

For our purposes in this chapter, I thought a Harmony of the Ascension of Jesus would be helpful. I have taken the various passages on the Ascension from Matthew, Mark, and Acts and threaded them together for you. Here is the fuller narrative:

Then the eleven disciples went to Galilee, to the mountain where Jesus had told them to go. When they saw him, they worshiped him; but some doubted. ...when they met together, they asked him, "Lord, are you at this time going to restore the kingdom to Israel?"

He said to them: "It is not for you to know the times or dates the Father has set by his own authority. But you will receive power when the Holy Spirit comes on you; and you will be my witnesses in Jerusalem, and in all Judea and Samaria, and to the ends of the earth."

Then Jesus ... said [to them], "All authority in heaven and on earth has been given to me. Therefore, ...Go into all the world and preach the good news to all creation. Whoever believes and is baptized will be saved, but whoever does not believe will be condemned. And these signs will accompany those who believe: In my name they will drive out demons; they will speak in new tongues; they will pick up snakes with their hands; and when they drink deadly poison, it will not hurt them at all; they will place their hands on sick people, and they will get well."

"...Make disciples of all nations, baptizing them in the name of the Father and of the Son and of the Holy Spirit, and teaching them to obey everything I have commanded you. And surely I am with you always, to the very end of the age." After the Lord Jesus had spoken to them, he was taken up into heaven... before their very eyes, and a cloud hid him from their sight... and he sat at the right hand of God.

They were looking intently up into the sky as he was going, when suddenly two men dressed in white stood beside them. "Men of Galilee," they said, "why do you stand here looking o the sky? This same Jesus, who has been taken from you into heaven, will come back in the same way you have seen him go into heaven."

Then the disciples went out and preached everywhere, and the Lord worked with them and confirmed his word by the signs that accompanied it. (Matthew 28:18-20; Mark 16:14-18; Acts 1:6-11)

So that's how Jesus' ascension unfolds. Now let's talk about what it means.

WHAT JESUS' ASCENSION MEANS FOR US

Jesus' ascension and session are just as vital for us as his resurrection. But while many Christians may be able to describe the ascension event, few can tell you why the ascension and session are so essential.

Jesus' ascension and session made the sending of the Holy Spirit possible. Simply put, the Holy Spirit is given to the church upon the risen Jesus' arrival to heaven. As Jesus teaches his disciples about the vital connection between love and obedience, he talks about the coming of the Holy Spirit and his role with them.

Anyone who doesn't love me will not obey me. And remember, my words are not my own. What I am telling you is from the Father who sent me. I am telling you these things now while I am still with you. But when the Father sends the Advocate as my representative—that is, the Holy Spirit—he will teach you everything and will remind you of everything I have told you. (John 14:24-26)

The Holy Spirit will remain with the Church (universal) until Christ's return. He will have a dynamic role with believers, helping them in every aspect of their spiritual formation and their witness. Later, as Jesus is about to ascend, he tells his followers about the empowerment of the Holy Spirit they will receive to continue Jesus' mission and ministry.

> *John baptized with water, but in just a few days you will be bap-tized with the Holy Spirit." ...But you will receive power when the Holy Spirit comes upon you. And you will be my witnesses, telling people about me everywhere—in Jerusalem, throughout Judea, in Samaria, and to the ends of the earth."* (Acts 1:5, 8)

Luke gives us additional details. In his commentary on the events of Pentecost and Peter's subsequent sermon, he describes the coming of the Holy Spirit.

> *On the day of Pentecost all the believers were meeting together in one place. Suddenly, there was a sound from heaven like the roaring of a mighty windstorm, and it filled the house where they were sitting. Then, what looked like flames or tongues of fire appeared and settled on each of them. And everyone present was filled with the Holy Spirit and began speaking in other lan-guages, as the Holy Spirit gave them this ability.*
>
> *At that time there were devout Jews from every nation living in Jerusalem. When they heard the loud noise, everyone came running, and they were bewildered to hear their own languages being spoken by the believers.*
>
> *They were completely amazed. "How can this be?" they ex-claimed. "These people are all from Galilee, and yet we hear them speaking in our own native languages! Here we are—Parthians, Medes, Elamites, people from Mesopotamia, Judea, Cappadocia, Pontus, the province of Asia, Phrygia, Pamphylia, Egypt, and the areas of Libya around Cyrene, visitors from Rome (both Jews and converts to Judaism), Cretans, and Arabs. And we all hear these people speaking in our own languages about the wonderful things God has done!" They stood there amazed and perplexed. "What can this mean?" they asked each other.*

But others in the crowd ridiculed them, saying, "They're just drunk, that's all!" (Acts 2:1-13)

Now he is exalted to the place of highest honor in heaven, at God's right hand. And the Father, as he had promised, gave him the Holy Spirit to pour out upon us, just as you see and hear today. (Acts 2:33)

Jesus' ascension and session initiated the outpouring of spiritual gifts. With the coming of the Holy Spirit – the Helper, the Comforter – are also his spiritual gifts. These special expressions of grace operate under the rule and reign of Jesus from heaven. Jesus previously told his disciples,

He is the Holy Spirit, who leads into all truth. The world cannot receive him, because it isn't looking for him and doesn't recognize him. But you know him, because he lives with you now and later will be in you. (John 14:17)

As he carries out his apostolic teaching, Paul regularly describes the spiritual gifts and their working in his ministry among the churches.

Now, dear brothers and sisters, regarding your question about the special abilities the Spirit gives us. I don't want you to misunderstand this. You know that when you were still pagans, you were led astray and swept along in worshiping speechless idols. So I want you to know that no one speaking by the Spirit of God will curse Jesus, and no one can say Jesus is Lord, except by the Holy Spirit.

There are different kinds of spiritual gifts, but the same Spirit is the source of them all. There are different kinds of service, but we serve the same Lord. God works in different ways, but it is the same God who does the work in all of us.

A spiritual gift is given to each of us so we can help each other. To one person the Spirit gives the ability to give wise advice; to another the same Spirit gives a message of special knowledge. The same Spirit gives great faith to another, and to someone else the one Spirit gives the gift of healing. He gives one person the power to perform miracles, and another the ability to prophesy.

He gives someone else the ability to discern whether a message is from the Spirit of God or from another spirit. Still another person is given the ability to speak in unknown languages, while another is given the ability to interpret what is being said. It is the one and only Spirit who distributes all these gifts. He alone decides which gift each person should have. (1 Corinthians 12:1-11)

Now these are the gifts Christ gave to the church: the apostles, the prophets, the evangelists, and the pastors and teachers. Their responsibility is to equip God's people to do his work and build up the church, the body of Christ. This will continue until we all come to such unity in our faith and knowledge of God's Son that we will be mature in the Lord, measuring up to the full and complete standard of Christ.

Then we will no longer be immature like children. We won't be tossed and blown about by every wind of new teaching. We will not be influenced when people try to trick us with lies so clever they sound like the truth. Instead, we will speak the truth in love, growing in every way more and more like Christ, who is the head of his body, the church. He makes the whole body fit together perfectly. As each part does its own special work, it helps the other parts grow, so that the whole body is healthy and growing and full of love. (Ephesians 4:11-16)

These special spiritual abilities are primarily used in the context of the body – the church. They are not for our own glory, but for the blessing and help of others. The leadership gifts listed in Ephesians 4 above are to prepare and lead God's people in his ministry. Paul says that gifts are given to each follower of Christ. Peter, too, tells us that *every* believer has been given spiritual gifts.

God has given each of you a gift from his great variety of spiritual gifts. Use them well to serve one another. Do you have the gift of speaking? Then speak as though God himself were speaking through you. Do you have the gift of helping others? Do it with all the strength and energy that God supplies. Then everything you do will bring glory to God through Jesus Christ. All glory and power to him forever and ever! Amen. (1 Peter 4:10-11)

Jesus' ascension and session guarantee the imparting of spiritual power. Jesus promised his followers that they would be endued with power from on high to be his agents, his witnesses, from Jerusalem to the ends of the earth! Jesus told his followers that they would accomplish even greater things than he accomplished during his earthly ministry! This spiritual power is how that happens. We are on the same mission, under the authority of the Messiah, but are greater in number. We are quite literally Christ's ambassadors – his authorized representatives (2 Corinthians 5:20), wielding the power and authority of our King as long as we are on his mission.

I love that Jesus reminded his followers of his ongoing powerful presence just before he ascended.

> *"And be sure of this: I am with you always, even to the end of the age."* (Matthew 28:20b)

In fact, Luke tells us that Jesus promised that power with the coming of the Holy Spirit.

> *"And now I will send the Holy Spirit, just as my Father promised. But stay here in the city until the Holy Spirit comes and fills you with power from heaven."* (Luke 24:49)

John tells us that we are to keep doing the very work Jesus did, and we can expect even greater results.

> *"I tell you the truth, anyone who believes in me will do the same works I have done, and even greater works, because I am going to be with the Father. You can ask for anything in my name, and I will do it, so that the Son can bring glory to the Father. Yes, ask me for anything in my name, and I will do it!* (John 14:12-14)

And again, Luke describes Jesus' teaching about this power to his followers right before he ascended into heaven.

Once when he was eating with them, he commanded them, "Do not leave Jerusalem until the Father sends you the gift he promised, as I told you before. John baptized with water, but in just a few days you will be baptized with the Holy Spirit."

So when the apostles were with Jesus, they kept asking him, "Lord, has the time come for you to free Israel and restore our kingdom?"

He replied, "The Father alone has the authority to set those dates and times, and they are not for you to know. But you will receive power when the Holy Spirit comes upon you. And you will be my witnesses, telling people about me everywhere—in Jerusalem, throughout Judea, in Samaria, and to the ends of the earth." (Acts 1:4-8)

We are empowered for Jesus' mission – to carry the witness of his gospel throughout the world.

Jesus' ascension and session continue his mediation between God and man. This is so important for us to understand personally. Because Jesus is at God's right hand, he is the perfect mediator and intercessor for us before the Father. Paul says there is one mediator between God and us – that's Jesus!

For,

There is one God and one Mediator who can reconcile God and humanity—the man Christ Jesus. He gave his life to purchase freedom for everyone. This is the message God gave to the world at just the right time. And I have been chosen as a preacher and apostle to teach the Gentiles this message about faith and truth. I'm not exaggerating—just telling the truth. (1 Timothy 2:5-7)

There were many priests under the old system, for death prevented them from remaining in office. But because Jesus lives forever, his priesthood lasts forever. Therefore he is able, once and forever, to save those who come to God through him. He lives forever to intercede with God on their behalf. (Hebrews 7:23-25)

Jesus' ascension and session have made our eternal destiny a reality. Jesus said he went before us to prepare a place for us in the Father's house (John 14:1-6). Paul tells us that believers appear *with Christ* in glory (Colossians 3:3). Paul also tells us that our citizenship is not here on Earth but in heaven (Philippians 3:20). He says that we have been raised up *with Christ* and seated *with him* in the heavenly places (Ephesians 2:6). Paul even says we will judge angels (1 Corinthians 6:3)! Believers are ultimately *elevated* with Christ – If we are in Christ, we have a heavenly destiny with him!

Finally, Jesus' ascension and session ultimately realign everything. Are you ready for all the garbage of this life to be over? No more crime. No more corruption. No more deceit. No more powerbrokers. No more abuse. No more cancer. No more disease. No more fear. It is Jesus who makes all things new again – the way they were intended to be – leading us all back to God's definition of "very good" from the Creation (see Genesis 1:31)!

Jesus vanquished Satan, his dark dominion, and all the collateral damage he has wreaked.

> *"The time for judging this world has come, when Satan, the ruler of this world, will be cast out. And when I am lifted up from the earth, I will draw everyone to myself."* (John 12:31-32)

For those who are in Christ, all shame and disgrace is obliterated.

> *As the Scriptures tell us, "Anyone who trusts in him will never be disgraced." Jew and Gentile are the same in this respect. They have the same Lord, who gives generously to all who call on him. For "Everyone who calls on the name of the Lord will be saved."* (Romans 10:11-13)

Jesus destroys all the rulers, authorities, and powers of darkness.

> *But there is an order to this resurrection: Christ was raised as the first of the harvest; then all who belong to Christ will be raised when he comes back.*

After that the end will come, when he will turn the Kingdom over to God the Father, having destroyed every ruler and authority and power. For Christ must reign until he humbles all his enemies beneath his feet. And the last enemy to be destroyed is death. For the Scriptures say, "God has put all things under his authority." (Of course, when it says "all things are under his authority," that does not include God himself, who gave Christ his authority.) Then, when all things are under his authority, the Son will put himself under God's authority, so that God, who gave his Son authority over all things, will be utterly supreme over everything everywhere. (1 Corinthians 15:23-28)

There is no power greater than that of our God, demonstrated through Jesus Christ.

I also pray that you will understand the incredible greatness of God's power for us who believe him. This is the same mighty power that raised Christ from the dead and seated him in the place of honor at God's right hand in the heavenly realms. Now he is far above any ruler or authority or power or leader or anything else—not only in this world but also in the world to come. God has put all things under the authority of Christ and has made him head over all things for the benefit of the church. And the church is his body; it is made full and complete by Christ, who fills all things everywhere with himself. (Ephesians 1:20-23)

God gave Jesus the highest name – the highest honor.

Therefore, God elevated him to the place of highest honor and gave him the name above all other names, that at the name of Jesus every knee should bow, in heaven and on earth and under the earth, and every tongue declare that Jesus Christ is Lord, to the glory of God the Father. (Philippians 2:9-11)

The holy angels and authorities of heaven recognize and accept Jesus' ruling authority.

Now Christ has gone to heaven. He is seated in the place of honor next to God, and all the angels and authorities and powers accept his authority. (1 Peter 3:22)

The bottom line is that Jesus – the mighty God and our Savior – is worthy!

Then I saw a scroll in the right hand of the one who was sitting on the throne. There was writing on the inside and the outside of the scroll, and it was sealed with seven seals. And I saw a strong angel, who shouted with a loud voice: "Who is worthy to break the seals on this scroll and open it?" But no one in heaven or on earth or under the earth was able to open the scroll and read it.

Then I began to weep bitterly because no one was found worthy to open the scroll and read it. But one of the twenty-four elders said to me, "Stop weeping! Look, the Lion of the tribe of Judah, the heir to David's throne, has won the victory. He is worthy to open the scroll and its seven seals."

Then I saw a Lamb that looked as if it had been slaughtered, but it was now standing between the throne and the four living beings and among the twenty-four elders. He had seven horns and seven eyes, which represent the sevenfold Spirit of God that is sent out into every part of the earth. He stepped forward and took the scroll from the right hand of the one sitting on the throne. And when he took the scroll, the four living beings and the twenty-four elders fell down before the Lamb. Each one had a harp, and they held gold bowls filled with incense, which are the prayers of God's people. And they sang a new song with these words:

"You are worthy to take the scroll and break its seals and open it.

For you were slaughtered, and your blood has ransomed people for God from every tribe and language and people and nation.

And you have caused them to become a Kingdom of priests for our God.

And they will reign on the earth."

Then I looked again, and I heard the voices of thousands and millions of angels around the throne and of the living beings and the elders. And they sang in a mighty chorus:

"Worthy is the Lamb who was slaughtered— to receive power and riches and wisdom and strength and honor and glory and blessing."

And then I heard every creature in heaven and on earth and under the earth and in the sea. They sang:

"Blessing and honor and glory and power belong to the one sitting on the throne and to the Lamb forever and ever."

And the four living beings said, "Amen!" And the twenty-four elders fell down and worshiped the Lamb. (Revelation 5:1-14)

All of this is wrapped up in Jesus' ascension and session. "I believe in Jesus Christ...that he ascended into heaven, and sits at the right hand of God, the Father Almighty..." Can you agree with me that these doctrinal truths are essential to our Christian faith? The ascension and session of Christ are a big deal.

STUDY GUIDE

IT MAKES A DIFFERENCE

Christians who understand what the scriptures say about the ascension and session of Jesus celebrate his Lordship. They realize that Jesus' ascension and session are just as important to our Christian Faith and lifestyle as are his death and resurrection. By ascending and ruling from God's right hand, Jesus makes provision for God's Holy Spirit to dwell with believers, equipping them for life and ministry. He also guarantees the gift of spiritual power to those on his mission. Finally, Jesus' rule and reign from heaven ultimately works to make every-thing right again.

Those who don't understand the biblical teaching about Jesus' ascension and session nearly always resist Jesus' Lordship and may even argue about the sovereignty of God. They question why God has not already eradicated evil, disease, war, and more from the earth. Their trust in God is minimal at best, so they seek social and political answers to human problems over Christian ministry. They are often like the first-century Jews to whom Jesus said, "So why do you keep calling me 'Lord, Lord!' when you don't do what I say?" (Luke 6:46).

The biblical record is clear: Jesus reigns!

HOW DO I LIVE OUT WHAT I HAVE JUST LEARNED IN MY OWN LIFE?

1. Take a moment to stop and pray. Ask God, through the Holy Spirit, to increase your understanding of the essentials of the Christian Faith. Ask Him to reveal and clarify any points which have been confusing or unclear.

2. After reading the chapter, meditate about the significance of the Ascension and Session of Jesus in your own life.

3. Take several days to consider: Who can help you apply what you learn to put it into an ongoing life's practice?

4. How are you living this out right now? How is your life reflective of your understanding of this truth?

HOW DO I IMPART WHAT I HAVE JUST LEARNED TO CHILDREN?

Preparing to teach this lesson to children: As part of the study of Chapter 8 (the Ascension and Session), it is suggested that the children create a three-panel story page. You may want to go to the following website to download a free template. Run off enough for each child to have one, plus a couple of extras in case the children want to start again. https://www.papertraildesign.com/wp-content/uploads/2020/08/Comic-Book-Template-4.jpg. Also, please gather the following materials: pencils and markers or crayons. Optionally, you may choose to offer cotton balls, shiny bits of wrapping paper, or foil and glue.

1. Continue to work on memorizing the Apostle's Creed. Be sure they have memorized through this part: *I believe in God, the Father almighty, creator of heaven and earth. I believe in Jesus Christ, his only Son, our Lord, who was conceived*

by the Holy Spirit and born of the virgin Mary. He suffered under Pontius Pilate, was crucified, died, and was buried; he descended into hell. The third day he rose again from the dead. He ascended to heaven and is seated at the right hand of God the Father almighty.

2. Tell the children that after Jesus rose from the dead and appeared to many people to prove he was alive, his work on earth was complete. He was ready to return to heaven where he had lived with God before he came to earth. This return is called *the Ascension.* You may need to define the term *ascend* for them. They may be more familiar with *descend,* the opposite term. God caused Jesus to be taken up to heaven in a cloud of glory.

3. Explain that after Jesus left earth to return to heaven, he sent the Holy Spirit to live in the hearts of the disciples. This gives us power to do God's work. We will learn more about the Holy Spirit and his work in a future chapter.

4. Talk to the children about where Jesus is now, in heaven, ruling over all creation with God the Father. This is called *Session,* another term with which the children probably will not be familiar. You may need to revisit what is meant by the term *almighty* as it is used to describe God. We call Jesus "Lord" because he is the ruler.

5. Have the children create a pictorial representation of the *Ascension*, the sending of the Holy Spirit, and the *Session*, one in each block. Before they start, talk about how they might represent each concept. If you chose to supply cotton balls, they could be glued under the feet of the ascending Jesus. If you have shiny paper, it could be used to fashion a crown on the head of Jesus as he sits at the right side of Father God.

6. If you have kids in your group who have not yet surrendered to Jesus, continue praying for the Holy Spirit to open that conversational door so you can explain the gospel. Once they receive Christ, the indwelling presence of the Holy Spirit will make the lessons in this book much more accessible to them.

HOW DO I IMPART WHAT I HAVE JUST LEARNED TO TEENS?

1. Pray at the beginning of the session, asking God to increase understanding. You can do this or ask a volunteer.

2. Read the Apostles' Creed out loud. Either read it yourself or ask for a volunteer.

3. Repeat the first several lines: *I believe in God, the Father almighty, creator of heaven and earth. I believe in Jesus Christ, his only Son, our Lord, who was conceived by the Holy Spirit and born of the virgin Mary. He suffered under Pontius Pilate, was crucified, died, and was buried; he descended into hell. The third day he rose again from the dead. He ascended to heaven and is seated at the right hand of God the Father almighty.* Encourage the teens to commit this to memory.

4. Have the teens pull out their notes from the first session. Ask them to jot down the answers to any questions that may be answered during this session, and to share those discoveries as they happen. Provide sufficient time to record any thoughts they may wish to capture. Assure them that they will have the opportunity to ask any remaining questions about this section at the end of the session.

5. Be sure the teens understand the terms *Ascension* and *Session* as they are used theologically.

6. Discuss reasons Jesus talked about his *Ascension and Session* ahead of their occurrence.

7. Talk about the importance of Jesus being described as sitting at the right hand of God the Father almighty.

8. Review the reasons the *Ascension and Session* are important. These are enumerated in the section What Jesus's Ascension means for us.

9. Ask the teens how the *Ascension and Session* of Jesus affect their life.

10. If time permits, allow teens to divide the final scripture passage (Revelation 5:1-14) into speaking parts and read it with expression as a form of worship. Ask them to imagine how the scene in heaven might actually look.

11. Allow teens to ask any questions about Jesus' *Ascension and Session* that they had noted in their journals that were not addressed in this discussion. Ask them if/how their understanding of Jesus changed through what they learned in this session.

12. If you have teens in your group who have not yet surrendered to Jesus, continue praying for the Holy Spirit to open that conversational door so you can explain the gospel. Once they receive Christ, the indwelling presence of the Holy Spirit will make the lessons in this book much more accessible to them.

HOW DO I IMPART WHAT I HAVE JUST LEARNED TO ADULTS?

1. Challenge your adults to take a moment to stop and pray, asking God, through the Holy Spirit, to increase their understanding of the essentials of the Christian Faith. Ask Him to reveal and clarify any points which have been confusing or unclear.

2. Review the Apostles' Creed, emphasizing the first several lines: *I believe in God, the Father almighty, creator of heaven and earth. I believe in Jesus Christ, his only Son, our Lord, who was conceived by the Holy Spirit and born of the virgin Mary. He suffered under Pontius Pilate, was crucified, died, and was buried; he descended into hell. The third day he rose again from the dead. He ascended to heaven and is seated at the right hand of God the Father almighty.* If they have not done so, encourage them to memorize the Creed in its entirety, reminding them that it is a summary of the essentials of the Christian Faith.

3. Have participants pull out the notes they made during the first session. Ask them to jot down the answers to any questions about the first few lines that may be answered during this session, and to share those discoveries as they happen.

Provide sufficient time to record any thoughts they may wish to capture. Assure them that they will have the opportunity to ask any questions that were not answered in this session at the end of the session.

4. Review the definitions of the terms *Ascension* and *Session* as are used in this chapter.

5. Dr. Kimball asserts that Jesus' ascension and session are just as vital for us as his resurrection. What are the reasons for this assertion?

6. Ask participants why the writers of the Creed would think it important to describe Jesus as sitting at the right hand of the Father almighty.

7. Allow participants to ask any questions about Jesus' *Ascension and Session* they had noted previously that were not addressed in this discussion. Participants may have questions about the work of the Holy Spirit. While the subject is addressed here, it will be revisited in more detail in Chapter 10.

8. Close the session by reading Revelation 5:1-14 aloud in unison as a form of worship, asking participants to create the scene in their minds as they do so.

9. If you have folks in your group who have not yet surrendered to Jesus, continue praying for the Holy Spirit to open that conversational door so you can explain the gospel. Once they receive Christ, the indwelling presence of the Holy Spirit will make the lessons in this book much more accessible to them.

CHAPTER 9
Jesus: The Righteous Judge

"I believe in Jesus Christ...He will come to judge the living and the dead..."

Then I saw heaven opened, and a white horse was standing there. Its rider was named Faithful and True, for he judges fairly and wages a righteous war. His eyes were like flames of fire, and on his head were many crowns. A name was written on him that no one understood except himself. He wore a robe dipped in blood, and his title was the Word of God. The armies of heaven, dressed in the finest of pure white linen, followed him on white horses. From his mouth came a sharp sword to strike down the nations. He will rule them with an iron rod. He will release the fierce wrath of God, the Almighty, like juice flowing from a winepress. On his robe at his thigh was written this title: King of all kings and Lord of all lords.

Then I saw an angel standing in the sun, shouting to the vultures flying high in the sky: "Come! Gather together for the great banquet God has prepared. Come and eat the flesh of kings, generals, and strong warriors; of horses and their riders; and of all humanity, both free and slave, small and great."

Then I saw the beast and the kings of the world and their armies gathered together to fight against the one sitting on the horse

181

and his army. And the beast was captured, and with him the false prophet who did mighty miracles on behalf of the beast— miracles that deceived all who had accepted the mark of the beast and who worshiped his statue. Both the beast and his false prophet were thrown alive into the fiery lake of burning sulfur. Their entire army was killed by the sharp sword that came from the mouth of the one riding the white horse. And the vultures all gorged themselves on the dead bodies. (Revelation 19:11-21)

"I believe in Jesus Christ... He will come to judge the living and the dead." I know so many Christians who fear the end times. They do not like to read Bible books like Revelation because they do not understand that, for the followers of Christ, Revelation is a book of hope. I had a conversation not long ago with someone who had read a post on the internet that described current events in terms of the battle of Armageddon (Revelation 16:12-16). The Apostle John describes a great and final battle with the demon-led worldly rulers and their armies rallying against the Lord. My friend was positive that we are on the brink of Armageddon and has quite literally worked himself into a panic. I tried to explain that Jesus said none of us could actually know the day or hour of his return (Matthew 24:36), but that when it does happen, it's a *good* thing for Jesus' people. I also explained that, as seen in our passage above, the battle itself would be very short: Jesus immediately ends it with the sharp sword of his mouth (Revelation 19:21).

I think part of the angst about the end times is because the apocalyptic genre of Bible literature (like Revelation, parts of Isaiah, Ezekiel, Daniel, and Zechariah) is truly hard to follow and understand. Another contributing factor may be that there are so many different "camps" when it comes to eschatology (the study of the end times): Premillennialism, Amillennialism, Postmillennialism, and various views on the timing of the Great Tribulation. But regardless of what one has surmised with respect to the Biblical millennium and tribulation, the Apostles' Creed brings us back to the simplicity of two unifying truths: Jesus is indeed coming again, and when he comes, he will judge humanity. I assure you that, on both counts, this is absolutely glorious news for the believer!

JESUS' RETURN

Jesus' return will be sudden and unexpected. While Jesus does give us some signs to warn us that the end is near, he also says that only the Father in heaven knows the day and hour. We are to live in a continuously prepared state. Jesus' return will be sudden and immediate – like a thief in the night or a flash of lightning. As his people, we need to be ready for his return, and we need to prepare others as well.

> *"However, no one knows the day or hour when these things will happen, not even the angels in heaven or the Son himself. Only the Father knows.*
>
> *"When the Son of Man returns, it will be like it was in Noah's day. In those days before the flood, the people were enjoying banquets and parties and weddings right up to the time Noah entered his boat. People didn't realize what was going to happen until the flood came and swept them all away. That is the way it will be when the Son of Man comes.*
>
> *"Two men will be working together in the field; one will be taken, the other left. Two women will be grinding flour at the mill; one will be taken, the other left.*
>
> *"So you, too, must keep watch! For you don't know what day your Lord is coming. Understand this: If a homeowner knew exactly when a burglar was coming, he would keep watch and not permit his house to be broken into. You also must be ready all the time, for the Son of Man will come when least expected.*
> (Matthew 24:36-44)

Not only do we need to live a life of preparedness, but we must also be truly patient as we wait for Jesus' return. Jesus' half-brother James, the lead apostle in the Church at Jerusalem, writes to the saints about this.

> *Dear brothers and sisters, be patient as you wait for the Lord's return. Consider the farmers who patiently wait for the rains in the fall and in the spring. They eagerly look for the valuable harvest to ripen. You, too, must be patient. Take courage, for the coming of the Lord is near.* (James 5:7-8)

And Peter continues the thought as he writes to Christians dealing with false teachers – including bad teaching about Jesus' return. He tells us how to "wait."

> But you must not forget this one thing, dear friends: A day is like a thousand years to the Lord, and a thousand years is like a day. The Lord isn't really being slow about his promise, as some people think. No, he is being patient for your sake. He does not want anyone to be destroyed, but wants everyone to repent. But the day of the Lord will come as unexpectedly as a thief. Then the heavens will pass away with a terrible noise, and the very elements themselves will disappear in fire, and the earth and everything on it will be found to deserve judgment.
>
> Since everything around us is going to be destroyed like this, what holy and godly lives you should live, looking forward to the day of God and hurrying it along. On that day, he will set the heavens on fire, and the elements will melt away in the flames. But we are looking forward to the new heavens and new earth he has promised, a world filled with God's righteousness.
>
> And so, dear friends, while you are waiting for these things to happen, make every effort to be found living peaceful lives that are pure and blameless in his sight. (2 Peter 3:8-14)

Jesus' return will be personal. His *parousia,* or Jesus' second coming, will not be some kind of mystical or ghostly event. Jesus will return personally. He, himself, will come to claim his people. And mark my words, the whole world will know it is *him* when this happens. Even those who have disbelieved or rejected him – they will know him. Remember, Paul tells us

> ...that at the name of Jesus every knee should bow, in heaven and on earth and under the earth, and every tongue declare that Jesus Christ is Lord, to the glory of God the Father. (Philippians 2:10-11)

Jesus promised a personal return to his disciples. It's actually a promise to all those who know and follow him as Christ.

"Don't let your hearts be troubled. Trust in God, and trust also in me. There is more than enough room in my Father's home. If this were not so, would I have told you that I am going to pre-pare a place for you? **When everything is ready, I will come and get you, so that you will always be with me where I am.** *And you know the way to where I am going."* (John 14:1-4, **emphasis mine**)

And Paul describes it as a personal return to the Christians at Thessalonica as he writes to them about the hope they have in the resurrection.

And now, dear brothers and sisters, we want you to know what will happen to the believers who have died so you will not grieve like people who have no hope. For since we believe that Jesus died and was raised to life again, we also believe that when Jesus returns, God will bring back with him the believers who have died.

We tell you this directly from the Lord: We who are still living when the Lord returns will not meet him ahead of those who have died. **For the Lord himself will come down from heaven** *with a commanding shout, with the voice of the archangel, and with the trumpet call of God. First, the believers who have died will rise from their graves. Then, together with them, we who are still alive and remain on the earth will be caught up in the clouds to meet the Lord in the air. Then we will be with the Lord forever. So encourage each other with these words.* (1 Thessalonians 4:13-18, **emphasis mine**)

Jesus' return will be visible. In the last chapter, we talked about the angels' proclamation that "...someday he will return from heaven in the same way you saw him go" (Acts 1:10-11). Jesus ascended in front of everyone. Jesus will return in the same way. In fact, one day as Jesus sat on the Mount of Olives, he told his disciples how his return would unfold.

And then at last, the sign that the Son of Man is coming will appear in the heavens, and there will be deep mourning among all the peoples of the earth. And they will see the Son of Man

coming on the clouds of heaven with power and great glory. And
he will send out his angels with the mighty blast of a trumpet, and
they will gather his chosen ones from all over the world—from
the farthest ends of the earth and heaven. (Matthew 24:30-31)

He will gather all those who have trusted in him. There is only judgment
for those who refused God's gift of salvation in Jesus. But for believers,
there is the glorious fruit of their salvation. The writer of Hebrews says:

And just as each person is destined to die once and after that
comes judgment, so also Christ was offered once for all time as
a sacrifice to take away the sins of many people. He will come
again, not to deal with our sins, but to bring salvation to all who
are eagerly waiting for him. (Hebrews 9:27-28)

And Peter talks about how, even though we might suffer now, it will be
glorious for us when Jesus returns and is revealed to the whole world!

So be truly glad. There is wonderful joy ahead, even though
you must endure many trials for a little while. These trials will
show that your faith is genuine. It is being tested as fire tests and
purifies gold—though your faith is far more precious than mere
gold. So when your faith remains strong through many trials, it
will bring you much praise and glory and honor on the day when
Jesus Christ is revealed to the whole world.

You love him even though you have never seen him. Though you
do not see him now, you trust him; and you rejoice with a glo-
rious, inexpressible joy. The reward for trusting him will be the
salvation of your souls.

This salvation was something even the prophets wanted to know
more about when they prophesied about this gracious salvation
prepared for you. They wondered what time or situation the Spirit
of Christ within them was talking about when he told them in
advance about Christ's suffering and his great glory afterward.

They were told that their messages were not for themselves, but
for you. And now this Good News has been announced to you

by those who preached in the power of the Holy Spirit sent from heaven. It is all so wonderful that even the angels are eagerly watching these things happen.

So prepare your minds for action and exercise self-control. Put all your hope in the gracious salvation that will come to you when Jesus Christ is revealed to the world. (1 Peter 1:6-13)

Jesus' return will be bodily. Again, he doesn't return in spirit – in some kind of ghostly form – but in his own real body. John writes in his first letter to the Church:

> *See how very much our Father loves us, for he calls us his children, and that is what we are! But the people who belong to this world don't recognize that we are God's children because they don't know him. Dear friends, we are already God's children, but he has not yet shown us what we will be like when Christ appears. But we do know that we will be like him, **for we will see him as he really is**.* (1 John 3:1-2, **emphasis mine**)

Paul tells the Philippian Christians that even our own lowly bodies will be transformed when he returns – our bodies will be like his heavenly body!

> *But we are citizens of heaven, where the Lord Jesus Christ lives. And we are eagerly waiting for him to return as our Savior. He will take our weak mortal bodies and change them into glorious bodies like his own, using the same power with which he will bring everything under his control.* (Philippians 3:20-21)

No more aches. No more pain. No more sickness. No more injury. No more suffering or shame. (Revelation 21:1-5).

Jesus' return will be like his ascension – it's bodily.

Jesus' return will be glorious. Jesus will be coming on the "clouds" – as I've said before, this references God's shekinah glory! He will be accompanied by the angelic host – the angel armies. It will be a joyous wonder to behold for all who belong to him. But it will be a terrible wonder for everyone else. Jesus even says that the nations will mourn on that day (Matthew 24:30). The first time he came as Savior. The next time he comes as Judge.

> *"But when the Son of Man comes in his glory, and all the angels with him, then he will sit upon his glorious throne. All the nations will be gathered in his presence, and he will separate the people as a shepherd separates the sheep from the goats.* (Matthew 25:31-32)

Once again, I must emphasize that, for all those who have surrendered to Jesus as King and Master (Lord) and have had their sins completely forgiven because of his shed blood on the cross of Calvary, this is a good and glorious event. We have nothing at all to fear! Jesus tells us that he has come to gather us from all over the world.

> *Then everyone will see the Son of Man coming on the clouds with great power and glory. And he will send out his angels to gather his chosen ones from all over the world—from the farthest ends of the earth and heaven.* (Mark 13:26-27)

> *Then everyone will see the Son of Man coming on a cloud with power and great glory. So when all these things begin to happen, stand and look up, for your salvation is near!"* (Luke 21:27-28)

It will be an event of great hope and expectation!

> *For the grace of God has been revealed, bringing salvation to all people. And we are instructed to turn from godless living and sinful pleasures. We should live in this evil world with wisdom, righteousness, and devotion to God, while we look forward with hope to that wonderful day when the glory of our great God and Savior, Jesus Christ, will be revealed. He gave his life to free us from every kind of sin, to cleanse us, and to make us his very own people, totally committed to doing good deeds.* (Titus 2:11-14)

One final word of warning. Many believers today seem consumed in looking for signs of the end times. Some of those believers are way too focused on trying to identify the Beast, the False Prophet, and the Antichrist from Revelation. One of my mentors recently posted a powerful meme on social media. It reads, "Theology 101: No passage of Scripture directs Christians to prep for the Antichrist, but numerous passages instruct them to await Christ's return. It's a real problem if your end-times expectations are Antichrist-centered (fear) rather than Christ-centered (hope) (1 Thessalonians 1:9-10)."[23] The passage referenced here is an important one:

> *...for they keep talking about the wonderful welcome you gave us and how you turned away from idols to serve the living and true God. And they speak of how you are looking forward to the coming of God's Son from heaven—Jesus, whom God raised from the dead. He is the one who has rescued us from the terrors of the coming judgment.* (1 Thessalonians 1:9-10)

Jesus' return is sudden, personal, visible, bodily, and glorious. And we, as his people, need to be vigilant in watching for it. This is how Jesus' second coming unfolds. Now let's look at what happens when he comes.

JESUS' JUDGMENT

The most important point we can make here is that Jesus is the Judge. The judgment to which I'm referring is not upon believers but upon all those who have rejected King Jesus. There is coming a time when it will be too late to surrender. I find the words of Paul to the Philippians wonderful for those who follow Christ but sobering for those who don't.

> *Therefore, God elevated him to the place of highest honor and gave him the name above all other names, that at the name of Jesus every knee should bow, in heaven and on earth **and under the earth**, and every tongue declare that Jesus Christ is Lord, to the glory of God the Father.* (Philippians 2:9-11, **emphasis mine**)

The phrase "under the earth" certainly refers to those who are dead and buried, but could it also refer to those in hell? The terminology of allegiance is comprehensive. *Every* knee will bow. *Every* tongue will declare

---

23   Meme from Dr. Michael J. Svigel, online, *Twitter*, @Svigel 4/14/21.

that Jesus is Lord. It is my view that this is precisely what Paul is saying. Even those who have rejected Christ – and have thereby been rejected by him – will ultimately bow their knee and declare with their own tongue that Jesus Christ is LORD. But for them, it will be forever too late. Jesus came the first time to save us. All those who reject that offer will meet him the second time as Judge.

> *"Then the King will turn to those on the left and say, 'Away with you, you cursed ones, into the eternal fire prepared for the devil and his demons. For I was hungry, and you didn't feed me. I was thirsty, and you didn't give me a drink. I was a stranger, and you didn't invite me into your home. I was naked, and you didn't give me clothing. I was sick and in prison, and you didn't visit me.'*
>
> *"Then they will reply, 'Lord, when did we ever see you hungry or thirsty or a stranger or naked or sick or in prison, and not help you?'*
>
> *"And he will answer, 'I tell you the truth, when you refused to help the least of these my brothers and sisters, you were refusing to help me.'*
>
> *"And they will go away into eternal punishment, but the righteous will go into eternal life."* (Matthew 25:41-46)

Some like to believe that the "God of the Old Testament" is angry and vengeful, but the "Jesus of the New Testament" is meek and kind. While Jesus truly shows us what real meekness looks like, make no mistake that he is also the one who dishes out God's wrath at the end. The world has tended to portray Jesus as a great teacher, a wonderful man, a true prophet, a gentle Messiah, and a loving shepherd. All of these things are true, but so is the fact of his holiness, his justice, and his absolute righteousness.

We love to quote John 3:16 – you even see placards of this verse at various sporting events. But we must take that verse in context. The verses that follow are equally important (and remember, when Jesus spoke these words he had come as Savior – but he's looking forward in time).

"For this is how God loved the world: He gave his one and only Son, so that everyone who believes in him will not perish but have eternal life. God sent his Son into the world not to judge the world, but to save the world through him.

"There is no judgment against anyone who believes in him. ***But anyone who does not believe in him has already been judged for not believing in God's one and only Son. And the judgment is based on this fact: God's light came into the world, but people loved the darkness more than the light, for their actions were evil. All who do evil hate the light and refuse to go near it for fear their sins will be exposed.*** *But those who do what is right come to the light so others can see that they are doing what God wants."* (John 3:16-21, **emphasis mine**)

Jesus warns his disciples that he has the authority to judge everyone.

"I tell you the truth, those who listen to my message and believe in God who sent me have eternal life. They will never be condemned for their sins, but they have already passed from death into life.

"And I assure you that the time is coming, indeed it's here now, when the dead will hear my voice—the voice of the Son of God. And those who listen will live. The Father has life in himself, and he has granted that same life-giving power to his Son. And he has given him authority to judge everyone because he is the Son of Man. Don't be so surprised! Indeed, the time is coming when all the dead in their graves will hear the voice of God's Son, and they will rise again. Those who have done good will rise to experience eternal life, and those who have continued in evil will rise to experience judgment. (John 5:24-29)

And Paul warns the people in Athens about the authority of Jesus' judgment.

"God overlooked people's ignorance about these things in earlier times, but now he commands everyone everywhere to repent of

their sins and turn to him. For he has set a day for judging the world with justice by the man he has appointed, and he proved to everyone who this is by raising him from the dead." (Acts 17:30-31)

Jesus is the Judge. And it is good that *he* is the Judge because he is unflappable, he is incorruptible, he is the essence of good, and he already knows every fact of every person's case. Jesus cannot be deceived. Jesus cannot be swayed. Either a person's sins have already been paid for by Jesus' own blood, or they have not. And Jesus himself will be the Judge of that!

Jesus' judgment is real. People today live like there will be no reckoning. How foolish! The judgment is not a myth. And I've found that all but the most-seared hearts still know this to be true. We can discern good from evil. Even children have an innate sense of justice. Have you heard a child decry, "That isn't fair!"? Jesus tells us in Matthew's gospel that his judgment includes everything – From unrepentant hearts right down to every careless word we have said.

Then Jesus began to denounce the towns where he had done so many of his miracles, because they hadn't repented of their sins and turned to God. "What sorrow awaits you, Korazin and Bethsaida! For if the miracles I did in you had been done in wicked Tyre and Sidon, their people would have repented of their sins long ago, clothing themselves in burlap and throwing ashes on their heads to show their remorse. I tell you, Tyre and Sidon will be better off on judgment day than you.

"And you people of Capernaum, will you be honored in heaven? No, you will go down to the place of the dead. For if the miracles I did for you had been done in wicked Sodom, it would still be here today. ²⁴ I tell you, even Sodom will be better off on judgment day than you." (Matthew 11:20-24)

"A good person produces good things from the treasury of a good heart, and an evil person produces evil things from the treasury of an evil heart. And I tell you this, you must give an account on judgment day for every idle word you speak. The words you say will either acquit you or condemn you." (Matthew 12:35-37)

Peter warns that God's judgment will not be delayed when it comes to those who deceive, the immoral, those who practice twisted sexuality, and those who despise authority.

But there were also false prophets in Israel, just as there will be false teachers among you. They will cleverly teach destructive heresies and even deny the Master who bought them. In this way, they will bring sudden destruction on themselves. Many will follow their evil teaching and shameful immorality. And because of these teachers, the way of truth will be slandered. In their greed they will make up clever lies to get hold of your money. But God condemned them long ago, and their destruction will not be delayed.

For God did not spare even the angels who sinned. He threw them into hell, in gloomy pits of darkness, where they are being held until the day of judgment. And God did not spare the ancient world—except for Noah and the seven others in his family. Noah warned the world of God's righteous judgment. So God protected Noah when he destroyed the world of ungodly people with a vast flood. Later, God condemned the cities of Sodom and Gomorrah and turned them into heaps of ashes. He made them an example of what will happen to ungodly people. But God also rescued Lot out of Sodom because he was a righteous man who was sick of the shameful immorality of the wicked people around him. Yes, Lot was a righteous man who was tormented in his soul by the wickedness he saw and heard day after day. So you see, the Lord knows how to rescue godly people from their trials, even while keeping the wicked under punishment until the day of final judgment. He is especially hard on those who follow their own twisted sexual desire, and who despise authority. (2 Peter 2:1-10)

Jesus' judgment is righteous. While those on the receiving end will weep and mourn, all creation will know that Jesus' judgment is right. It is correct. It is good. There is a heavenly record for every human being that has ever lived. Jesus' judgment is not arbitrary – but both the prophecies of Daniel and Revelation tell us that his judgment is based upon our own lives – what we have done in life as recorded.

Truthfully, in a sense, Jesus does not condemn any human being: if condemned, we have condemned ourselves. Remember the words of Jesus himself from John's gospel we read above:

God sent his Son into the world not to judge the world, but to save the world through him.

> *"There is no judgment against anyone who believes in him. **But anyone who does not believe in him has already been judged for not believing in God's one and only Son.** And the judgment is based on this fact: God's light came into the world, but people loved the darkness more than the light, for their actions were evil.* (John 3:17-19, **emphasis mine**)

The Apostle Paul writes to the Christians in Rome about their own stubbornness.

> *But because you are stubborn and refuse to turn from your sin, you are storing up terrible punishment for yourself. For a day of anger is coming, when God's righteous judgment will be revealed. He will judge everyone according to what they have done. He will give eternal life to those who keep on doing good, seeking after the glory and honor and immortality that God offers. But he will pour out his anger and wrath on those who live for themselves, who refuse to obey the truth and instead live lives of wickedness. There will be trouble and calamity for everyone who keeps on doing what is evil—for the Jew first and also for the Gentile. But there will be glory and honor and peace from God for all who do good—for the Jew first and also for the Gentile. For God does not show favoritism.* (Romans 2:5-11)

Our God does what is right – he does not show favoritism. We bring the calamity of his judgment upon ourselves.

Paul writes to persecuted Christians in Thessalonica about how God will judge those who are unrighteously making them suffer.

> *And God will provide rest for you who are being persecuted and also for us when the Lord Jesus appears from heaven. He will*

> *come with his mighty angels, in flaming fire, bringing judgment on those who don't know God and on those who refuse to obey the Good News of our Lord Jesus. They will be punished with eternal destruction, forever separated from the Lord and from his glorious power.* (2 Thessalonians 1:7-9)

In John's apocalyptic vision of Revelation, he confirms what Daniel saw. There really is a record. There are books – the Lamb's Book of Life, which has the names recorded of every person in human history that has surrendered in faith to King Jesus, and additional books which appear to be the record of our lives. If one's name is in the Book of Life, it no longer matters what is on our record because the blood of Christ has wiped away all of our sins. In fact, King David yearned for this many generations before Jesus was even born (Psalm 51:1-2).

> *At that time Michael, the archangel who stands guard over your nation, will arise. Then there will be a time of anguish greater than any since nations first came into existence. But at that time every one of your people whose name is written in the book will be rescued. Many of those whose bodies lie dead and buried will rise up, some to everlasting life and some to shame and everlasting disgrace.* (Daniel 12:1-2)

> *I saw the dead, both great and small, standing before God's throne. And the books were opened, including the Book of Life. And the dead were judged according to what they had done, as recorded in the books. The sea gave up its dead, and death and the grave gave up their dead. And all were judged according to their deeds. Then death and the grave were thrown into the lake of fire. This lake of fire is the second death. And anyone whose name was not found recorded in the Book of Life was thrown into the lake of fire.* (Revelation 20:12-15)

> *Now repent of your sins and turn to God, so that your sins may be wiped away.* (Acts 3:19)

Jesus' judgment is just. Jesus' judgment on sin is the very essence of what is ultimately morally right and fair. I'm going to provide a lot of additional scripture references here to emphasize this point. God's love and justice were demonstrated in Christ's death and resurrection. God made a way for every human being to be redeemed, including people of forward-looking faith who lived before Jesus was even born (Hebrews 11). In fact, this is God's desire (Ezekiel 18:23; 2 Peter 3:9).

God has also revealed himself and his nature to humanity through creation (Romans 1:18-20), the Holy Spirit, and the Bible (1 Corinthians 2:10-16; 2 Timothy 3:15-17), and ultimately through Jesus Christ (John 14:6-7; Colossians 1:15-20; Hebrews 1:1-3). There is no reason for any human being to remain ignorant about God and rejecting him is always done by choice. There can no longer be any doubt that God's judgment levied by Jesus will be just – for we know God does not show favoritism (Acts 10:34; Romans 2:11).

God has been incredibly patient with humanity. When the time comes for the judgment, no one can say God did not give people enough time. Paul proclaims to many pagans in Athens,

"God overlooked people's ignorance about these things in earlier times, but now he commands everyone everywhere to repent of their sins and turn to him. For he has set a day for judging the world with justice by the man he has appointed, and he proved to everyone who this is by raising him from the dead." (Acts 17:30-31)

Warning his readers to "stay the course," Peter writes,

And remember that the heavenly Father to whom you pray has no favorites. He will judge or reward you according to what you do. So you must live in reverent fear of him during your time here as "temporary residents." For you know that God paid a ransom to save you from the empty life you inherited from your ancestors. And it was not paid with mere gold or silver, which lose their value. It was the precious blood of Christ, the sinless, spotless Lamb of God. (1 Peter 1:17-19)

From the standpoint of those in heaven who celebrate the fall of Babylon and all that this sinful city represents throughout biblical history, God's judgment is indeed just. Eternal justice has once and for all been served.

After this, I heard what sounded like a vast crowd in heaven shouting,

> *"Praise the Lord!*
> *Salvation and glory and power belong to our God.*
> *His judgments are true and just.*
> *He has punished the great prostitute who corrupted the earth with her immorality.*
> *He has avenged the murder of his servants."*
> *And again their voices rang out:*
> *"Praise the Lord!*

The smoke from that city ascends forever and ever!"
(Revelation 19:1-3)

Jesus' judgment is thorough. There is nothing that will remain hidden when it comes to the judgment. Nothing. Jesus' judgment covers everything.

> *As for me, it matters very little how I might be evaluated by you or by any human authority. I don't even trust my own judgment on this point. My conscience is clear, but that doesn't prove I'm right. It is the Lord himself who will examine me and decide.*
>
> *So don't make judgments about anyone ahead of time—before the Lord returns. For he will bring our darkest secrets to light and will reveal our private motives. Then God will give to each one whatever praise is due.* (1 Corinthians 4:3-5)

Jesus' judgment includes fallen angels. His judgment includes all those principalities, powers, authorities, and angels – the demonic realm – that followed Satan in rebellion against God. Unlike humanity, there is absolutely no redemption for angels because they were never deceived. They finally get what is coming to them.

> *For God did not spare even the angels who sinned. He threw them into hell, in gloomy pits of darkness, where they are being held until the day of judgment.* (2 Peter 2:4)

And I remind you of the angels who did not stay within the limits of authority God gave them but left the place where they belonged. God has kept them securely chained in prisons of darkness, waiting for the great day of judgment. (Jude 6)

Jesus' judgment technically begins with both believers and non-believers, but it doesn't end that way. This is both glorious news and horrible news…it depends on who you are! A friend of mine recently asked about Christians being judged by Jesus. Let me describe it this way: *everyone* stands before Jesus on that day (2 Corinthians 5:9-10). The heavenly record is opened, and *everyone* has to face their own record. *Everyone.* But for those who are in Christ – for all those who have surrendered to him as Savior and King – they have a PAID IN FULL stamp across their page! Their sins are already dealt with. They've experienced the atonement we talked about in Chapter 5. By putting their faith in Christ and accepting his sacrifice on their behalf, their names are written in the Lamb's (Jesus') Book of Life. *Their* judgment has already been levied fully at the cross on Jesus. God's wrath for them has already been poured out – God is satisfied. It's glorious news!

But for those who have not received Christ – for those who have not believed – for those who have rejected God's offer that leads to full and complete forgiveness – none of these things we just celebrated are true: which leads to my next point.

Jesus' judgment has two destinations. We've already looked at the following passages. But please take some time to read them again slowly and intently.

"At that time Michael, the archangel who stands guard over your nation, will arise. Then there will be a time of anguish greater than any since nations first came into existence. But at that time every one of your people whose name is written in the book will be rescued. Many of those whose bodies lie dead and buried will rise up, some to everlasting life and some to shame and everlasting disgrace. (Daniel 12:1-2)

But when the Son of Man comes in his glory, and all the angels with him, then he will sit upon his glorious throne. All the nations will be gathered in his presence, and he will separate the people as a shepherd separates the sheep from the goats. He will place the sheep at his right hand and the goats at his left.

"Then the King will say to those on his right, 'Come, you who are blessed by my Father, inherit the Kingdom prepared for you from the creation of the world. For I was hungry, and you fed me. I was thirsty, and you gave me a drink. I was a stranger, and you invited me into your home. I was naked, and you gave me clothing. I was sick, and you cared for me. I was in prison, and you visited me.'

"Then these righteous ones will reply, 'Lord, when did we ever see you hungry and feed you? Or thirsty and give you something to drink? Or a stranger and show you hospitality? Or naked and give you clothing? When did we ever see you sick or in prison and visit you?'

"And the King will say, 'I tell you the truth, when you did it to one of the least of these my brothers and sisters, you were doing it to me!'

"Then the King will turn to those on the left and say, 'Away with you, you cursed ones, into the eternal fire prepared for the devil and his demons. For I was hungry, and you didn't feed me. I was thirsty, and you didn't give me a drink. I was a stranger, and you didn't invite me into your home. I was naked, and you didn't give me clothing. I was sick and in prison, and you didn't visit me.'

"Then they will reply, 'Lord, when did we ever see you hungry or thirsty or a stranger or naked or sick or in prison, and not help you?'

"And he will answer, 'I tell you the truth, when you refused to help the least of these my brothers and sisters, you were refusing to help me.'

"And they will go away into eternal punishment, but the righteous will go into eternal life." (Matthew 25:31-46)

But because you are stubborn and refuse to turn from your sin, you are storing up terrible punishment for yourself. For a day of anger is coming, when God's righteous judgment will be revealed. He will judge everyone according to what they have done. He will give eternal life to those who keep on doing good, seeking after the glory and honor and immortality that God offers. But he will pour out his anger and wrath on those who live for themselves, who refuse to obey the truth and instead live lives of wickedness. There will be trouble and calamity for everyone who keeps on doing what is evil—for the Jew first and also for the Gentile. But there will be glory and honor and peace from God for all who do good—for the Jew first and also for the Gentile. For God does not show favoritism. (Romans 2:5-11)

And I saw a great white throne and the one sitting on it. The earth and sky fled from his presence, but they found no place to hide. I saw the dead, both great and small, standing before God's throne. And the books were opened, including the Book of Life. And the dead were judged according to what they had done, as recorded in the books. The sea gave up its dead, and death and the grave gave up their dead. And all were judged according to their deeds. Then death and the grave were thrown into the lake of fire. This lake of fire is the second death. And anyone whose name was not found recorded in the Book of Life was thrown into the lake of fire. (Revelation 20:11-15)

Sobering words, aren't they? There are two eternal destinies. For those who are in Christ – with all of our sins and flaws forgiven – there is a resurrection to eternal life and glory with him. But for those who are not in Christ – whose names are NOT found written in the Lamb's (Jesus') book of life – there is another resurrection. It is a resurrection to *eternal* contempt. It is a resurrection to *eternal* suffering. It is a resurrection to *eternal* anguish. This is what we call damnation. And this is no fairy tale. It's the real deal. It doesn't matter one bit if you completely reject the idea of eternal punishment – if you die without Christ, you'll learn the truth.

Faith in Christ is nothing to play around with. It's not some "religious experience." It's the offer of the eternal God for real salvation. And people ridicule and reject it to their own personal peril.

Jesus' judgment is final. There is no second chance when it finally comes to the judgment. Humanity's second chance is right now in Jesus Christ. Paul writes to the Christians in Corinth,

> *As God's partners, we beg you not to accept this marvelous gift*
> *of God's kindness and then ignore it. For God says,*
>
> *"At just the right time, I heard you.*
> *On the day of salvation, I helped you."*
>
> **Indeed, the "right time" is now. Today is the day of salvation.**
> (2 Corinthians 6:1-2, *emphasis mine*)

Today is the day of salvation. The time to seek God's gift of redemption is during *this* life. We either accept God's offer or we don't. It's really that simple. When the judgment comes, it's final.

As you can see, there is a lot wrapped up in Jesus' return and judgment. "I believe in Jesus Christ...that he will come again to judge both the living and the dead..." Can you agree with me that these doctrinal truths are absolutely essential to our faith? Friend, where do you stand? What do you actually believe when it comes to Jesus' return as the final Judge of all things? If you have surrendered to Jesus as Savior and Lord (King, Master), then this whole chapter is reason for great rejoicing! But if you haven't – or perhaps you're not sure – then there is a reason for concern. Why not settle that today? Don't make the mistake of waiting. We need to live in a state of preparedness for Jesus' return every moment of every day.

STUDY GUIDE

IT MAKES A DIFFERENCE

Christians who rely on what the Bible teaches about Jesus' glorious return have no fear of the end of time. They know Jesus' return will be sudden and unexpected, so they strive to live a prepared life. They also know that Jesus' return will be visible – no one on earth will miss it. They look forward to Jesus' return with excitement and anticipation. They have already bowed to his lordship and know that it will be a wonderful thing for all his followers when he comes again. The only people who need to fear his return are those who have rejected his rule and reign.

Those who do not rely on – or do not even know – that biblical teaching are fearful of both Jesus' return and his judgment. They do not realize that Jesus' judgment is righteous and that those who are washed by his blood have been made righteous and have nothing to fear. They look at apocalyptic literature like that in Daniel, Ezekiel, and Revelation with trepidation because they believe they will be a target. And because they tend to avoid bible books like these, they end up missing so much of the *good* news God has for his people.

HOW DO I LIVE OUT WHAT I HAVE JUST LEARNED IN MY OWN LIFE?

1. Take a moment to stop and pray. Ask God, through the Holy Spirit, to increase your understanding of the essentials of the Christian Faith. Ask Him to reveal and clarify any points which have been confusing or unclear.

2. After reading the chapter, evaluate your own feeling about Jesus' return as Righteous Judge. Is your "gut reaction" mostly one of fear, dread, concern, or rejoicing? What causes you to feel this way?

3. Have you surrendered your own life to Jesus as Lord and Savior?

4. Review all that the Creed has to say about Jesus, his purpose, and his work. Spend some time meditating on what difference all of that has made, and will make, in your own life.

5. Take several days to consider: Who can help you apply what you learn to put it into an ongoing life's practice?

6. How are you living this out right now? How is your life reflective of your understanding of this truth?

HOW DO I IMPART WHAT I HAVE JUST LEARNED TO CHILDREN?

Preparing to teach this lesson to children: *The children will be making a craft to review Jesus' work and purpose as stated in the Creed. Choose one of the suggestions (see #6 below) and gather the appropriate materials.*

1. Begin by praying with the children. Ask God, through the Holy Spirit, to help the children understand more about the Christian faith. Ask God to help them clearly understand the new things they are about to learn.

2. Continue to work with the children on memorizing the Apostle's Creed. Be sure they have memorized through this part:

    I believe in God, the Father almighty, creator of heaven and earth.

    I believe in Jesus Christ, his only Son, our Lord, who was conceived by the Holy Spirit and born of the virgin Mary. He suffered under Pontius Pilate, was crucified, died, and was buried; he descended into hell. The third day he rose again from the dead. He ascended to heaven and is seated at the right hand of God the Father almighty. From there he will come to judge the living and the dead.

3. Discuss the concept of *eternity* – forever and ever. Explain that our decision about Jesus is for eternity.

4. Talk to the children about choices and consequences. When we make poor choices, poor consequences often follow. They will likely be familiar with the possible consequences of breaking rules, like running into the street without looking. Talk about why parents and others in authority would make such rules – because that is best for them, and those who love them want the best for them. God is like that. He makes rules for us to live by so that we can have the best possible life. He created us, so he knows what's best for us. However, he also understands that humans sometimes make bad decisions,

even when we try to do what is right. That is why he sent Jesus to take the eternal consequences of our poor choices if we accept him as Lord and Savior.

5. Explain to the children that sin has *eternal* consequences that must be paid. Jesus paid them for those who accept him as Lord and Savior so they can go to heaven to live with him forever when they die. Heaven is a beautiful, happy place where nothing bad ever happens, and we can be forever with Jesus and those we love who died before us if they chose Jesus as their Savior.

6. We have already talked about the fact that most people do not come back to earth when they die, but Jesus is very special, as we know. This part of the Creed tells us that Jesus will come back to Earth one last time. When he does, he will know who to take with him to heaven (all those who surrendered to him as Lord and Savior), whether they are still alive or have already died. If we give our hearts to Jesus, remember that he has already forgiven everything we have done wrong, so we do not need to fear his judgment. He will also know who did not surrender to him, so he knows they chose not to go to heaven. Then time will end forever, and our decisions will be final. That is what the Creed means when it says he will judge the living and the dead. Jesus knows what decision people have made since he knows everything.

7. Review the activities choices. Choose one.

    a. CUBE
    Materials needed: Per child: stiff paper, cube pattern available at this website *http://printables.atozteacher-stuff.com/wp-content/uploads/2011/08/cubeoutline.png*. Run off a few extras in case someone cuts where they shouldn't. Also needed: scissors, pencils, markers or crayons, glue or tape.

    Procedure: Write each of the six creedal statements regarding Jesus (listed below) – one per side of the cube.

Allow children to illustrate each. Cut out the cube – taking care not to cut off tabs. Fold on dotted lines. Tape or glue sides together. Review each event briefly.

b.   BEACH BALL

Materials needed: Per child: Beach ball, sharpie marker. Beach balls have six sides. Most dollar stores have them.

Procedure: Write each of the six creedal statements regarding Jesus – one per section of the ball. Write the name, Jesus on the circle at the bottom. Remember that sharpie markers take a few seconds to dry before they should be touched to fingers or any surface you don't want permanently marked. Review each event briefly.

Creedal Statements:
* Jesus born to Mary
* Died and was buried
* Went to hell
* Came to life after 3 days
* Went to heaven with God
* Comes back to judge

8.   Take some time to talk about how the children could ask Jesus to be their Lord and to forgive their sins.

9.   If you have children in your group who have not yet surrendered to Jesus, continue to pray for the Holy Spirit to open that conversational door so you can explain the gospel. Once they receive Christ, the indwelling presence of the Holy Spirit will make the lessons in this book much more accessible to them.

HOW DO I IMPART WHAT I HAVE JUST LEARNED TO TEENS?

1.   Begin by praying with the teens. Ask God, through the Holy Spirit, to increase understanding. You can do this or ask a volunteer.

2.   Read the Apostles' Creed out loud. Read it yourself, ask for a volunteer, or read it in unison.

3. Repeat the first several lines:

   I believe in God, the Father almighty, creator of heaven and earth.

   I believe in Jesus Christ, his only Son, our Lord, who was conceived by the Holy Spirit and born of the virgin Mary. He suffered under Pontius Pilate, was crucified, died, and was buried; he descended into hell. The third day he rose again from the dead. He ascended to heaven and is seated at the right hand of God the Father almighty. From there he will come to judge the living and the dead.

4. Have the teens pull out their Question Journals. Ask them to jot down the answers to any questions about the Creed that are answered in this session. Have them share those discoveries, giving them sufficient time to record any thoughts they wish to capture. Assure them that they can ask any remaining questions about this section at the end of the session.

5. Review the italicized statements in the section *Jesus' Return on page x.* Discuss any questions or misunderstandings they have about this event.

6. Review the italicized statements in the section *Jesus' Judgment on page 183.* Ask them whether Jesus' Judgment seems to them to be more frightening or more a cause for rejoicing. Stress that for those who have put their faith in Jesus as Lord and Savior there is no reason to fear his judgment.

7. Consider if this is a good time to explain how teens can ask Jesus to forgive their sins, accept him as their Lord and Savior, and be certain of their eternal destiny at the judgment.

8. Ask the teens if they have heard people say that *everyone* will go to heaven when they die. Discuss how that could not be true if the statements in the Creed are true. One or the other is the truth. They cannot both be so. Ask them to think about how they might answer someone who says that a loving God has to be willing to forgive everyone and take everyone to heaven. Actually, that statement is true. God *is* willing, but he

cannot accept those into heaven who refuse to be in relationship with him. Be prepared for teens to struggle with this concept. Review John 3:16-18. Help them see that humanity is already hell-bound (v. 18) and that our loving God did indeed intervene by sending Jesus.

9. Allow the teens to ask any questions about Jesus' second coming and judgment that they had noted in their journals that were not addressed in this discussion. Ask them if/how their understanding of Jesus changed through what they learned in this session.

10. If you have teens in your group who have not yet surrendered to Jesus, continue praying for the Holy Spirit to open that conversational door so you can explain the gospel. Once they receive Christ, the indwelling presence of the Holy Spirit will make the lessons in this book much more accessible to them.

HOW DO I IMPART WHAT I HAVE JUST LEARNED TO ADULTS?

1. Challenge your adults to take a moment to stop and pray, asking God, through the Holy Spirit, to increase their understanding of the essentials of the Christian Faith. Encourage them to ask Him to reveal and clarify any points which have been confusing or unclear.

2. Review the Apostle's Creed. Repeat the first several lines of the Creed with emphasis. If they have not done so, encourage them to memorize the Creed, reminding them that this is a summary of the essentials of the Christian faith:

    I believe in God, the Father almighty, creator of heaven and earth.

    I believe in Jesus Christ, his only Son, our Lord, who was conceived by the Holy Spirit and born of the virgin Mary. He suffered under Pontius Pilate, was crucified, died, and was buried; he descended into hell. The third day he rose again from the dead. He ascended to heaven and is seated at the right hand of God the Father almighty. From there he will come to judge the living and the dead.

3. Have participants pull out the notes they made during previous sessions. Ask them to jot down the answers to any questions about the Creed that may be answered during this session and to share those discoveries as they happen. Provide sufficient time to record any thoughts they may wish to capture. Assure them that they will have the opportunity to ask any questions that were not answered in this session at the end of the session.

4. Review the italicized statements in the section *Jesus' Return on page 183*. Discuss any questions or misunderstandings they have about this event.

5. Review the italicized statements in the section *Jesus' Judgment* on page x. Ask them what their reaction is to the reality of the judgment. Does it inspire fear? Awe? Rejoicing? A mixture? Ask them to elaborate on their reactions.

6. Prayerfully consider if this is a good time to explain to participants that it is never too late to ask Jesus to forgive their sins, surrender to him as their Lord and Savior, and be certain of their eternal destiny at the judgment.

7. Ask participants if they have heard people say that everyone will go to heaven when they die. Discuss how that could not be true if the statements in the Creed are true. One or the other is the truth. They cannot both be so. Ask them to think about how they might answer someone who makes the statement that a loving God would not want to condemn anyone to hell. Actually, that statement is true. God *is not willing that any should perish (2 Peter 3:9)*, but he cannot accept those into heaven who refuse to be in relationship with him. Review John 3:16-18. Help them see that humanity is already hell-bound (v. 18) and that our loving God did indeed intervene by sending Jesus.

8. The Creed's paragraph about Jesus is the longest and most detailed of the creedal statements. Discuss why this would be true. Ask participants to reflect on what difference these truths about Jesus have made in their lives. Have them share if they are willing.

9. Allow participants to ask any questions about Jesus' second coming and judgment they had noted previously that were not addressed in this discussion.

10. If you have people in your group who have not yet surrendered to Jesus, continue to pray for the Holy Spirit to open that conversational door so you can explain the gospel. Once they receive Christ, the indwelling presence of the Holy Spirit will make the lessons in this book much more accessible to them.

CHAPTER 10
The Holy Spirit

"I believe in the Holy Spirit..."

If you love me, obey my commandments. And I will ask the Father, and he will give you another Advocate, who will never leave you. He is the Holy Spirit, who leads into all truth. The world cannot receive him, because it isn't looking for him and doesn't recognize him. But you know him, because he lives with you now and later will be in you. No, I will not abandon you as orphans—I will come to you. Soon the world will no longer see me, but you will see me. Since I live, you also will live. When I am raised to life again, you will know that I am in my Father, and you are in me, and I am in you. Those who accept my commandments and obey them are the ones who love me. And because they love me, my Father will love them. And I will love them and reveal myself to each of them."

Judas (not Judas Iscariot, but the other disciple with that name) said to him, "Lord, why are you going to reveal yourself only to us and not to the world at large?"

Jesus replied, "All who love me will do what I say. My Father will love them, and we will come and make our home with each of them. Anyone who doesn't love me will not obey me. And remember, my words are not my own. What I am telling you is from the Father who sent me. I am telling you these things now while I am still with you. But when the Father sends the Advocate as my representative—that is, the Holy Spirit—he will teach you everything and will remind you of everything I have told you. (John 14:15-26)

"But now I am going away to the one who sent me, and not one of you is asking where I am going. Instead, you grieve because of what I've told you. But in fact, it is best for you that I go away, because if I don't, the Advocate won't come. If I do go away, then I will send him to you. And when he comes, he will convict the world of its sin, and of God's righteousness, and of the coming judgment. The world's sin is that it refuses to believe in me. Righteousness is available because I go to the Father, and you will see me no more. Judgment will come because the ruler of this world has already been judged.

"There is so much more I want to tell you, but you can't bear it now. When the Spirit of truth comes, he will guide you into all truth. He will not speak on his own but will tell you what he has heard. He will tell you about the future. He will bring me glory by telling you whatever he receives from me. All that belongs to the Father is mine; this is why I said, 'The Spirit will tell you whatever he receives from me.' (John 16:5-15)

HE'S NOT THE "SILENT PARTNER"

"I believe in the Holy Spirit..." If one does not have a full and *right* understanding of the person and work of the Holy Spirit, they probably have a very limited relationship with God. God the Father is God. God the Son (Jesus) is God. And God the Holy Spirit is God. All three persons of our Triune God are of the same essence. No one person is more important or less important than the others. It is critically important that our Christian Faith includes a genuine relationship with the Holy Spirit of God.

The Holy Spirit is not the "Silent Partner" of the Trinity. As we will see in this chapter, the Holy Spirit is very active in the life and ministry of individual Christians and Jesus' Church.

THE PERSON OF THE HOLY SPIRIT

The Holy Spirit is not an inanimate energy like The Force in Star Wars. The Holy Spirit is a distinct person. The scriptures show us that he possesses the attributes of personhood.

The Holy Spirit has intellect. The Holy Spirit knows and understands God's thoughts and can help us gain wisdom and insight from God. The Spirit's intellect blesses you and me as he makes us able to understand and apply spiritual truths to our lives. Paul writes,

> *No one can know a person's thoughts except that person's own spirit, and no one can know God's thoughts except God's own Spirit. And we have received God's Spirit (not the world's spirit), so we can know the wonderful things God has freely given us.* (1 Corinthians 2:11-12)

Those who are in Christ, having surrendered to Jesus as Savior and King, have been given God's Holy Spirit! We are able to understand the things of God even when they seem foolish to the rest of the world. It's not helpful to get frustrated with worldly people who act and think worldly; Paul says they truly cannot understand.

> *But people who aren't spiritual can't receive these truths from God's Spirit. It all sounds foolish to them and they can't understand it, for only those who are spiritual can understand what the Spirit means.* (1 Corinthians 2:14)

The Holy Spirit has wisdom and revelation. The Holy Spirit, being God, has the full and complete wisdom of God and can share some of that wisdom and revelation with us so that we know God the Father better. We understand the Father's heart through the wisdom and revelation of the Holy Spirit. We understand the Father's plans through the wisdom and revelation of the Holy Spirit. The Holy Spirit makes *us* wise beyond our own human ability so that we can be fruitful partners with God in his mission.

> *Ever since I first heard of your strong faith in the Lord Jesus and your love for God's people everywhere, I have not stopped thanking God for you. I pray for you constantly, asking God, the glorious*

Father of our Lord Jesus Christ, **to give you spiritual wisdom
and insight so that you might grow in your knowledge of God.**
(Ephesians 1:15-17, **emphasis mine**)

The New Living Translation reads, "...to give you spiritual wisdom
and insight..." Another way to translate this might be, "...to give you
the Spirit of wisdom and insight..." or even "...to give you the Spirit of
wisdom and revelation..."[24]

The Holy Spirit has emotions. It is here that we really see the Holy
Spirit's personhood. An inanimate or impersonal force does not have
emotions as the Holy Spirit does. We're told that the Holy Spirit loves.

*Dear brothers and sisters, I urge you in the name of our Lord
Jesus Christ to join in my struggle by praying to God for me. Do
this because of your love for me, given to you by the Holy Spirit.*
(Romans 15:30)

The Holy Spirit grieves.

I will tell of the Lord's unfailing love.
I will praise the Lord for all he has done.
*I will rejoice in his great goodness to Israel, which he has
granted according to his mercy and love.*
He said, "They are my very own people.
Surely they will not betray me again."
And he became their Savior.
*In all their suffering he also suffered, and he personally rescued
them.*
In his love and mercy he redeemed them.
He lifted them up and carried them through all the years.
But they rebelled against him and grieved his Holy Spirit.

So he became their enemy and fought against them.
(Isaiah 63:7-10, **emphasis mine**)

---

24   Both the New American Standard Bible (Lockman Foundation, 1971) and the English
Standard Version (Crossway, 2001) translate the passage this way.

And do not bring sorrow to God's Holy Spirit by the way you live. Remember, he has identified you as his own, guaranteeing that you will be saved on the day of redemption. (Ephesians 4:30)

The Holy Spirit can be insulted.

Dear friends, if we deliberately continue sinning after we have received knowledge of the truth, there is no longer any sacrifice that will cover these sins. There is only the terrible expectation of God's judgment and the raging fire that will consume his enemies. For anyone who refused to obey the law of Moses was put to death without mercy on the testimony of two or three witnesses. Just think how much worse the punishment will be for those who have trampled on the Son of God, and have treated the blood of the covenant, which made us holy, as if it were common and unholy, **and have insulted and disdained the Holy Spirit** *who brings God's mercy to us.* (Hebrews 10:26-29, **emphasis mine**)

The Holy Spirit yearns for God.

But when the right time came, God sent his Son, born of a woman, subject to the law. God sent him to buy freedom for us who were slaves to the law, so that he could adopt us as his very own children. And because we are his children, **God has sent the Spirit of his Son into our hearts, prompting us to call out, "Abba, Father."** *Now you are no longer a slave but God's own child. And since you are his child, God has made you his heir.* (Galatians 4:4-7, **emphasis mine**)

By the way, in case you didn't know, *Abba* is the word for "Daddy." This is not just any yearning for God, but an intimate yearning for our Heavenly Father in all the things we learned about in Chapter 2.

But perhaps, for us, the most vital thing with respect to the Spirit's emotions is that he shares the fruit of the Spirit with us. I could have listed these in the next section, but because they so clearly have an emotional component, I think they are better understood here.

But the Holy Spirit produces this kind of fruit in our lives: love, joy, peace, patience, kindness, goodness, faithfulness, gentleness, and self-control. There is no law against these things!

Those who belong to Christ Jesus have nailed the passions and desires of their sinful nature to his cross and crucified them there. Since we are living by the Spirit, let us follow the Spirit's leading in every part of our lives. Let us not become conceited, or provoke one another, or be jealous of one another. (Galatians 5:22-26)

- **Love** – we've already talked about this one, but the Holy Spirit shares what is called *agape* love with us. There are many different Greek words that are translated into English as "love." That makes understanding some passages in the New Testament challenging. But *agape* love is unique: it's Jesus' other-oriented, self-sacrificing love.

- **Joy** – the Holy Spirit shares joy with us. Whereas happiness is based upon one's circumstances, joy is not. Joy is a source of God's unshakable strength that transcends happiness and circumstances.

- **Peace** – the Holy Spirit shares his peace with us. This ties us back to the whole blessing of real *shalom* (the Hebrew word translated as "peace"). Shalom is more than just the absence of conflict in our lives: the whole concept is God's peace, health, wholeness, comfort, and completeness.

- **Patience** – the Holy Spirit shares his long-suffering nature with us. Just as our heavenly Father patiently waits for humanity to accept Christ, we also can be patient as his representatives – his ambassadors.

- **Kindness** – the Holy Spirit shares his kindness with us so that we can be authentic and considerate with all those who are still "in process."

- **Goodness** – the Holy Spirit shares his goodness with us, that our righteousness and morality are true echoes of God's goodness.

- **Faithfulness** – the Holy Spirit shares his faithfulness with us, that we show Christ's character in us through steadfastness and loyalty both to him and his mission.

- **Gentleness** – the Holy Spirit shares his gentleness with us, a holy tenderness or compassion demonstrated in all our relationships.

- **Self-control** – the Holy Spirit shares his self-control with us, that all our emotions and behavior are in full submission – full surrender – to the Father for his purposes.

The Holy Spirit has intellect. He has wisdom and revelation. He has emotion: the Holy Spirit loves, grieves, can be insulted, yearns, and shares all the fruit of the Spirit with us. The personhood of the Holy Spirit is indisputable. But just as important for us to understand is what the person of the Holy Spirit does for God's people.

THE EMPOWERING WORK OF THE HOLY SPIRIT

Perhaps the most salient point of this chapter is that the Holy Spirit resides with the Church.

> *"Look, I am coming soon, bringing my reward with me to repay all people according to their deeds. I am the Alpha and the Omega, the First and the Last, the Beginning and the End."*
>
> *Blessed are those who wash their robes. They will be permitted to enter through the gates of the city and eat the fruit from the tree of life. Outside the city are the dogs—the sorcerers, the sexually immoral, the murderers, the idol worshipers, and all who love to live a lie.*
>
> *"I, Jesus, have sent my angel to give you this message for the churches. I am both the source of David and the heir to his throne. I am the bright morning star."*
>
> **The Spirit and the bride say, "Come."** *Let anyone who hears this say, "Come." Let anyone who is thirsty come. Let anyone who desires drink freely from the water of life.* (Revelation 22:12-17, **emphasis mine**)

The bride of Christ is the Church. Throughout the Book of Revelation, every time we see a reference to the Holy Spirit, he is with God's people – the Church. The indication is that, when Jesus ascended to the right hand of the Father, the Father sent the Holy Spirit to be with us. We discussed that in Chapter 8 on Jesus' ascension and session.

And so the Holy Spirit, walking with the Church on Jesus' mission to the very end, does many incredible things for us both personally and for the sake of Christ's mission through us.

If we don't understand the empowering work of the Holy Spirit as Christians, we are greatly hampered in our ability to be faithful and obedient to Christ and his mission – and we may even have an inadequate understanding of our Triune God! So, what does the Holy Spirit do?

The Holy Spirit teaches. The Holy Spirit empowers us by teaching us to lead us into all truth. Jesus told us that he would send the Spirit to teach his followers.

> *But when the Father sends the Advocate as my representative— that is, the Holy Spirit—he will teach you everything and will remind you of everything I have told you.* (John 14:26)

> *When the Spirit of truth comes, he will guide you into all truth. He will not speak on his own but will tell you what he has heard. He will tell you about the future. He will bring me glory by telling you whatever he receives from me. All that belongs to the Father is mine; this is why I said, 'The Spirit will tell you whatever he receives from me.'* (John 16:13-15)

The Holy Spirit ensures that we learn and understand everything we need to know, and he reminds us of what Jesus has already taught his people. He teaches us.

The Holy Spirit testifies. The Holy Spirit empowers us through the inner witness he provides to our hearts because of our faith in Jesus. The writer of Hebrews calls this "evidence of things we cannot see" (Hebrews 11:1).

> *"But I will send you the Advocate—the Spirit of truth. He will come to you from the Father and will testify all about me. And you must also testify about me because you have been with me from the beginning of my ministry..."* (John 15:26-27)

The Holy Spirit is the chief witness about Jesus. He is the greatest witness to the reality of who Christ is. He speaks to us on both the intellectual and also the heart level. And this leads to our next point.

The Holy Spirit convicts. It is God's Holy Spirit that works in us to transform our hearts and our minds.

> *"And when he comes, he will convict the world of its sin, and of God's righteousness, and of the coming judgment. The world's sin is that it refuses to believe in me. Righteousness is available because I go to the Father, and you will see me no more. Judgment will come because the ruler of this world has already been judged.* (John 16:8-11)

This is an important passage for understanding how the Holy Spirit works within us – he does so with conviction. He convicts us of our own sinfulness and of the sinful deeds and attitudes that flow from it. He convicts us about the utter holiness of God – how completely different he is and how far our hearts are away from him. He convicts us regarding the coming judgment of the whole world – that in his mercy and grace, God has made a way for full and complete forgiveness of our sinfulness, and that those who do not receive Jesus (for he is the one and only way of salvation – John 14:6) are destined for judgment (see Chapter 9).

The Holy Spirit works within us. He breaks our hearts. He convicts us of our sinfulness. He shows us ourselves in the mirror of Christ's character and we are broken. He doesn't beat us down with guilt (this is what Satan does); instead, he motivates us with conviction to change and move forward. The Holy Spirit convicts.

The Holy Spirit comforts. The Holy Spirit empowers us by easing the distress we feel from suffering, grief, persecution, and other opposition we face.

> *"But now I am going away to the one who sent me, and not one of you is asking where I am going. Instead, you grieve because of what I've told you. But in fact, it is best for you that I go away, because if I don't, the Advocate won't come. If I do go away, then I will send him to you.* (John 16:5-7)

The word translated as "Advocate" here is the Greek word *paraclete* – one who comes alongside another. A mediator. A counselor.

The Holy Spirit is the greatest counselor. He does not need to discern anything – not our needs, not our pain, not our motives – he knows all these full well. He cannot be fooled or deceived. The Holy Spirit speaks the truth to us – in the inmost parts of our hearts and minds. He raises us up in Christ.

The Holy Spirit empowers. God does not just give us our assignment in his mission to redeem the world – he also gives us the tools and empowerment to get the job done. He does both of these things through the indwelling presence of his Holy Spirit.

> *So when the apostles were with Jesus, they kept asking him, "Lord, has the time come for you to free Israel and restore our kingdom?"*
>
> *He replied, "The Father alone has the authority to set those dates and times, and they are not for you to know. But you will receive power when the Holy Spirit comes upon you. And you will be my witnesses, telling people about me everywhere—in Jerusalem, throughout Judea, in Samaria, and to the ends of the earth." (Acts 1:6-8)*

The fulfillment of Jesus' promise came on the Day of Pentecost, while Jewish people from all over the known world were celebrating in the Holy City of Jerusalem.

> *On the day of Pentecost all the believers were meeting together in one place. Suddenly, there was a sound from heaven like the roaring of a mighty windstorm, and it filled the house where they were sitting. Then, what looked like flames or tongues of fire appeared and settled on each of them. And everyone present was filled with the Holy Spirit and began speaking in other languages, as the Holy Spirit gave them this ability.*
>
> *At that time there were devout Jews from every nation living in Jerusalem. When they heard the loud noise, everyone came running, and they were bewildered to hear their own languages being spoken by the believers.*
>
> *They were completely amazed. "How can this be?" they exclaimed. "These people are all from Galilee, and yet we hear*

*them speaking in our own native languages! Here we are—
Parthians, Medes, Elamites, people from Mesopotamia, Judea,
Cappadocia, Pontus, the province of Asia, Phrygia, Pamphylia,
Egypt, and the areas of Libya around Cyrene, visitors from
Rome (both Jews and converts to Judaism), Cretans, and Arabs.
And we all hear these people speaking in our own languages
about the wonderful things God has done!" They stood there
amazed and perplexed. "What can this mean?" they asked each
other.* (Acts 2:1-12)

It is no surprise that the very first thing the believers in Jesus did when
filled with the Holy Spirit was to proclaim to those from all over the world
the wonderful things God has done. The Holy Spirit indues Christ's people
with power and boldness for the task they have been given. And part of
that empowerment is equipping as well. The Holy Spirit is the source of
spiritual gifts – the tools and resources we need to complete Christ's mission. We'll look more at this in the pages that follow.

The Holy Spirit unifies. The Holy Spirit empowers us by uniting us.
As the singular Holy Spirit indwells Christ's people, the multiplicity
of personalities is made one in Christ.

*All the believers devoted themselves to the apostles' teaching,
and to fellowship, and to sharing in meals (including the Lord's
Supper), and to prayer.*

*A deep sense of awe came over them all, and the apostles per-
formed many miraculous signs and wonders. And all the believers met together in one place and shared everything they
had. They sold their property and possessions and shared the
money with those in need. They worshiped together at the Temple
each day, met in homes for the Lord's Supper, and shared their
meals with great joy and generosity—all the while praising God
and enjoying the goodwill of all the people. And each day the
Lord added to their fellowship those who were being saved.*
(Acts 2:42-47)

This unity is a direct answer to our Savior's intercessory prayer for his
apostles and all those who will come to faith because of their witness.

After saying all these things, Jesus looked up to heaven and said, "Father, the hour has come. Glorify your Son so he can give glory back to you. For you have given him authority over everyone. He gives eternal life to each one you have given him. And this is the way to have eternal life—to know you, the only true God, and Jesus Christ, the one you sent to earth. I brought glory to you here on earth by completing the work you gave me to do. Now, Father, bring me into the glory we shared before the world began.

"I have revealed you to the ones you gave me from this world. They were always yours. You gave them to me, and they have kept your word. Now they know that everything I have is a gift from you, for I have passed on to them the message you gave me. They accepted it and know that I came from you, and they believe you sent me.

"My prayer is not for the world, but for those you have given me, because they belong to you. All who are mine belong to you, and you have given them to me, so they bring me glory. Now I am departing from the world; they are staying in this world, but I am coming to you. Holy Father, you have given me your name; now protect them by the power of your name so that they will be united just as we are. During my time here, I protected them by the power of the name you gave me. I guarded them so that not one was lost, except the one headed for destruction, as the Scriptures foretold.

"Now I am coming to you. I told them many things while I was with them in this world so they would be filled with my joy. I have given them your word. And the world hates them because they do not belong to the world, just as I do not belong to the world. I'm not asking you to take them out of the world, but to keep them safe from the evil one. They do not belong to this world any more than I do. Make them holy by your truth; teach them your word, which is truth. Just as you sent me into the world, I am sending them into the world. And I give myself as a holy sacrifice for them so they can be made holy by your truth.

"I am praying not only for these disciples but also for all who will ever believe in me through their message. I pray that they

will all be one, just as you and I are one—as you are in me, Father, and I am in you. And may they be in us so that the world will believe you sent me.

"I have given them the glory you gave me, so they may be one as we are one. I am in them and you are in me. May they experience such perfect unity that the world will know that you sent me and that you love them as much as you love me. Father, I want these whom you have given me to be with me where I am. Then they can see all the glory you gave me because you loved me even before the world began!

"O righteous Father, the world doesn't know you, but I do; and these disciples know you sent me. I have revealed you to them, and I will continue to do so. Then your love for me will be in them, and I will be in them." (John 17:1-26, **emphasis mine**)

We are unified – of one mind, one heart, one mission, serving one God! All of our multiple agendas are washed away, being overtaken by the singular *Immanuel Agenda*.[25] We are commonly devoted to the same teaching, the same relationships, the same lifestyle, the same prayer – and this unity changes the world around us. Remember that Jesus said the world would know that we belong to him by the way we love one another (John 13:35). It is the Holy Spirit that fosters that unifying love.

The Holy Spirit calls and commissions. The Holy Spirit acts as a recruiter for Jesus' mission. Jesus established the Great Commission on the lives of all believers – past, present, and future.

Jesus came and told his disciples, "I have been given all authority in heaven and on earth. Therefore, go and make disciples of all the nations, baptizing them in the name of the Father and the Son and the Holy Spirit. Teach these new disciples to obey all the commands I have given you. And be sure of this: I am with you always, even to the end of the age." (Matthew 28:28:18-20)

---

25   Just for clarity, when I say *Immanuel Agenda* I am referring to Christ's mission to redeem the world. *Immanuel* (Hebrew for "God with us") is one of Jesus' titles (see Isaiah 7:14 & Matthew 1:23). Jesus' agenda unifies us all – even with our unique personalities, gifts and talents – on one incredible mission. It's the Holy Spirit that does that.

And then he told them, "Go into all the world and preach the Good News to everyone. Anyone who believes and is baptized will be saved. But anyone who refuses to believe will be condemned. These miraculous signs will accompany those who believe: They will cast out demons in my name, and they will speak in new languages. They will be able to handle snakes with safety, and if they drink anything poisonous, it won't hurt them. They will be able to place their hands on the sick, and they will be healed."

When the Lord Jesus had finished talking with them, he was taken up into heaven and sat down in the place of honor at God's right hand. And the disciples went everywhere and preached, and the Lord worked through them, confirming what they said by many miraculous signs. (Mark 16:15-20)

So when the apostles were with Jesus, they kept asking him, "Lord, has the time come for you to free Israel and restore our kingdom?"

He replied, "The Father alone has the authority to set those dates and times, and they are not for you to know. But you will receive power when the Holy Spirit comes upon you. And you will be my witnesses, telling people about me everywhere—in Jerusalem, throughout Judea, in Samaria, and to the ends of the earth." (Acts 1:6-8)

After Jesus' ascension to the right hand of the Father in heaven, it is the Holy Spirit that continues calling people into that mission.

Among the prophets and teachers of the church at Antioch of Syria were Barnabas, Simeon (called "the black man"), Lucius (from Cyrene), Manaen (the childhood companion of King Herod Antipas), and Saul. One day as these men were worshiping the Lord and fasting, the Holy Spirit said, "Appoint Barnabas and Saul for the special work to which I have called them." So after more fasting and prayer, the men laid their hands on them and sent them on their way. (Acts 13:1-3)

The Holy Spirit knows the mission. He knows the tasks. He knows the resources. He knows the needs of those we are trying to reach. He

224

knows the opposition we will face – both spiritual and human. And he knows who God has best equipped for each and every facet of that work. Sometimes when we least expect it, the Spirit calls us – heart to heart. And we can't find peace until we take that step of faith in the direction of his wooing. He commissions the right people, at the right time, to the right kingdom works.

The Holy Spirit guides. And the Spirit's guidance is holistic – it's not just for the mission but for all of life!

> *But you are not controlled by your sinful nature. You are controlled by the Spirit if you have the Spirit of God living in you. (And remember that those who do not have the Spirit of Christ living in them do not belong to him at all.) And Christ lives within you, so even though your body will die because of sin, the Spirit gives you life because you have been made right with God. The Spirit of God, who raised Jesus from the dead, lives in you. And just as God raised Christ Jesus from the dead, he will give life to your mortal bodies by this same Spirit living within you.*
>
> *Therefore, dear brothers and sisters, you have no obligation to do what your sinful nature urges you to do. For if you live by its dictates, you will die. But if through the power of the Spirit you put to death the deeds of your sinful nature, you will live. For all who are led by the Spirit of God are children of God.*
>
> *So you have not received a spirit that makes you fearful slaves. Instead, you received God's Spirit when he adopted you as his own children. Now we call him, "Abba, Father." For his Spirit joins with our spirit to affirm that we are God's children.* (Romans 8:9-16)

The Holy Spirit is our guide for life and mission. Sometimes we can't see the way forward. Sometimes our own sinful habits get in the way – they derail us. But to be led by the Holy Spirit is to always stay on the right path – the one of God's ordaining. And even when we step off of the path (which we always will from time to time), it is the leading of the Spirit that corrects us and gets us back on track.

The Holy Spirit assures. There is great empowerment in the Holy Spirit's confirmation that we are indeed God's precious, beloved, and redeemed children. Let's face it: there are days when we just don't *feel* like Jesus has redeemed us. There are days when we can't muster the motivation for Jesus' mission. We stand in our own way. This is when we rely on the Holy Spirit's assurance.

> *Therefore, since we have been made right in God's sight by faith, we have peace with God because of what Jesus Christ our Lord has done for us. Because of our faith, Christ has brought us into this place of undeserved privilege where we now stand, and we confidently and joyfully look forward to sharing God's glory.*
>
> *We can rejoice, too, when we run into problems and trials, for we know that they help us develop endurance. And endurance develops strength of character, and character strengthens our confident hope of salvation. And this hope will not lead to disappointment. For we know how dearly God loves us, because he has given us the Holy Spirit to fill our hearts with his love.* (Romans 5:1-5)
>
> *So you have not received a spirit that makes you fearful slaves. Instead, you received God's Spirit when he adopted you as his own children. Now we call him, "Abba, Father." For his Spirit joins with our spirit to affirm that we are God's children.* (Romans 8:15-16)

Circumstances around us scream more loudly than the still, small voice of God within our hearts. There are days when we even may question our own salvation, let alone our unique part in Christ's mission to save the world. And then the Holy Spirit speaks – and we know we are God's beloved children. He assures.

The Holy Spirit intercedes. This one is personally overwhelming for me. We already talked about Jesus' ministry of mediation and intercession for us at the right hand of the Father back in Chapter 8. Now we learn that the Holy Spirit also intercedes – but his work is particularly precious because he steps in when we do not know how to pray.

> *And the Holy Spirit helps us in our weakness. For example, we don't know what God wants us to pray for. But the Holy Spirit prays for us with groanings that cannot be expressed in words.*

226

And the Father who knows all hearts knows what the Spirit is saying, for the Spirit pleads for us believers in harmony with God's own will. And we know that God causes everything to work together for the good of those who love God and are called according to his purpose for them. (Romans 8:26-28)

When we are on our last nerve, when we don't even know how to pray, the Holy Spirit picks up the slack and intercedes with us – and even on our behalf. In doing so, he aligns our hearts and prayers with the will of God.

The Holy Spirit sanctifies. The word holy means "set apart." Whenever we talk about a person, place, or thing being holy, we mean it is set apart for God's purposes. To "sanctify" something means we make it holy. So, when the Holy Spirit sanctifies a person, place, or thing, he is actively and purposefully setting it apart for God's purposes.

As Paul talks about his missionary ministry, taking the gospel to new people and lands, he writes to the Christians in Rome,

I am fully convinced, my dear brothers and sisters, that you are full of goodness. You know these things so well you can teach each other all about them. Even so, I have been bold enough to write about some of these points, knowing that all you need is this reminder. For by God's grace, I am a special messenger from Christ Jesus to you Gentiles. **I bring you the Good News so that I might present you as an acceptable offering to God, made holy by the Holy Spirit.** *So I have reason to be enthusiastic about all Christ Jesus has done through me in my service to God. Yet I dare not boast about anything except what Christ has done through me, bringing the Gentiles to God by my message and by the way I worked among them.* **They were convinced by the power of miraculous signs and wonders and by the power of God's Spirit.** *In this way, I have fully presented the Good News of Christ from Jerusalem all the way to Illyricum.* (Romans 15:14-19)

Paul's enthusiasm is not in his own accomplishments but in what he repeatedly sees the Holy Spirit do in the lives of those among whom he ministers. He is eager to see these Roman Christians experience what has happened in his other missionary journeys – that they would be made holy (set apart for God's purposes) by the Holy Spirit and become "an acceptable offering to God."

The Holy Spirit sanctifies us. The Holy Spirit uses us to sanctify others. Even when people are misaligned with the heart of God – derailed by their own sin and worldliness – it's the Holy Spirit that makes them utterly holy. We cannot change or convince a human heart – but the Holy Spirit can work from within that person to accomplish the miracle of holiness.

The Holy Spirit speaks and enlightens. The Holy Spirit empowers us by giving us critical understanding on spiritual things. We already alluded to this in discussing the Holy Spirit's intellect above, but the Holy Spirit expresses to us the heart and the wisdom of God. Paul writes to the Corinthians,

> *When I first came to you, dear brothers and sisters, I didn't use lofty words and impressive wisdom to tell you God's secret plan. For I decided that while I was with you I would forget everything except Jesus Christ, the one who was crucified. I came to you in weakness—timid and trembling. And my message and my preaching were very plain. Rather than using clever and persuasive speeches, I relied only on the power of the Holy Spirit. I did this so you would trust not in human wisdom but in the power of God.*
>
> *Yet when I am among mature believers, I do speak with words of wisdom, but not the kind of wisdom that belongs to this world or to the rulers of this world, who are soon forgotten. No, the wisdom we speak of is the mystery of God—his plan that was previously hidden, even though he made it for our ultimate glory before the world began. But the rulers of this world have not understood it; if they had, they would not have crucified our glorious Lord. That is what the Scriptures mean when they say,*
>
> *"No eye has seen, no ear has heard, and no mind has imagined what God has prepared for those who love him."*

But it was to us that God revealed these things by his Spirit. For his Spirit searches out everything and shows us God's deep secrets. No one can know a person's thoughts except that person's own spirit, and no one can know God's thoughts except God's own Spirit. And we have received God's Spirit (not the world's spirit), so we can know the wonderful things God has freely given us.

When we tell you these things, we do not use words that come from human wisdom. Instead, we speak words given to us by the Spirit, using the Spirit's words to explain spiritual truths. *But people who aren't spiritual can't receive these truths from God's Spirit. It all sounds foolish to them and they can't understand it, for only those who are spiritual can understand what the Spirit means.* (1 Corinthians 2:1-14, **emphasis mine**)

The Holy Spirit gives us the understanding of things we once thought were utterly foolish. We can know and enjoy the "wonderful things God has freely given us" because the Holy Spirit enlightens us.

The Holy Spirit justifies. We also previously talked about justification, where God, as the ultimate Judge, declares us righteous on account of the shed blood of Jesus. The declaration is by the heavenly Father, but the Holy Spirit leads the process that brings us to Christ.

Don't you realize that those who do wrong will not inherit the Kingdom of God? Don't fool yourselves. Those who indulge in sexual sin, or who worship idols, or commit adultery, or are male prostitutes, or practice homosexuality, or are thieves, or greedy people, or drunkards, or are abusive, or cheat people—none of these will inherit the Kingdom of God. Some of you were once like that. But you were cleansed; you were made holy; ***you were made right with God by calling on the name of the Lord Jesus Christ and by the Spirit of our God.*** (1 Corinthians 6:9-11, **emphasis mine**)

The Holy Spirit leads us through the cleansing flood of Jesus' blood so that God declares us righteous (justified) in his own sight.

The Holy Spirit works and equips. The Holy Spirit empowers us by giving us the personal tools and abilities we need to fulfill our part in Christ's mission.

Each of us has a divine design. We are each "fearfully and wonderfully made" in the image of God to carry out his divine purposes for us (Psalm 139:13-16; Genesis 1:26-28). Before sin entered the picture (Genesis 3), humanity was created to rule and reign over creation with God. When humanity fell, and Satan usurped that authority, our divine design and *imago Dei* (or image of God) were tainted. But in Christ, all this is restored and expanded – expanded because we not only will reign again with Christ (Ephesians 2:6), but we are also now partners in his mission to redeem the rest of humanity (Matthew 28:18-20)! For this, the Holy Spirit works in us and through us to prepare and equip us for our renewed destiny in Christ. Paul writes,

> *Now, dear brothers and sisters, regarding your question about the special abilities the Spirit gives us. I don't want you to misunderstand this. You know that when you were still pagans, you were led astray and swept along in worshiping speechless idols. So I want you to know that no one speaking by the Spirit of God will curse Jesus, and no one can say Jesus is Lord, except by the Holy Spirit.*
>
> *There are different kinds of spiritual gifts, but the same Spirit is the source of them all. There are different kinds of service, but we serve the same Lord. God works in different ways, but it is the same God who does the work in all of us.*
>
> *A spiritual gift is given to each of us so we can help each other. To one person the Spirit gives the ability to give wise advice; to another the same Spirit gives a message of special knowledge. The same Spirit gives great faith to another, and to someone else the one Spirit gives the gift of healing. He gives one person the power to perform miracles, and another the ability to prophesy. He gives someone else the ability to discern whether a message is from the Spirit of God or from another spirit. Still another person is given the ability to speak in unknown languages, while another*

is given the ability to interpret what is being said. It is the one and only Spirit who distributes all these gifts. He alone decides which gift each person should have. (1 Corinthians 12:1-11)

Paul tells us that *each person* is given a spiritual gift (often more than one). Peter concurs,

God has given each of you a gift from his great variety of spiritual gifts. Use them well to serve one another. Do you have the gift of speaking? Then speak as though God himself were speaking through you. Do you have the gift of helping others? Do it with all the strength and energy that God supplies. Then everything you do will bring glory to God through Jesus Christ. All glory and power to him forever and ever! Amen. (1 Peter 4:10-11)

Some special giftedness is given by the Spirit for the leading of God's people. Those who lead with these five special abilities (see below) enable Christ's church to function at its optimum. Likewise, when any of these are missing, the work of Christ in that local body is hampered.

Now these are the gifts Christ gave to the church: the apostles, the prophets, the evangelists, and the pastors and teachers. Their responsibility is to equip God's people to do his work and build up the church, the body of Christ. This will continue until we all come to such unity in our faith and knowledge of God's Son that we will be mature in the Lord, measuring up to the full and complete standard of Christ.

Then we will no longer be immature like children. We won't be tossed and blown about by every wind of new teaching. We will not be influenced when people try to trick us with lies so clever they sound like the truth. Instead, we will speak the truth in love, growing in every way more and more like Christ, who is the head of his body, the church. He makes the whole body fit together perfectly. As each part does its own special work, it helps the other parts grow, so that the whole body is healthy and growing and full of love. (Ephesians 4:11-16)

The Holy Spirit distributes the gifts as he sees fit. The Spirit is the one who knows who has been designed by God for what parts of Christ's mission. Everyone has a part to play. We actually *need* each other! It is wrong to say we don't need certain gifts today. It takes all of us working together – using the unique equipping we have each been given together as a family – to glorify God by completing the mission.

The human body has many parts, but the many parts make up one whole body. So it is with the body of Christ. Some of us are Jews, some are Gentiles, some are slaves, and some are free. But we have all been baptized into one body by one Spirit, and we all share the same Spirit.

Yes, the body has many different parts, not just one part. If the foot says, "I am not a part of the body because I am not a hand," that does not make it any less a part of the body. And if the ear says, "I am not part of the body because I am not an eye," would that make it any less a part of the body? If the whole body were an eye, how would you hear? Or if your whole body were an ear, how would you smell anything?

But our bodies have many parts, and God has put each part just where he wants it. How strange a body would be if it had only one part! Yes, there are many parts, but only one body. The eye can never say to the hand, "I don't need you." The head can't say to the feet, "I don't need you."

In fact, some parts of the body that seem weakest and least important are actually the most necessary. And the parts we regard as less honorable are those we clothe with the greatest care. So we carefully protect those parts that should not be seen, while the more honorable parts do not require this special care. So God has put the body together such that extra honor and care are given to those parts that have less dignity. This makes for harmony among the members, so that all the members care for each other. If one part suffers, all the parts suffer with it, and if one part is honored, all the parts are glad.

All of you together are Christ's body, and each of you is a part of it. Here are some of the parts God has appointed for the church: first are apostles, second are prophets, third are teachers, then those who do miracles, those who have the gift of healing, those who can help others, those who have the gift of leadership, those who speak in unknown languages.

Are we all apostles? Are we all prophets? Are we all teachers? Do we all have the power to do miracles? Do we all have the gift of healing? Do we all have the ability to speak in unknown languages? Do we all have the ability to interpret unknown languages? Of course not! So you should earnestly desire the most helpful gifts. (1 Corinthians 12:12-31)

The Holy Spirit transforms. There is great empowerment as the Holy Spirit, daily, makes us more like Jesus. Sin has tainted who we are. Sin has derailed who we were meant to be. But once we are in Christ, that divine design is fully restored along with the image of God. The glory humanity once had in the Garden of Eden (Genesis 1 & 2) is restored! Paul likens this to a veil being removed to show the manifest beauty underneath.

But whenever someone turns to the Lord, the veil is taken away. For the Lord is the Spirit, and wherever the Spirit of the Lord is, there is freedom. So all of us who have had that veil removed can see and reflect the glory of the Lord. And the Lord—who is the Spirit—makes us more and more like him as we are changed into his glorious image. (2 Corinthians 3:16-18)

The Holy Spirit is the one who walks with each of us in Christ's Church so that we, more and more, are being transformed into the likeness of our Savior. "Christian" means "Christlike" or "Like Christ." It's the Spirit of the Living God that makes that likeness in us a reality. The Holy Spirit transforms us.

I began by saying that the Holy Spirit is *not* the "silent partner" of our Triune God. Do you now understand why I say that? Do you see all that the Holy Spirit is up to? All of these things are wrapped up in our relationship with God's Holy Spirit. And when Christians do not know the person and work of the Holy Spirit, it is no wonder they struggle in so many areas of their lives and their mission!

"I believe in the Holy Spirit..." The Holy Spirit is God. The Holy Spirit is a person. The Holy Spirit works incredibly within us. The Holy Spirit is *real* and working in and among Christ's people to this day.

STUDY GUIDE

IT MAKES A DIFFERENCE

It amazes me how little most Christians know about the person and work of the Holy Spirit. The Christian who learns about the Spirit's partnership with us in life and ministry has a distinct advantage over everyone else. They know that the Holy Spirit is a distinct person of our Triune God who has intellect, wisdom, and emotions. Moreover, they know the Holy Spirit lives with them to equip and empower them for holiness and Jesus' mission until the Lord returns. He teaches. He testifies. He convicts of sin. He comforts. He unifies. He calls and commissions. He guides. He assures and intercedes. He sanctifies. He speaks and enlightens. He justifies. He fills out our divine design with tools and abilities – including spiritual gifts – to accomplish all God has laid before us for his glory. If we are to experience personal transformation, ever growing to be more like Jesus, we must rely on the work of the Holy Spirit to accomplish this in us, for we cannot do it on our own.

Those with little or no understanding of the person and work of the Holy Spirit are deeply hampered in their Christian walk. They cannot take advantage of all the Spirit offers because of ignorance. Some recognize the Holy Spirit's part in salvation and leave it at that. Others have developed a theological framework that dramatically minimizes the role of the Holy Spirit today. Considering the long list of works of the Spirit in the paragraph above, it's easy to understand why these folks struggle so much in their Christian life. They resist the Spirit's efforts to sanctify them and wonder why they have such a personal struggle with holiness. They may experience similar setbacks concerning learning the Scripture, dealing with suffering and grief, biblical peacemaking, praying, and especially when it comes to equipping for ministry. If one minimizes the work of the Spirit in spiritual gifts and other aspects of God's divine design, they miss critical tools and helps for life and ministry.

God the Father and God the Son sent God the Holy Spirit to reside with the Church until Jesus returns for a reason. We cannot live fully in victory, bearing kingdom fruit, without a vibrant relationship with the Spirit.

HOW DO I LIVE OUT WHAT I HAVE JUST LEARNED IN MY OWN LIFE?

1. Take a moment to stop and pray. Ask God, through the Holy Spirit, to increase your understanding of the essentials of the Christian Faith. Ask Him to reveal and clarify any points which have been confusing or unclear.

2. Read the section *The Person of the Holy Spirit*. Ask yourself if you have truly considered the Holy Spirit part of the Triune God as he is represented in this section. If not, how might a change of perspective change your spiritual life?

3. Consider each of the empowering works of the Holy Spirit as they are listed in this chapter. Which of these do you most need to see evidenced in your life? Ask the Holy Spirit to help.

4. Review the list of fruits of the Spirit. Meditate on which of these you most need to develop in your life. Ask the Holy Spirit to help you do so.

5. Spend time contemplating which gifts of the Spirit you have been given and how you might use them to serve your church body best. If you are unsure what your gifts are, ask your pastor or other church leader to help you discover your gifts and then brainstorm ways to use them for the good of your church.

6. Take several days to consider: Who can help you apply what you learn to put it into an ongoing life's practice?

7. How are you living this out right now? How is your life reflective of your understanding of this truth?

HOW DO I IMPART WHAT I HAVE JUST LEARNED TO CHILDREN?

***Preparing to teach this lesson to children:** Decide whether you want to have the children make this visual individually or as a group.*

If they are making individual representations, gather the following materials: large (approximately 11 x 16) sheet of blank paper per child, pencils, markers and/or crayons, scissors, and glue. Run off 9 apple patterns, such as the ones suggested here: https://www.first-palette.com/printable/apple.html *per child. Choose the template with multiple apples per sheet. Run off 9 leaf patterns, such as the one suggested here:* https://onelittleproject.com/leaf-template/ *per child. Again, choose the template with multiple leaves per page. Run off a tree pattern, such as this one:* https://www.loveourreallife.com/print-able-trees-without-leaves/ *. If your copier enlarges, you may want to run off the tree pattern directly onto the larger paper.*

If they are making a group representation, choose a room where you have the space to display the visual on the wall or a bulletin board. Draw or run off an outline of a tree on large brown paper. Run off 9 leaf and apple patterns, such as the ones suggested above, choosing the larger templates.

1. Begin by praying with the children. Ask God, through the Holy Spirit, to help the children understand more about the Christian faith. Ask God to help them clearly understand the new things they are about to learn.

2. Continue to work on memorizing the Apostle's Creed. Be sure they have memorized through this part:

   I believe in God, the Father almighty, creator of heaven and earth.
   I believe in Jesus Christ, his only Son, our Lord, who was conceived by the Holy Spirit and born of the virgin Mary. He suffered under Pontius Pilate, was crucified, died, and was buried; he descended into hell. The third day he rose again from the dead. He ascended to heaven and is seated at the right hand of God the Father almighty. From there he will come to judge the living and the dead.
   I believe in the Holy Spirit...

3. Tell the children that when Jesus left the disciples to ascend to heaven, they needed someone to be with them and guide them, so Jesus sent the Holy Spirit. Jesus sent the Holy Spirit not only to help the disciples but to help those of us who follow Jesus today. The Holy Spirit is also God, just like Jesus and God the Father. We cannot see the Holy Spirit, but we can know about him through his work. In this lesson we are going to make a picture of some of the things the Holy Spirit does for us.

4. If the children are making individual pictures:

    a. Have the children draw a large tree trunk with branches, using the tree pattern as a model if you were unable to run off an enlargement on a copier. Color the trunk and branches brown. Label the inside of the trunk *Holy Spirit.* You may want to have the children turn the paper sideways to write. If you are making a tree on the wall or bulletin board, hand out the patterns for leaves and apples as needed.

    b. Have the children write the fruits of the Spirit: love, joy, peace, patience, goodness, kindness, faithfulness, gentleness, and self-control on the nine apples. Color the apples red and yellow. Give examples of what each of these looks like in our lives today. Paste the "fruits" onto the tree branches. Explain that good fruit comes from a good tree – after its kind – apples from apple trees, oranges from orange trees, and so forth. As we become more like God, we show his fruit.

    c. Explain that the Holy Spirit has other jobs as well. He is our helper. His jobs: teaches, comforts, gives power, invites us to God, guides, gives spiritual gifts, helps us get along, helps us grow, helps us pray. Have the children write these jobs on the leaves, color them green, and glue them on the trees. Explain that these are just some of the jobs of the Spirit. Briefly talk about each one.

4. If the children are making one large tree, have the tree and trunk pinned to the bulletin board or stuck to the wall with

sticky tack. Allow the children to create the apples and leaves as described above and attach them to the tree using pins or sticky tack.

5.   If you have children in your group who have not yet surrendered to Jesus, continue to pray for the Holy Spirit to open that conversational door so you can explain the gospel. Once they receive Christ, the indwelling presence of the Holy Spirit will make the lessons in this book much more accessible to them.

HOW DO I IMPART WHAT I HAVE JUST LEARNED TO TEENS?

Advance preparation suggested: Run off a four-column chart per teen. Here is an example: https://www.smartdraw.com/education-work-sheet/examples/four-column-chart/ . If you are comfortable using word processing software, you could create your own by designing and printing a table with four columns. A legal-sized sheet (long) of paper run off with a landscape (sideways) orientation will work best.

1.   Begin by praying with the teens. Ask God, through the Holy Spirit, to increase understanding. You can do this or ask a volunteer.

2.   Read the Apostles' Creed out loud. Read it yourself, ask for a volunteer, or read it in unison.

3.   Repeat these lines:

I believe in God, the Father almighty, creator of heaven and earth.

I believe in Jesus Christ, his only Son, our Lord, who was conceived by the Holy Spirit and born of the virgin Mary. He suffered under Pontius Pilate, was crucified, died, and was buried; he descended into hell. The third day he rose again from the dead. He ascended to heaven and is seated at the right hand of God the Father almighty. From there he will come to judge the living and the dead.

I believe in the Holy Spirit...

4.   Have the teens pull out their Question Journals. Ask them to jot down the answers to any questions about the Creed that are

answered in this session. Have them share those discoveries, giving them sufficient time to record any thoughts they wish to capture. Assure them that they can ask any remaining questions about this section at the end of the session.

5. Ask the teens what they know about the Holy Spirit. Don't be surprised if their knowledge is limited or inaccurate. Rather than attempting to answer/correct this now, assure the teens that limited knowledge of the person and work of the Holy Spirit is common, and that will be addressed in this lesson. Assure them that they will have the opportunity to ask any questions that remain after this lesson.

6. Have the teens create a four-column chart (see example above). Across the top write *Holy Spirit.* Title the first column *Characteristics*, the second column *Fruit*, the third column *Roles* and the fourth column *Gifts.*

7. Read the section entitled *The Person of the Holy Spirit* and list his characteristics in the Characteristics column. Finish with *Producer of Fruit.* There are seven characteristics listed, including the one mentioned above. Ask the teens which of these surprised them. Discuss as needed.

8. The nine fruits of the Spirit are in a bulleted list under that section. Have teens list them in the Fruits column. Have teens give examples of what those fruits look like in the life of the Christian.

9. There are fifteen roles of the Spirit listed by Dr. Kimball in the section, *The Empowering Work of the Holy Spirit,* so warn the teens to write small in this column. Discuss the ways the Holy Spirit empowers the Christian. Ask the teens if there are any that are new to them. As necessary, explain further.

10. There are as many as seventeen gifts (depending on how you divide them) of the Spirit listed under the role, *The Holy Spirit Works and Equips,* so the "write small" advice applies here too. You may want to let the teens know that most scholars agree that these lists are not even a complete listing. Some of the gifts

listed here will be easy for the teens to identify (such as teacher), others more controversial or complex to explain. Rather than spending too much time trying to give a full explanation of every gift listed, concentrate on the *purposes* for gifting. If there is sufficient interest, there are numerous gift inventories available for teens to explore at another time.

11. Allow the teens to ask any questions about the Holy Spirit that they had noted in their journals that were not addressed in this discussion. Ask them if/how their understanding changed through what they learned in this session.

12. If you have teens in your group who have not yet surrendered to Jesus, continue praying for the Holy Spirit to open that conversational door so you can explain the gospel. Once they receive Christ, the indwelling presence of the Holy Spirit will make the lessons in this book much more accessible to them.

HOW DO I IMPART WHAT I HAVE JUST LEARNED TO ADULTS?

1. Challenge your adults to take a moment to stop and pray, asking God, through the Holy Spirit, to increase their understanding of the essentials of the Christian Faith. Encourage them to ask Him to reveal and clarify any points which have been confusing or unclear.

2. Review the Apostle's Creed. Repeat the first several lines of the Creed with emphasis. If they have not done so, encourage them to memorize the Creed, reminding them that this is a summary of the essentials of the faith:

I believe in God, the Father almighty, creator of heaven and earth.

I believe in Jesus Christ, his only Son, our Lord, who was conceived by the Holy Spirit and born of the virgin Mary. He suffered under Pontius Pilate, was crucified, died, and was buried; he descended into hell. The third day he rose again from the dead. He ascended to heaven and is seated at the right hand of God the Father almighty. From there he will come to judge the living and the dead.

I believe in the Holy Spirit...

3. Have participants pull out the notes they made during previous sessions. Ask them to jot down the answers to any questions about the Creed that may be answered during this session and to share those discoveries as they happen. Provide sufficient time to record any thoughts they may wish to capture. Assure them that they will have the opportunity to ask any questions that were not answered in this session at the end of the session.

4. Ask participants what they think of when they hear the words, *Holy Spirit*. Limited knowledge of the person and work of the Holy Spirit is common in the North American Church. Discuss to what extent this might be true in their experience and/or why they believe this might be the case. Assure them that they will have the opportunity to ask any questions that remain after this lesson.

5. This chapter has four major facets of truth about the Holy Spirit. The first are his *characteristics*. Discuss the characteristics listed in italics in the section entitled *The Person of the Holy Spirit*, setting aside for now the section on the fruits, which are listed last. Were any of these surprising? How did this listing add to your understanding of what the Spirit is like?

6. Next, examine the list of the *fruits* the Spirit shares with the believer. For which of these are you most grateful? Which do you feel the need to have more abundant in your own life?

7. Now take a look at the active, empowering *work* of the Spirit, which is discussed in the section entitled, *The Empowering Work of the Holy Spirit*. Dr. Kimball says, "If we don't understand the empowering work of the Holy Spirit as Christians, we are greatly hampered in our ability to be faithful and obedient to Christ and his mission – and we may even have an inadequate understanding of our Triune God!" Look at the discussion of his work in this light. How do the actions of the Holy Spirit help us to be "faithful and obedient" to the mission?

8. Return, for a moment, to the section *The Holy Spirit works and equips*. The list of gifts here, most theologians agree, is an

incomplete list. The purpose of the gifts is undoubtedly to equip us to do the mission to which we have been assigned. There are perhaps more disagreements about the nature of some of these gifts than about many other passages of scripture. Rather than focusing on the exact definition and description of each gift in the list, encourage participants to take a few moments to think about *why* the gifts are assigned and *what* their particular gifts may be. If they have questions about their gifts and their purpose, there are many gift inventories available. A pastor or denominational leader will probably be acquainted with at least one of these should participants desire to follow up with the quest to best understand how the Spirit has gifted them and how these gifts might best be used in their local church.

9. Allow participants to ask any questions about Holy Spirit they had noted previously that were not addressed in this discussion.

10. If you have people in your group who have not yet surrendered to Jesus, continue to pray for the Holy Spirit to open that conversational door so you can explain the gospel. Once they receive Christ, the indwelling presence of the Holy Spirit will make the lessons in this book much more accessible to them.

CHAPTER 11
The Universal Church

"I believe in one holy, catholic Church..."

Once you were dead because of your disobedience and your many sins. You used to live in sin, just like the rest of the world, obeying the devil—the commander of the powers in the unseen world. He is the spirit at work in the hearts of those who refuse to obey God. All of us used to live that way, following the passionate desires and inclinations of our sinful nature. By our very nature we were subject to God's anger, just like everyone else.

But God is so rich in mercy, and he loved us so much, that even though we were dead because of our sins, he gave us life when he raised Christ from the dead. (It is only by God's grace that you have been saved!) For he raised us from the dead along with Christ and seated us with him in the heavenly realms because we are united with Christ Jesus. So God can point to us in all future ages as examples of the incredible wealth of his grace and kindness toward us, as shown in all he has done for us who are united with Christ Jesus.

God saved you by his grace when you believed. And you can't take credit for this; it is a gift from God. Salvation is not a reward for the good things we have done, so none of us can boast about it. For we are God's masterpiece. He has created us anew in Christ Jesus, so we can do the good things he planned for us long ago.

Don't forget that you Gentiles used to be outsiders. You were called "uncircumcised heathens" by the Jews, who were proud of their circumcision, even though it affected only their bodies and not their hearts. In those days you were living apart from Christ. You were excluded from citizenship among the people of Israel, and you did not know the covenant promises God had made to them. You lived in this world without God and without hope. But now you have been united with Christ Jesus. Once you were far away from God, but now you have been brought near to him through the blood of Christ.

For Christ himself has brought peace to us. He united Jews and Gentiles into one people when, in his own body on the cross, he broke down the wall of hostility that separated us. He did this by ending the system of law with its commandments and regulations. He made peace between Jews and Gentiles by creating in himself one new people from the two groups. Together as one body, Christ reconciled both groups to God by means of his death on the cross, and our hostility toward each other was put to death.

He brought this Good News of peace to you Gentiles who were far away from him, and peace to the Jews who were near. Now all of us can come to the Father through the same Holy Spirit because of what Christ has done for us.

So now you Gentiles are no longer strangers and foreigners. You are citizens along with all of God's holy people. You are members of God's family. Together, we are his house, built on the foundation of the apostles and the prophets. And the cornerstone is Christ Jesus himself. We are carefully joined together in him, becoming a holy temple for the Lord. Through him you Gentiles are also being made part of this dwelling where God lives by his Spirit. (Ephesians 2:1-22)

TWO SIDES OF THE SAME COIN

"I believe in one holy, catholic church..." As noted before, holy means "set apart for God's purposes." And the word "catholic" here is not referring to Roman Catholicism but is a term that means "universal." So the Apostles' Creed here is calling us to believe in Jesus' Church that is both separated unto God for his special purposes and universal in nature. We'll discuss more about that universal nature in this chapter.

It's important here to note that any discussion of Christ's universal church must also be taken together with the next stanza of the Creed: "...the communion of the saints..." As with other paired stanzas we've previously studied in the Creed, these two ideas are two sides of the same coin. While we will be delineating them as separate chapters in this book, they are actually two critical aspects of the same reality. The Church Jesus has created is comprised of both Jews and Gentiles (non-Jews – i.e., *all* ethnicities) and is timeless, composed of saints (holy ones) from the past, the present, and the future.

THE CHURCH DEFINED

Dr. Wayne Grudem defines the Church as "the community of all true believers for all time."[26] In today's world, many Christians and non-Christians alike confuse the church as a believing community with the church as an organization or a building. But Jesus' church has never been an organization or a building – it's always been a people!

The Church is comprised of the saved. The "Church" refers to the Greek word *ekklesia*, which is a compound term made up of the word *ek* ("out of" or "out from") and the word *kaleo* ("to call"). *Ekklesia* literally means "the called-out ones."

> *But you are not like that, for you are a chosen people. You are royal priests, a holy nation, God's very own possession. As a result, you can show others the goodness of God, **for he called you out of the darkness into his wonderful light.***

---

26   Wayne Grudem, *Systematic Theology: An Introduction to Biblical Doctrine,* Grand Rapids, MI: Zondervan Academic, p. 1048.

"Once you had no identity as a people; now you are God's people. Once you received no mercy; now you have received God's mercy." (1 Peter 2:9-10, **emphasis mine**)

Theologically, Jesus' Church is that community of believers who have been called out of Satan's dominion of darkness and into Jesus' dominion of light. As he stood before King Agrippa, explaining his encounter with the risen Jesus, the apostle Paul quotes Christ's calling on his life,

Yes, I am sending you to the Gentiles to open their eyes, **so they may turn from darkness to light and from the power of Satan to God.** *Then they will receive forgiveness for their sins and be given a place among God's people, who are set apart by faith in me.'* (Acts 26:17-18, **emphasis mine**)

This called-out nature is very important. In today's local churches, it is sometimes possible to become a member of a congregation *without* having been "called out of the darkness and into his wonderful light." It is sometimes possible for people to obtain full membership privileges in a local congregation without having been truly "turned from darkness to light and from the power of Satan to God." These people may regularly attend services in a building called a "church" and may be members of an organization called a "church," but we must clearly understand that they are not yet part of the Church we are describing. Surrender to and salvation by Jesus are mandatory – it's unfortunate that some local congregations have made them optional.

This community of the saved is the *body* of Christ. Paul writes to the Romans,

Because of the privilege and authority God has given me, I give each of you this warning: Don't think you are better than you really are. Be honest in your evaluation of yourselves, measuring yourselves by the faith God has given us. Just as our bodies have many parts and each part has a special function, so it is with Christ's body. We are many parts of one body, and we all belong to each other. (Romans 12:3-5)

The body of Christ is made up of many people, just like a human body is made up of many parts (see also 1 Corinthians 10:17; 12:27; Ephesians 5:23; Colossians 1:24; Hebrews 13:3). Using "body" terminology helps us understand that all of the life and activity of Jesus' Church is lived out on behalf of our Savior. We are Jesus' body. Jesus came in a physical body so that he could carry out his redeeming mission on earth. Jesus came in a physical body to demonstrate the love of God to humanity. Jesus came in a physical body to *touch* people with love and healing. Jesus came in a physical body to be a tangible instrument of God's *shalom* to a world that desperately needed it. As the body of Christ, the Church continues all these things under the power of the Holy Spirit to this day.

This community of the saved is the *bride* of Christ. As Paul writes to the Ephesian Christians about Christ-honoring marriage, he invokes this beautiful bride imagery to make his point.

> *And further, submit to one another out of reverence for Christ.*
>
> *For wives, this means submit to your husbands as to the Lord. For a husband is the head of his wife as Christ is the head of the church. He is the Savior of his body, the church. As the church submits to Christ, so you wives should submit to your husbands in everything.*
>
> *For husbands, this means love your wives, just as Christ loved the church. He gave up his life for her to make her holy and clean, washed by the cleansing of God's word. He did this to present her to himself as a glorious church without a spot or wrinkle or any other blemish. Instead, she will be holy and without fault. In the same way, husbands ought to love their wives as they love their own bodies. For a man who loves his wife actually shows love for himself. No one hates his own body but feeds and cares for it, just as Christ cares for the church. And we are members of his body.* (Ephesians 5:21-30)

Understanding the Church as Jesus' bride speaks of the level of intimacy we enjoy with our Savior (see also 2 Corinthians 11:2; Revelation 19:7-9; 21:1-2). Jesus loves his Church like a husband loves his bride. This is actually a continuing theme from the Old Testament describing

God's relationship to Israel. There are profound images in the prophecies of Isaiah and Hosea where God demonstrates his redeeming love
for his people. Further, Jesus' Church loves him as a bride loves her
husband. The relationship is not coerced in any way – we love, and we
are faithful because we *want* to be.

As Jesus talks to his disciples about his departure to heaven, he uses
well-known betrothal language to convey his love.

> *"Don't let your hearts be troubled. Trust in God, and trust also
> in me. There is more than enough room in my Father's home. If
> this were not so, would I have told you that I am going to prepare
> a place for you? When everything is ready, I will come and get
> you, so that you will always be with me where I am.* (John 14:1-3)

When a young Jewish man in the first century would receive the
blessing of his beloved's father to marry his daughter, that was just
the beginning of the relationship. The young suitor would then have
to build a home for them. Quite often, this home would be an addition
to the family compound (or "his father's house"). In such a situation,
there might be many such chambers, one for each of the family's sons.
The last words the young man would say to his bride before the wedding would be, "I go to prepare a place for you." She would then not
see him again until the chamber was done to his father's satisfaction
and the wedding celebration could begin (think about the bridegroom
coming with a shout and the parable of the ten virgins in Matthew 25
– it's all tied together!). Jesus' entire ministry communicated this kind
of love to his followers.

The Church is the *ekklesia*, the called-out ones – the body and bride
of Christ.

The Church is the gathered people of God. To be holy is to be separated unto God for his purposes. We must never mistake this to mean
that we completely separate from pre-Christian people around us as
that would eliminate our ability to be a witness and blessing to them!
But we are to be separate – holy, sacred, *different.* We are separated
from the worldly and gathered together unto God. Paul writes to the
Corinthian Christians,

Don't team up with those who are unbelievers. How can righteousness be a partner with wickedness? How can light live with darkness? What harmony can there be between Christ and the devil? How can a believer be a partner with an unbeliever? And what union can there be between God's temple and idols? For we are the temple of the living God. As God said:

"I will live in them and walk among them. I will be their God, and they will be my people. Therefore, come out from among unbelievers, and separate yourselves from them, says the Lord. Don't touch their filthy things, and I will welcome you. And I will be your Father, and you will be my sons and daughters, says the Lord Almighty." (2 Corinthians 6:14-18)

We've already talked about the word *ekklesia*, meaning "called-out ones," but its common usage in Greek culture also means "assembly" or "called-together ones." We are not just called out of the realm of sin and darkness; we are also called *to* the realm of glory and light! This gathered Church is composed of *anyone* who has surrendered to Christ – Jewish and Gentile (non-Jewish) believers alike. This gathered Church is made up of all peoples – all nations. Jesus established this in his Great Commission:

*Jesus came and told his disciples, "I have been given all authority in heaven and on earth. Therefore, go and make disciples **of all the nations**, baptizing them in the name of the Father and the Son and the Holy Spirit. Teach these new disciples to obey all the commands I have given you. And be sure of this: I am with you always, even to the end of the age."* (Matthew 28:18-20, **emphasis mine**)

Nations here is the Greek word *ethne*, from which we get our English word *ethnic*. *Ethne* describes a people distinguished by language, dialect, and/or culture. It's the Greek equivalent of our missionary phrase "people group." Jesus did not call his followers to disciple only Jews, but people from every people group. And when one includes his instructions in Acts 1:8, his expectation is for us to make disciples for him from every people group to the very ends of the earth! This gathered Church is to be global!

The gathered Church worships. Again, let's return to 2 Peter 2:9,

> *But you are not like that, for you are a chosen people. You are royal priests, a holy nation, God's very own possession. As a result,* **you can show others the goodness of God**, *for he called you out of the darkness into his wonderful light.* (1 Peter 2:9)

The Greek phrase here can also be rendered, "...that you may proclaim the excellencies of God..." or "...that you may declare the praises of God..." Notice that what the called-out ones do is *worship!* This makes sense because as the Holy Spirit fell upon the believers in Jerusalem on the Day of Pentecost, the very first thing they did under his power was to declare the wonderful things God has done.

> *At that time there were devout Jews from every nation living in Jerusalem. When they heard the loud noise, everyone came running, and they were bewildered to hear their own languages being spoken by the believers.*
>
> *They were completely amazed. "How can this be?" they exclaimed. "These people are all from Galilee, and yet we hear them speaking in our own native languages! Here we are— Parthians, Medes, Elamites, people from Mesopotamia, Judea, Cappadocia, Pontus, the province of Asia, Phrygia, Pamphylia, Egypt, and the areas of Libya around Cyrene, visitors from Rome (both Jews and converts to Judaism), Cretans, and Arabs.* ***And we all hear these people speaking in our own languages about the wonderful things God has done!"*** (Acts 2:5-11, **emphasis mine**)

There was a powerful witness. There was unadulterated praise. There was worship of God.

The Church is a great and timeless cloud of witnesses. This cloud of witnesses is not just all people groups, but it's actually also all believers of all time. This gives us a hint into the next chapter on the Communion of the Saints. Hebrews 11 provides a "hall of faith" made up of all those who were known for their forward-looking faith generations before Jesus was even born!

Faith shows the reality of what we hope for; it is the evidence of things we cannot see. Through their faith, the people in days of old earned a good reputation.

By faith we understand that the entire universe was formed at God's command, that what we now see did not come from anything that can be seen.

It was by faith that Abel brought a more acceptable offering to God than Cain did. Abel's offering gave evidence that he was a righteous man, and God showed his approval of his gifts. Although Abel is long dead, he still speaks to us by his example of faith.

It was by faith that Enoch was taken up to heaven without dying—"he disappeared, because God took him." For before he was taken up, he was known as a person who pleased God. And it is impossible to please God without faith. Anyone who wants to come to him must believe that God exists and that he rewards those who sincerely seek him.

It was by faith that Noah built a large boat to save his family from the flood. He obeyed God, who warned him about things that had never happened before. By his faith Noah condemned the rest of the world, and he received the righteousness that comes by faith.

It was by faith that Abraham obeyed when God called him to leave home and go to another land that God would give him as his inheritance. He went without knowing where he was going. And even when he reached the land God promised him, he lived there by faith—for he was like a foreigner, living in tents. And so did Isaac and Jacob, who inherited the same promise. Abraham was confidently looking forward to a city with eternal foundations, a city designed and built by God.

It was by faith that even Sarah was able to have a child, though she was barren and was too old. She believed that God would keep his promise. And so a whole nation came from this one man who was as good as dead—a nation with so many people that, like the stars in the sky and the sand on the seashore, there is no way to count them.

All these people died still believing what God had promised them. They did not receive what was promised, but they saw it all from a distance and welcomed it. They agreed that they were foreigners and nomads here on earth. Obviously people who say such things are looking forward to a country they can call their own. If they had longed for the country they came from, they could have gone back. But they were looking for a better place, a heavenly homeland. That is why God is not ashamed to be called their God, for he has prepared a city for them. (Hebrews 11:1-16)

And this is only half of the passage! The writer of Hebrews ends this review with these words:

All these people earned a good reputation because of their faith, yet none of them received all that God had promised. For God had something better in mind for us, so that they would not reach perfection without us. (Hebrews 11:39-40)

All of these Old Testament "saints" gained God's approval because of their faith. Paul actually says that Abraham believed God and "it was credited to him as righteousness" (Galatians 3:6)! This is the language of justification! This cloud of witnesses proclaims the praises of God – there is great thanksgiving. This cloud of witnesses declares the wonders of God – celebrating all that he has done. We'll learn more in the next chapter.

The Church is the *witness to the Kingdom of God.* The Church herself is not the kingdom but is produced by the kingdom (or maybe better to say, is produced by the King). The idea of a kingdom is largely misunderstood today – at least in North America. When many people see the word "kingdom," they assume it refers to the land over which a king exercises his authority. However, in most cases, the biblical usage is not referring to the *realm* of the king, but the *reign* of the king.

The term translated "kingdom" in the New Testament is the Greek word *basilean*. The way this term is used is based on its context. While there are instances where the word refers to Christ's domain, in most cases, the references are to Christ's dominion – his kingship. George

Eldon Ladd gives an excellent background on this in his book, *The Gospel of the Kingdom*.[27] It is precisely this idea of kingship that Paul has in mind when he writes to the Church at Colossae,

> *For he has rescued us from the kingdom of darkness and transferred us into the Kingdom of his dear Son, who purchased our freedom and forgave our sins.* (Colossians 1:13-14)

The Church is not the reign of Jesus, but is *under* the reign of Jesus. As people are called out, as people are called together, they surrender to King Jesus and enter into his kingdom.

The Church is the *instrument* of Christ's kingdom rule and reign. We have the person, power, and presence of the Holy Spirit. We have been commissioned (Matthew 28:18-20). We are Christ's ambassadors (2 Corinthians 5:20). Through the Holy Spirit, we manifest the power of the kingdom – seeing answered prayer, healing ministry, deliverance, and teaching with authority. We proclaim the gospel of the kingdom – the good news about Jesus' ultimate rule and reign. We are the witnesses of the kingdom, called to advance that rule and reign under the power of the Holy Spirit, heart by heart, soul by soul, throughout the whole world. And this brings us to our next point.

The Church is called to a mission. That mission, the Great Commission, is to make disciples of all people groups and thereby extend the kingdom of God. This is the great purpose of Jesus' church. It is the "prime directive" under which every local congregation operates. We exist to make disciples, extending the rule and reign of Jesus. And every believer is to be about that effort.

The Church is a community of the saved. The Church is gathered as a great cloud of timeless witnesses on the mission to be Jesus' instrument, leading the world to surrender to him as their Savior and their King. Knowing this, it becomes easy to see that the Church of Jesus Christ is expressed or functions both locally and universally.

---

27   George Eldon Ladd, *The Gospel of the Kingdom: Scriptural Studies in the Kingdom of God*, Grand Rapids, MI: Eerdmans, 1990.

THE CHURCH LOCAL AND UNIVERSAL ("CATHOLIC")

Many Christians don't think about it, but Jesus' Church is an amazing body. Every local expression of the Church is the Church, and yet, all of us down through the ages are *one* Church in Christ. This is the essence of *communion* – our common union with each other in Christ is reflected in The Lord's Table. Paul writes to the Corinthians,

> *When we bless the cup at the Lord's Table, aren't we sharing in the blood of Christ? And when we break the bread, aren't we sharing in the body of Christ? And though we are many, we all eat from one loaf of bread, showing that we are one body.* (1 Corinthians 10:16-17)

Jesus' Church is both *local* and *universal* at the same time. There is one singular Church, but it is distributed over multiple local congregations of different shapes, sizes, and locations – and even different eras!

The Church is the Church on every level. When our Lord refers to the Church, it is always singular, not plural. There is one universal church. Once, when Jesus and his disciples were at Caesarea Philippi, Peter had an authentic epiphany from the heavenly Father.

> *When Jesus came to the region of Caesarea Philippi, he asked his disciples, "Who do people say that the Son of Man is?"*
>
> *"Well," they replied, "some say John the Baptist, some say Elijah, and others say Jeremiah or one of the other prophets."*
>
> *Then he asked them, "But who do you say I am?"*
>
> *Simon Peter answered, "You are the Messiah, the Son of the living God."*
>
> *Jesus replied, "You are blessed, Simon son of John, because my Father in heaven has revealed this to you. You did not learn this from any human being. Now I say to you that you are Peter (which means 'rock'), and upon this rock I will build my church, and all the powers of hell will not conquer it.* (Matthew 16:13-18)

Jesus' declaration is not about a single, local congregation, but of the Church universal. Paul does the same. As he is giving his farewell to the elders in the Church at Ephesus, he writes,

"So guard yourselves and God's people. Feed and shepherd God's flock—his church, purchased with his own blood—over which the Holy Spirit has appointed you as leaders. (Acts 20:28)

Paul refers to Jesus' Church – in the singular – which Christ purchased with his own blood.

When it comes to the called-out ones, there is only one Church even though it is expressed in many different localities. We see this already in the New Testament:

1. House Churches

    Give my greetings to Priscilla and Aquila, my co-workers in the ministry of Christ Jesus. In fact, they once risked their lives for me. I am thankful to them, and so are all the Gentile churches. Also give my greetings to the church that meets in their home. (Romans 16:3-5 – see also 1 Corinthians 16:19)

    When Paul and Silas left the prison, they returned to the home of Lydia. There they met with the believers and encouraged them once more. Then they left town. (Acts 16:40)

2. City-wide Churches

    This letter is from Paul, chosen by the will of God to be an apostle of Christ Jesus, and from our brother Sosthenes. I am writing to God's church in Corinth, to you who have been called by God to be his own holy people. He made you holy by means of Christ Jesus, just as he did for all people everywhere who call on the name of our Lord Jesus Christ, their Lord and ours. May God our Father and the Lord Jesus Christ give you grace and peace. (1 Corinthians 1:1-3)

    This letter is from Paul, Silas, and Timothy. We are writing to the church in Thessalonica, to you who belong to God the Father and the Lord Jesus Christ. May God give you grace and peace. (1 Thessalonians 1:1)

"Write this letter to the angel of the church in Ephesus. This is the message from the one who holds the seven stars in his right hand, the one who walks among the seven gold lampstands...

"Write this letter to the angel of the church in Smyrna. This is the message from the one who is the First and the Last, who was dead but is now alive...

"Write this letter to the angel of the church in Pergamum. This is the message from the one with the sharp two-edged sword...

"Write this letter to the angel of the church in Thyatira. This is the message from the Son of God, whose eyes are like flames of fire, whose feet are like polished bronze...

"Write this letter to the angel of the church in Sardis. This is the message from the one who has the sevenfold Spirit of God and the seven stars...

"Write this letter to the angel of the church in Philadelphia.

This is the message from the one who is holy and true, the one who has the key of David.

What he opens, no one can close; and what he closes, no one can open...

"Write this letter to the angel of the church in Laodicea. This is the message from the one who is the Amen—the faithful and true witness, the beginning of God's new creation... (Revelation 2:1-3:22)

3. Regional Churches

But you will receive power when the Holy Spirit comes upon you. And you will be my witnesses, telling people about me everywhere—in Jerusalem, throughout Judea, in Samaria, and to the ends of the earth." (Acts 1:8)

This letter is from Paul, an apostle. I was not appointed by any group of people or any human authority, but by Jesus Christ himself and by God the Father, who raised Jesus from the dead.

All the brothers and sisters here join me in sending this letter to the churches of Galatia. (Galatians 1:1-2)

4.   The Worldwide Church

*"For this is how God loved the world: He gave his one and only Son, so that **everyone** who believes in him will not perish but have eternal life.* (John 3:16, **emphasis mine**)

For husbands, this means love your wives, just as Christ loved the church. He gave up his life for her to make her holy and clean, washed by the cleansing of God's word. He did this to present her to himself as a glorious church without a spot or wrinkle or any other blemish. Instead, she will be holy and without fault. In the same way, husbands ought to love their wives as they love their own bodies. For a man who loves his wife actually shows love for himself. No one hates his own body but feeds and cares for it, just as Christ cares for the church. And we are members of his body. (Ephesians 5:25-30)

God has put all things under the authority of Christ and has made him head over all things for the benefit of the church. And the church is his body; it is made full and complete by Christ, who fills all things everywhere with himself. (Ephesians 1:22-23)

Christ is also the head of the church, which is his body.

He is the beginning, supreme over all who rise from the dead.

So he is first in everything.

For God in all his fullness was pleased to live in Christ, and through him God reconciled everything to himself.

He made peace with everything in heaven and on earth by means of Christ's blood on the cross. (Colossians 1:18-20)

Here are some of the parts God has appointed for the church: first are apostles, second are prophets, third are teachers, then those who do miracles, those who have the gift of healing, those who can help others, those who have the gift of leadership, those who speak in unknown languages. (1 Corinthians 12:28)

You have come to the assembly [ekklesia or church] of God's firstborn children, whose names are written in heaven. You have come to God himself, who is the judge over all things. You have come to the spirits of the righteous ones in heaven who have now been made perfect. (Hebrews 12:22-23)

I was circumcised when I was eight days old. I am a pure-blooded citizen of Israel and a member of the tribe of Benjamin—a real Hebrew if there ever was one! I was a member of the Pharisees, who demand the strictest obedience to the Jewish law. I was so zealous that I harshly persecuted the church. And as for righteousness, I obeyed the law without fault.

I once thought these things were valuable, but now I consider them worthless because of what Christ has done. (Philippians 3:5-7)

The Church is made up of every ethnicity. Teaching his disciples about the end of time, Jesus describes the Church as being composed of all nations (or *ethne*).

Jesus told them, "Don't let anyone mislead you, for many will come in my name, claiming, 'I am the Messiah.' They will deceive many. And you will hear of wars and threats of wars, but don't panic. Yes, these things must take place, but the end won't follow immediately. Nation will go to war against nation, and kingdom against kingdom. There will be famines and earthquakes in many parts of the world. But all this is only the first of the birth pains, with more to come.

"Then you will be arrested, persecuted, and killed. You will be hated all over the world because you are my followers. And many will turn away from me and betray and hate each other. And many false prophets will appear and will deceive many people. Sin will be rampant everywhere, and the love of many will grow cold. But the one who endures to the end will be saved. And the Good News about the Kingdom will be preached throughout the whole world, so that all nations will hear it; and then the end will come. (Matthew 24:4-14)

And we see this fulfilled in John's Revelation:

And they sang a new song with these words:

"You are worthy to take the scroll and break its seals and open it. For you were slaughtered, and your blood has ransomed people for God from every tribe and language and people and nation. And you have caused them to become a Kingdom of priests for our God. And they will reign on the earth." (Revelation 5:9-10)

I love the description in Revelation most of all because it gives every nuance of humanity from the smallest to the largest gathering.

1. The Church is from every *tribe* – this is the smallest subgroup of a nation or people group (can even be biologically related like a clan or a larger family line).

2. The Church is from every *language* – this is every nuance of a group's communication, right down to the smallest dialect.

3. The Church is from every *people* – the term used here refers to the populace of a region, the masses, or crowds.

4. The Church is from every *nation* – once again, the term is *ethne*; every ethnicity, every people group with its own distinct culture.

The Church is beautifully diverse – from every tribe and language and people and nation, but at the same time, we are always talking about one church.

The Church is one. Jesus himself explains that he makes his people a singular "flock" even though they come from many diverse backgrounds.

"I am the good shepherd; I know my own sheep, and they know me, just as my Father knows me and I know the Father. So I sacrifice my life for the sheep. **I have other sheep, too, that are not in this sheepfold. I must bring them also. They will listen to my voice, and there will be one flock with one shepherd.** (John 10:14-16, **emphasis mine**)

Jesus prayed for this oneness among us, and that it would impact the world.

> *"I am praying not only for these disciples but also for all who will ever believe in me through their message. **I pray that they will all be one, just as you and I are one**—as you are in me, Father, and I am in you. And may they be in us so that the world will believe you sent me.*
>
> *"I have given them the glory you gave me, **so they may be one as we are one.** I am in them and you are in me. **May they experience such perfect unity that the world will know that you sent me and that you love them as much as you love me.** (John 17:20-23, **emphasis mine**)*

As Jesus' Church, we are to live out this oneness.

> *Therefore I, a prisoner for serving the Lord, beg you to lead a life worthy of your calling, for you have been called by God. Always be humble and gentle. Be patient with each other, making allowance for each other's faults because of your love. Make every effort to keep yourselves united in the Spirit, binding yourselves together with peace. For there is one body and one Spirit, just as you have been called to one glorious hope for the future. There is one Lord, one faith, one baptism, one God and Father of all, who is over all, in all, and living through all. (Ephesians 4:1-6)*

All of these things are wrapped up in the Church being universal. The Church is composed of the saints. The church is called out and called together on a mission. The church is the body of Christ – the bride of Christ. The Church is a timeless cloud of witnesses to the rule and reign of King Jesus. The Church is the Church no matter the size or location. The Church is made up of every ethnicity – and is at the very same time, *one church!* This is what we mean when we say, "I believe in one holy, catholic church..."

STUDY GUIDE

IT MAKES A DIFFERENCE

The universal church is the community of all true believers for all time. Those who understand the biblical description of this body have great clarity on the makeup and mission of Christ's church. The church is only comprised of born-again people. They have a real and intimate relationship with God through Christ. They are called out of the kingdom of sin and darkness and are gathered to the Lord Jesus to be holy (that is, separate). They have a witness – proclaiming Christ and his wonderful work. They declare the rule and reign of God. And they are all we have described, whether local or global. The universal church of Jesus Christ is unique and recognizable.

Unfortunately, there are many misunderstandings today about the essence of Jesus' church. Many see the church first as a building or a place to gather. And a large number, particularly in the West, have missed the exclusivity of the church's definition – including people who have never surrendered to Christ among the church's number. Many contemporary expressions of the church do not strive for holiness, choosing to embrace lifestyle choices that are contrary to biblical teaching. Others include diverse philosophies under the church's banner that cannot be found in Scripture. And it is difficult to find many denominations or local congregations that still embrace and promote the full and complete rule and reign of God. Those who do not hold to the biblical description of Jesus' church have and actually create more confusion about its life and ministry.

Understanding the universal church is the key to living out its mission.

HOW DO I LIVE OUT WHAT I HAVE JUST LEARNED IN MY OWN LIFE?

1. Take a moment to stop and pray. Ask God, through the Holy Spirit, to increase your understanding of the essentials of the Christian Faith. Ask Him to reveal and clarify any points which have been confusing or unclear.

2. Read the section, *The Church Defined.* Take time to prayerfully consider how closely your own definition of the church matches the true definition as portrayed here. Consider any attitudes you have seen in your own congregation of worshippers that would indicate how closely your congregation reflects this definition. In any area where your congregation falls short of this understanding, what might you be called do to move it in a more biblical direction?

3. Now read *The Church Universal.* Reflect on your place in the universal (catholic) church. Have you seen yourself as part of the body of Christ as it is described here? How so? What is the evidence that your congregation of believers sees itself as part of the holy catholic church? How might you lift this idea up to your fellow believers?

4. Take several days to consider: Who can help you apply what you learn to put it into an ongoing life's practice?

5. How are you living this out right now? How is your life reflective of your understanding of this truth?

HOW DO I IMPART WHAT I HAVE JUST LEARNED TO CHILDREN?

Preparing to teach this lesson to children: Gather the needed supplies ahead of the lesson. For each child: 1) A copy of a male and a female bible character. Here are examples to download. https://natashalh.com/bible-character-coloring-pages/ *If you choose to use these pictures, Jesus and Queen Esther are the best for this purpose. 2) A piece of light-colored paper (such as light pastels) large enough to hold the two figures pasted side by side, 3) Scissors, 4) Glue, 5) Markers, crayons, or colored pencils. If you have children in the group younger than third grade, you may want to run off paper with lines for them to write on, as younger children often have difficulty writing in a straight line.*

1. Begin by praying with the children. Ask God, through the Holy Spirit, to help the children understand more about the Christian faith. Ask God to help them clearly understand the new things they are about to learn.

2. Continue to work with the children on memorizing the Apostle's Creed. Be sure they have memorized through this part:

I believe in God, the Father almighty, creator of heaven and earth.

I believe in Jesus Christ, his only Son, our Lord, who was conceived by the Holy Spirit and born of the virgin Mary. He suffered under Pontius Pilate, was crucified, died, and was buried; he descended into hell. The third day he rose again from the dead. He ascended to heaven and is seated at the right hand of God the Father almighty. From there he will come to judge the living and the dead.

I believe in the Holy Spirit, the holy catholic church...

3. Pass out the copies of the male and female figures. Allow children to color them, then cut them out. Children may want to cut out the name of Jesus, but be sure to cut away and discard the name of Queen Esther, as she represents a bride, not herself.

4. Discuss with the children that Jesus is the head of the church, just as in a family with married parents, the man is the head of the home. Talk about how Jesus loves the church and cares for it just like a man who loves his wife would and that the church loves Jesus just like a bride loves her husband.

5. Turn the paper to the landscape orientation. Glue the Jesus figure on one side of the paper. Be sure to favor one edge or the other, as you will write beside the female figure. Paste or write Jesus' name above his figure. Write "Head of the Church" underneath.

6. Glue the female figure very close to the Jesus figure. Above her, write "Jesus' Bride, the Church." Be sure to explain to the children that the church we represent here is NOT a *building* where we gather to worship God on Sunday but consists of the *people* who love and worship Jesus.

7. Next to the female figure, we will write some of the characteristics of the church: ALL who are saved (explain what this means), ALL who worship Jesus, ALL who tell about his

love, ALL who obey his commands. Explain that we use the word "ALL" because the church is made up of everyone who does these things no matter what skin color they have, language they speak, or where they gather to worship. You may need to glue some lined paper to the side of the female figure for younger children to be able to write a legible list. Older children may be able to print four short lines under one another.

8. If you have children in your group who have not yet surrendered to Jesus, continue to pray for the Holy Spirit to open that conversational door so you can explain the gospel. Once they receive Christ, the indwelling presence of the Holy Spirit will make the lessons in this book much more accessible to them.

HOW DO I IMPART WHAT I HAVE JUST LEARNED TO TEENS?

1. Begin by praying with the teens. Ask God, through the Holy Spirit, to increase understanding. You can do this or ask a volunteer.

2. Read the Apostles' Creed out loud. Read it yourself, ask for a volunteer, or read it in unison.

3. Repeat these lines:

   I believe in God, the Father almighty, creator of heaven and earth.

   I believe in Jesus Christ, his only Son, our Lord, who was conceived by the Holy Spirit and born of the virgin Mary. He suffered under Pontius Pilate, was crucified, died, and was buried; he descended into hell. The third day he rose again from the dead. He ascended to heaven and is seated at the right hand of God the Father almighty. From there he will come to judge the living and the dead.

   I believe in the Holy Spirit, the holy catholic church,...

4. Have the teens pull out their Question Journals. Ask them to jot down the answers to any questions about the Creed that are answered in this session. Have them share those discoveries,

giving them sufficient time to record any thoughts they wish to capture. Assure them that they can ask any remaining questions about this section at the end of the session.

5. Ask the teens what they think of when they hear the word *"church."* Explain that we will be expanding the definition well beyond what most people think of when they use that word. Most people think of a building where people gather to worship, or perhaps of a certain group of people who worship there. When people say *"my church"* or *"the church on the corner of Elm and Main Streets,"* this is what they usually mean.

6. Be sure the teens understand the words *"holy"* and *"catholic"* as defined in the first paragraph under the subtitle *Two Sides of the Same Coin.*

7. Have the teens search out what the biblical church truly is, as explained in this chapter. Have them write THE CHURCH at the top of a piece of paper and challenge them to write the characteristics that define the church as they find them. Remind them to pay special attention to italicized phrases. They may work individually or as partners. Give them time to share their findings. Be prepared to add any they miss and to explain any terms they find confusing. Be aware that the upcoming chapter will further define *"the communion of saints."*

8. Working with the teens, spend some time fleshing out the metaphor of the church as the bride of Christ, starting with the statement, "This community of the saved is the *bride* of Christ." As part of the discussion, read John 14:1-3 again. You may also want to take time to read the Parable of the Ten Virgins (Matthew 25:1-13).

9. Talk with the teens about the church as "the gathered people of God." How can we be the Church to the world around us and yet be "separated unto God"? How important is fellowship with other believers? And who makes up that body of believers?

10. Allow the teens to ask any questions about the nature of the church they had noted previously that were not addressed in this discussion.

11. If you have teens in your group who have not yet surrendered to Jesus, continue praying for the Holy Spirit to open that conversational door so you can explain the gospel. Once they receive Christ, the indwelling presence of the Holy Spirit will make the lessons in this book much more accessible to them.

HOW DO I IMPART WHAT I HAVE JUST LEARNED TO ADULTS?

1. Challenge your adults to take a moment to stop and pray, asking God, through the Holy Spirit, to increase their understanding of the essentials of the Christian Faith. Encourage them to ask Him to reveal and clarify any points which have been confusing or unclear.

2. Review the Apostle's Creed. Re-read the lines below slowly and thoughtfully:

   I believe in God, the Father almighty, creator of heaven and earth.

   I believe in Jesus Christ, his only Son, our Lord, who was conceived by the Holy Spirit and born of the virgin Mary. He suffered under Pontius Pilate, was crucified, died, and was buried; he descended into hell. The third day he rose again from the dead. He ascended to heaven and is seated at the right hand of God the Father almighty. From there he will come to judge the living and the dead.

   I believe in the Holy Spirit, the holy catholic church...

3. If they have not done so, encourage them to memorize the Creed in its entirety, reminding them that it is a summary of the essentials of the Christian faith.

4. Have participants pull out the notes they made during previous sessions. Ask them to jot down the answers to any questions about the Creed that may be answered during this session and to share those discoveries as they happen. Provide sufficient time

to record any thoughts they may wish to capture. Assure them that they will have the opportunity to ask any questions that were not answered in this session at the end of the session.

5. Ask participants to review the characteristics of the *holy catholic church* as defined in this chapter. Which of these do they believe the groups of worshippers (what we often call "the church") in North America generally reflect? Are there departures they commonly see?

6. Ask participants to what do they attribute these departures (Example: The acceptance of non-believers as members or even leaders).

7. Ask participants: What should be done to encourage their own local body of believers to fully embrace these truths? Or if their own body of believers and its leadership does show evidence that they do embrace these truths, how might they be encouraged to continue or to expand their witness?

8. Ask participants: How can we be "called out," ""gathered," *and* "a witness to the Kingdom"?

9. Ask participants: How does the metaphor of the church as the bride of Christ add to the understanding of the relationship of Jesus to the Church?

10. Allow participants to ask any questions about the nature of the church they had noted previously that were not addressed in this discussion.

11. If you have people in your group who have not yet surrendered to Jesus, continue to pray for the Holy Spirit to open that conversational door so you can explain the gospel. Once they receive Christ, the indwelling presence of the Holy Spirit will make the lessons in this book much more accessible to them.

CHAPTER 12
The Communion of the Saints

"I believe in the communion of the saints…"

"I am praying not only for these disciples but also for all who will ever believe in me through their message. I pray that they will all be one, just as you and I are one—as you are in me, Father, and I am in you. And may they be in us so that the world will believe you sent me.

"I have given them the glory you gave me, so they may be one as we are one. I am in them and you are in me. May they experience such perfect unity that the world will know that you sent me and that you love them as much as you love me. Father, I want these whom you have given me to be with me where I am. Then they can see all the glory you gave me because you loved me even before the world began!

"O righteous Father, the world doesn't know you, but I do; and these disciples know you sent me. I have revealed you to them, and I will continue to do so. Then your love for me will be in them, and I will be in them." (John 17:20-26)

THE OTHER SIDE OF THE "COIN"

We began the last chapter by noting that one must study the topics of Christ's universal Church and the communion of the saints together. We hinted at this chapter as we discussed the universal Church as a great cloud of witnesses. The "communion of the saints," simply put, is that great cloud of Christ's faithful witnesses – past, present, and future – all in common union with our triune God because of faith in Jesus.

What is a Saint?

The word "saint" means "holy one." Many become confused by the term because of the special definition used by the Roman Catholic Church. For Catholics and certain other Christian traditions, a "saint" is a super holy person who is known for his or her "heroic sanctity" and who is thought to be in heaven.[28] For them, saints are special people to be venerated. But the biblical definition of a saint describes *anyone, alive or dead,* who has surrendered to Jesus, forgiven of their sin.

We have already defined the two terms "holy" and "sacred." A saint is one who is holy. A saint is a follower of Christ who is, thereby, set apart for God's sacred purposes. All of us who are in Christ are saints, God's special vessels. Saints are made sacred by Christ's blood. They are those who strive to live under the rule and reign of King Jesus and make up what we have described as Christ's universal Church. Paul refers to this as he writes to the Corinthians,

> *I am writing to God's church in Corinth, to you who have been called by God to be his own holy people.* **He made you holy by means of Christ Jesus**, *just as he did for all people everywhere who call on the name of our Lord Jesus Christ, their Lord and ours.*
>
> *May God our Father and the Lord Jesus Christ give you grace and peace.* (1 Corinthians 1:2-3, **emphasis mine**)

Christ's universal Church is holy because it is made up of holy people – saints. Christ's universal Church is holy because its head (Jesus) is holy.

---

28 "Roman Catholic Saints," entry by Melissa Petruzello in *Encyclopedia Britannica,* online, https://www.britannica.com/story/roman-catholic-saints-hallowed-from-the-other-side, 21 June 2023.

God has united you with Christ Jesus. For our benefit God made him to be wisdom itself. **Christ made us right with God; he made us pure and holy,** *and he freed us from sin.* (1 Corinthians 1:30, **emphasis mine**)

God has put all things under the authority of Christ and has made him head over all things for the benefit of the church. And the church is his body; it is made full and complete by Christ, who fills all things everywhere with himself. (Ephesians 1:21-23)

Christ's universal Church is holy because it is filled with the Holy Spirit.

Don't you realize that all of you together are the temple of God and that the Spirit of God lives in you? God will destroy anyone who destroys this temple. For God's temple is holy, and you are that temple. (1 Corinthians 3:16-17)

Christ's universal Church is separated unto God. We are made holy, separated from the dominion of darkness, and brought into the kingdom of light – the kingdom of God's Son. He went to great lengths to redeem (purchase) us. We are, thereby, set apart for *his* purposes.

Don't you realize that your body is the temple of the Holy Spirit, who lives in you and was given to you by God? You do not belong to yourself, for God bought you with a high price. So you must honor God with your body. (1 Corinthians 6:19-20 – see also 1 Corinthians 7:23)

For you know that God paid a ransom to save you from the empty life you inherited from your ancestors. And it was not paid with mere gold or silver, which lose their value. It was the precious blood of Christ, the sinless, spotless Lamb of God. (1 Peter 1:18-19)

But you are not like that, for you are a chosen people. You are royal priests, a holy nation, **God's very own possession. As a result, you can show others the goodness of God, for he called you out of the darkness into his wonderful light.**

"Once you had no identity as a people; now you are God's people. Once you received no mercy; now you have received God's mercy." (1 Peter 2:9-10, **emphasis mine**)

Christ's universal Church is separated out of the world. Once we have been released from our bondage to the domain of darkness, we are no longer bound to the world and its systems governed by Satan. We remain *in* the world to influence it for Jesus' kingdom, but we are no longer *of* the world. We are a separated community. Jesus prays for us,

> *"I have revealed you to the ones you gave me from this world. They were always yours. You gave them to me, and they have kept your word. Now they know that everything I have is a gift from you, for I have passed on to them the message you gave me. They accepted it and know that I came from you, and they believe you sent me.*
>
> *"My prayer is not for the world, but for those you have given me, because they belong to you. All who are mine belong to you, and you have given them to me, so they bring me glory. Now I am departing from the world; they are staying in this world, but I am coming to you. Holy Father, you have given me your name; now protect them by the power of your name so that they will be united just as we are. During my time here, I protected them by the power of the name you gave me. I guarded them so that not one was lost, except the one headed for destruction, as the Scriptures foretold.*
>
> *"Now I am coming to you. I told them many things while I was with them in this world so they would be filled with my joy. I have given them your word. And the world hates them because they do not belong to the world, just as I do not belong to the world. I'm not asking you to take them out of the world, but to keep them safe from the evil one. They do not belong to this world any more than I do. Make them holy by your truth; teach them your word, which is truth. Just as you sent me into the world, I am sending them into the world. And I give myself as a holy sacrifice for them so they can be made holy by your truth.* (John 17:6-19)

In Jesus' day, the Jewish leaders sought separation from the world. But Jesus' followers are to be fully engaged with the world for the sake of the gospel, just not participating in the activities of their former dark kingdom. Christians are to be in the world, affecting the world, demonstrating the greater kingdom's authority and agenda, and wooing people to Christ. We are to be about the Lord's mission in the midst of those who need to be impacted by it.

So "saints" are God's holy, separated people. We are reserved for his sacred purposes. We are redeemed for his worship and glory. Now let's see what is meant by the "communion of the saints."

WHAT IS THE "COMMUNION" OF THE SAINTS?

The word "Communion" here means "fellowship." At its most basic level, the communion of the saints is the solidarity of surrendered followers of Jesus. John writes,

> *We proclaim to you the one who existed from the beginning, whom we have heard and seen. We saw him with our own eyes and touched him with our own hands. He is the Word of life. This one who is life itself was revealed to us, and we have seen him. And now we testify and proclaim to you that he is the one who is eternal life. He was with the Father, and then he was revealed to us. We proclaim to you what we ourselves have actually seen and heard so that you may have fellowship with us. And our fellowship is with the Father and with his Son, Jesus Christ. We are writing these things so that you may fully share our joy.* (1 John 1:1-4)

John talks about the depth of this fellowship – that it began in person (they heard, they saw with their own eyes, they touched with their own hands), and now it even goes beyond the physical realm (it is with the Father and with his Son). He says he now writes this letter so that his readers may also share in this incredible joy!

The communion of the saints is the community of all believers throughout all time. This is huge!

> *For you are all children of God through faith in Christ Jesus. And all who have been united with Christ in baptism have put on Christ, like putting on new clothes. There is no longer Jew or Gentile, slave or free, male and female. For you are all one in Christ Jesus.*

And now that you belong to Christ, you are the true children of Abraham. You are his heirs, and God's promise to Abraham belongs to you. (Galatians 3:26-29)

We are children of God because of our faith in Jesus Christ. In Christ, we have total and complete – sweet – communion with each other. The walls that used to divide us are now removed in him. At the time that Paul is writing this, this idea is revolutionary. Jews and Gentiles are now *one* in Christ. Slaves and free people are now *one* in Christ. Male and female are now *one* in Christ. This has enormous implications down through human history – including today! The world around us is reacting to the oppression and injustices that have been placed on various people groups for generations. The problem is that the world – under the dominion of Satan in darkness – does not have the solution for which it is searching. And this is actually an indictment on the Church because the communion of the saints shows us the answer! If we were really engaging the world as we should, much would be different.

The world needs a united Church. Not one that is united around social reform, politics, or any other human agenda, but that is united around Jesus' mission as the communion of the saints. The world needs a Church where there are no divisions – one where there is no conflict. The world needs to see a Church that is united across ethnic, socio-economic, and denominational lines with a singular agenda – what I have already called the "Immanuel Agenda." Such a Church demonstrates the communion of the saints, celebrating the beautiful uniqueness and contribution of every ethnicity and background, but seeing the Church as one family, one race – the human race – redeemed by the blood of the Lamb. We say we believe in the communion of the saints – but we need to demonstrate its powerful beauty to the world.

The communion of the saints includes believers from the past. As noted in the last chapter, this even includes people from the Old Testament era who had genuine forward-looking faith.

Faith shows the reality of what we hope for; it is the evidence of things we cannot see. Through their faith, the people in days of old earned a good reputation.

By faith we understand that the entire universe was formed at God's command, that what we now see did not come from anything that can be seen.

It was by faith that Abel brought a more acceptable offering to God than Cain did. Abel's offering gave evidence that he was a righteous man, and God showed his approval of his gifts. Although Abel is long dead, he still speaks to us by his example of faith.

It was by faith that Enoch was taken up to heaven without dying—"he disappeared, because God took him." For before he was taken up, he was known as a person who pleased God. And it is impossible to please God without faith. Anyone who wants to come to him must believe that God exists and that he rewards those who sincerely seek him.

It was by faith that Noah built a large boat to save his family from the flood. He obeyed God, who warned him about things that had never happened before. By his faith Noah condemned the rest of the world, and he received the righteousness that comes by faith.

It was by faith that Abraham obeyed when God called him to leave home and go to another land that God would give him as his inheritance. He went without knowing where he was going. And even when he reached the land God promised him, he lived there by faith—for he was like a foreigner, living in tents. And so did Isaac and Jacob, who inherited the same promise. Abraham was confidently looking forward to a city with eternal foundations, a city designed and built by God.

It was by faith that even Sarah was able to have a child, though she was barren and was too old. She believed that God would keep his promise. And so a whole nation came from this one man who was as good as dead—a nation with so many people that, like the stars in the sky and the sand on the seashore, there is no way to count them.

All these people died still believing what God had promised them. They did not receive what was promised, but they saw it all from a distance and welcomed it. They agreed that they were foreigners and nomads here on earth. Obviously people who say such things are looking forward to a country they can call their own. If they had longed for the country they came from, they could have gone back. But they were looking for a better place, a heavenly home-land. That is why God is not ashamed to be called their God, for he has prepared a city for them. (Hebrews 11:1-16)

The communion of the saints includes believers today. We too have been called out of the kingdom of darkness and into the kingdom of light. We too have been redeemed by the blood of the Lamb. We too are included in this timeless gathering and its accompanying mission.

*But you are not like that, for you are a chosen people. You are royal priests, a holy nation, God's very own possession. As a result, you can show others the goodness of God, **for he called you out of the darkness into his wonderful light.***

"Once you had no identity as a people; now you are God's people. Once you received no mercy; now you have received God's mercy." (1 Peter 2:9-10, **emphasis mine**)

*Yes, I am sending you to the Gentiles to open their eyes, **so they may turn from darkness to light and from the power of Satan to God**. Then they will receive forgiveness for their sins and be given a place among God's people, who are set apart by faith in me.'* (Acts 26:17-18, **emphasis mine**)

The communion of the saints includes those who will confess Christ in the future. For generations to come, as long as we continue to wait for Jesus' return in glory, more and more people will surrender to the King and be included in the communion of the saints!

"I am the good shepherd; I know my own sheep, and they know me, just as my Father knows me and I know the Father. So I sac-rifice my life for the sheep. I have other sheep, too, that are not in this sheepfold. I must bring them also. They will listen to my voice, and there will be one flock with one shepherd. (John 10:14-16)

"I am praying not only for these disciples but also for all who will ever believe in me through their message. I pray that they

will all be one, just as you and I are one—as you are in me, Father, and I am in you. And may they be in us so that the world will believe you sent me. (John 17:20-21)

Timothy, my dear son, be strong through the grace that God gives you in Christ Jesus. You have heard me teach things that have been confirmed by many reliable witnesses. Now teach these truths to other trustworthy people who will be able to pass them on to others. (2 Timothy 2:1-2)

The communion of the saints is fellowship with God the Father, God the Son, and God the Holy Spirit. Again, at its heart, "communion" means "fellowship." The communion of the saints is not just a timeless fellowship with believers but also full fellowship with the triune God who draws us together.

*I always thank my God for you and for the gracious gifts he has given you, now that you belong to Christ Jesus. Through him, God has enriched your church in every way—with all of your eloquent words and all of your knowledge. This confirms that what I told you about Christ is true. Now you have every spiritual gift you need as you eagerly wait for the return of our Lord Jesus Christ. He will keep you strong to the end so that you will be free from all blame on the day when our Lord Jesus Christ returns. God will do this, for he is faithful to do what he says, **and he has invited you into partnership with his Son, Jesus Christ our Lord**.* (1 Corinthians 1:4-9, **emphasis mine**)

*We proclaim to you the one who existed from the beginning, whom we have heard and seen. We saw him with our own eyes and touched him with our own hands. He is the Word of life. This one who is life itself was revealed to us, and we have seen him. And now we testify and proclaim to you that he is the one who is eternal life. He was with the Father, and then he was revealed to us. We proclaim to you what we ourselves have actually seen and heard so that you may have fellowship with us. **And our fellowship is with the Father and with his Son, Jesus Christ**. We are writing these things so that you may fully share our joy.* (1 John 1:1-4, **emphasis mine**)

*May the grace of the Lord Jesus Christ, the love of God, **and the fellowship of the Holy Spirit be with you all.*** (2 Corinthians 13:14, **emphasis mine**)

And our communion with the Lord is fellowship in *everything*. It is fellowship with all the blessings and glory, and also fellowship with suffering.

Since you have been raised to new life with Christ, set your sights on the realities of heaven, where Christ sits in the place of honor at God's right hand. Think about the things of heaven, not the things of earth. For you died to this life, and your real life is hidden with Christ in God. And when Christ, who is your life, is revealed to the whole world, you will share in all his glory. (Colossians 3:1-4)

Yes, everything else is worthless when compared with the infinite value of knowing Christ Jesus my Lord. For his sake I have discarded everything else, counting it all as garbage, so that I could gain Christ and become one with him. I no longer count on my own righteousness through obeying the law; rather, I become righteous through faith in Christ. For God's way of making us right with himself depends on faith. I want to know Christ and experience the mighty power that raised him from the dead. I want to suffer with him, sharing in his death, so that one way or another I will experience the resurrection from the dead! (Philippians 3:8-11)

The communion of the saints is fellowship with each other. It matters not how different we each may be from each other; we who are redeemed are all part of the body of Christ. Jesus makes us *one*. And as we walk with him and live in him, personally experiencing daily transformation by the Holy Spirit under the rule and reign of Christ, our fellowship with one another grows deep.

The human body has many parts, but the many parts make up one whole body. So it is with the body of Christ. Some of us are

Jews, some are Gentiles, some are slaves, and some are free. But we have all been baptized into one body by one Spirit, and we all share the same Spirit. (1 Corinthians 12:12-13)

This is the message we heard from Jesus and now declare to you: God is light, and there is no darkness in him at all. So we are lying if we say we have fellowship with God but go on living in spiritual darkness; we are not practicing the truth. But if we are living in the light, as God is in the light, then we have fellowship with each other, and the blood of Jesus, his Son, cleanses us from all sin. (1 John 1:5-7)

You can see why this topic is important – and why it is best to study it in connection with the doctrine of Jesus' universal Church. There is a lot wrapped up in the phrase, "I believe in the communion of the saints"! The communion of the saints is made up of all those who have surrendered (and will yet surrender) to Christ, being made holy, separate, and sacred. The communion of the saints is an incredible fellowship – a fellowship of all believers over all time! The communion of the saints is a beautiful answer to what our world desperately needs right now – offering a united and powerful Church. The communion of the saints is full and uninterrupted fellowship with our triune God – Father, Son, and Holy Spirit. The communion of the saints is real, loving, and eternal fellowship with each other.

STUDY GUIDE

IT MAKES A DIFFERENCE

The communion of the saints is the great cloud of Christ's faithful witnesses, past, present, and future. It is made up of those who have been separated for God's purposes by surrendering to Jesus as King. There is no other way to become part of this communion. Those who understand what the Creed says about the communion of the saints have an authentic and everlasting fellowship with God – Father, Son, and Holy Spirit. They also have sweet communion with one another – regardless of ethnicity, economic standing, or any other factor. There is a powerful and timeless unity for everyone who is included.

Those who are unclear about the communion of the saints may not emphasize the necessity of being separated for God's purposes from the world and its agenda. This will lead them to unwittingly include people who have never surrendered to Jesus for salvation. They also may not recognize the timeless nature of the communion nor experience full and complete unity with believers from other backgrounds.

HOW DO I LIVE OUT WHAT I HAVE JUST LEARNED IN MY OWN LIFE?

1. Take a moment to stop and pray. Ask God, through the Holy Spirit, to increase your understanding of the essentials of the Christian Faith. Ask Him to reveal and clarify any points which have been confusing or unclear.

2. Meditate on the concept of "the communion of the saints" as described in this chapter. What part of this description is new to you? What part of this description is most precious to you?

3. Take some time to consider some specific persons or people groups that this communion includes. Recall some specific biblical characters, church fathers and/or mothers, and godly friends and family members (past and present) who have spoken into your spiritual life. Express your thanks to God for joining you with them in the communion of saints.

4. Now, take some time to give thanks to God for those who are currently part of your spiritual fellowship and nurture.

5. Next, ask God whom you should be drawing into "the communion" and just how He is asking you to go about this. Think into the future as well.

6. Finally, thank God that you are an heir who will, through accepting Jesus Christ's sacrifice on your behalf, remain part of the communion of the saints throughout eternity.

7. Take several days to consider: Who can help you apply what you learn to put it into an ongoing life's practice?

8. How are you living this out right now? How is your life reflective of your understanding of this truth?

HOW DO I IMPART WHAT I HAVE JUST LEARNED TO CHILDREN?

Preparing to teach this lesson to children: *Gather the needed supplies ahead of the lesson: Construction paper in various light colors. (One sheet should be yellow, the others can be any color light enough to legibly write on with a dark marker or crayon), scissors, markers or crayons, tape. Consider, for the sake of time, pre-cutting the construction paper into strips approximately 2" wide.*

1. Begin by praying with the children. Ask God, through the Holy Spirit, to help the children understand more about the Christian faith. Ask God to help them clearly understand the new things they are about to learn.

2. Continue to work with the children on memorizing the Apostle's Creed. Be sure they have memorized through this part:

   I believe in God, the Father almighty, creator of heaven and earth.

   I believe in Jesus Christ, his only Son, our Lord, who was conceived by the Holy Spirit and born of the virgin Mary. He suffered under Pontius Pilate, was crucified, died, and was buried; he descended into hell. The third day he rose again from the dead. He ascended to heaven and is seated at the right hand of God the Father almighty. From there he will come to judge the living and the dead.

   I believe in the Holy Spirit, the holy catholic church, the communion of saints...

3. Cut the construction paper into strips approximately 2" wide if you have not already done so. Give each child one strip of yellow paper and several strips of various other colors.

4. On the yellow strip, have them write "Jesus".

5. Brainstorm who else is included in "the communion of the saints". Be sure to prompt them to include people from the past, present, and future. Possibilities for the past might be

godly biblical characters, founders of your church fellowship, missionaries or other heroes of the faith, and/or relatives that have passed on that they might be aware of who were devoted to Jesus. Included in the present would be believers from other countries, races, languages, churches located nearby, pastors, elders, Sunday School teachers, etc. Be sure they also include a strip for those who will believe in Jesus as their Savior in the future. Have the children write each of these identifiers on a strip of paper.

6. Make a chain by looping the strips into circles that interlock. Begin the chain by taping the ends of the yellow "Jesus" strip together to form a circle. Insert each strip into the previous circle and tape the ends. The final strip should be inserted into the "Jesus" strip and the ends taped. This will form one circle of circles.

7. Point out that you have one big chain with Jesus at the center, just like you have one church of many parts.

8. An alternative, if time is an issue, is to have the group make a single chain, with each child writing a different idea on the strips. Be sure to include the Jesus strip!

9. If you have children in your group who have not yet surrendered to Jesus, continue praying for the Holy Spirit to open that conversational door so you can explain the gospel. Once they receive Christ, the indwelling presence of the Holy Spirit will make the lessons in this book much more accessible to them.

HOW DO I IMPART WHAT I HAVE JUST LEARNED TO TEENS?

Preparing to teach this lesson to teens: As part of this lesson, it is suggested that teens will create a "word cloud", which is a randomly arranged collection of words and phrases into a shape that roughly resembles a cloud. Decide if you want to have the teens create this cloud on paper or digitally. If you choose paper, each teen will need a blank sheet of paper and a pencil, plus a set of colored pencils or markers. There are several word cloud creation programs on line. Here is one: https://www.wordclouds.com/. To use this, or a similar program, teens will type their words and phrases into the word list and then hit "create". The lists and resulting clouds can then be compared.

1. Begin by praying with the teens. Ask God, through the Holy Spirit, to increase understanding. You can do this or ask a volunteer.

2. Read the Apostles' Creed out loud. Read it yourself, ask for a volunteer, or read it in unison.

3. Repeat these lines:

   I believe in God, the Father almighty, creator of heaven and earth.

   I believe in Jesus Christ, his only Son, our Lord, who was conceived by the Holy Spirit and born of the virgin Mary. He suffered under Pontius Pilate, was crucified, died, and was buried; he descended into hell. The third day he rose again from the dead. He ascended to heaven and is seated at the right hand of God the Father almighty. From there he will come to judge the living and the dead.

   I believe in the Holy Spirit, the holy catholic church, the communion of saints...

4. Have the teens pull out their Question Journals. Ask them to jot down the answers to any questions that may be answered during this session, and to share those discoveries as they happen. Provide sufficient time for them to record any thoughts they may wish to capture. Assure them that they will have the opportunity to ask any remaining questions about this section at the end of the session.

5. Create a "word cloud" using the words and phrases that describe the communion of saints. This can be done on paper by drawing a large cloud shape on a blank sheet and arranging the descriptive words and phrases randomly inside the cloud. Before they create the cloud, have them share the words and phrases aloud – adding to or modifying their lists as needed.

Check to make sure they include all of the important concepts. Suggest they write their words and phrases in pencil first, as this can be erased in case of misspelling or other errors. Then use the list to make the "word cloud". Allow teens to share their clouds with the group.

6. Digital version: https://www.wordclouds.com/ . Proceed as above, except that teens will type their lists into the program using their cell phones or other electronics. When they have shared their ideas and are satisfied with their lists, they simply hit "create" to make the cloud.

7. Ask the teens to consider how they are connected to the church of the past, present, and future. Ask them to share their insights. You may need to prompt their thoughts by asking questions like: How has your relationship with God been affected by the Apostle Paul? How has your relationship with God been affected by a relative or friend? How are we connected to believers in other churches, cultures, or countries? How might your relationship with Jesus affect those around you or those who come after you?

8. After sharing what they have discovered in the chapter, have a discussion about why we call the sacrament of the Lord's table "communion".

9. Allow the teens to ask any questions about the communion of saints they had noted previously that were not addressed in this discussion.

10. If you have teens in your group who have not yet surrendered to Jesus, continue praying for the Holy Spirit to open that conversational door so you can explain the gospel. Once they receive Christ, the indwelling presence of the Holy Spirit will make the lessons in this book much more accessible to them.

HOW DO I IMPART WHAT I HAVE JUST LEARNED TO ADULTS?

1. Challenge your adults to take a moment to stop and pray, asking God, through the Holy Spirit, to increase their

understanding of the essentials of the Christian Faith. Encourage them to ask Him to reveal and clarify any points which have been confusing or unclear.

2. Review the Apostle's Creed. Re-read the lines below slowly and thoughtfully:

I believe in God, the Father almighty, creator of heaven and earth.

I believe in Jesus Christ, his only Son, our Lord, who was conceived by the Holy Spirit and born of the virgin Mary. He suffered under Pontius Pilate, was crucified, died, and was buried; he descended into hell. The third day he rose again from the dead. He ascended to heaven and is seated at the right hand of God the Father almighty. From there he will come to judge the living and the dead.

I believe in the Holy Spirit, the holy catholic church, the communion of saints...

3. If they have not done so, encourage them to memorize the Creed in its entirety, reminding them that it is a summary of the essentials of the Christian faith.

4. Have participants pull out the notes they made during previous sessions. Ask them to jot down the answers to any questions about the Creed that may be answered during this session and to share those discoveries as they happen. Provide sufficient time to record any thoughts they may wish to capture. Assure them that they will have the opportunity to ask any questions that were not answered in this session at the end of the session.

5. Discuss with participants why it is important to understand the definition of "saints" as it is used in the Apostle's Creed. Ask them why understanding this definition is important to understanding the intent of the Creed?

6. Discuss how the characteristics of the universal church support the ideas that the church is *holy* and *sacred* as these words are defined in this chapter (and previously in the book).

7. Discuss how the definition of the communion of the saints relates to the reason the celebration of the sacrament of the Lord's Table is referred to as "communion".

8. Encourage participants to meditate on the awesome concept of the communion of saints past, present, and future. Guide this meditation by asking them to think of godly men and women they know about in the past that have had an effect on shaping the church – men like Peter and Paul, women like Tabitha (Dorcus), or Mary, the mother of Jesus. Ask them to consider those who personally shaped their own relationship with Jesus. Now consider those who are still doing so. Ask them to look at the lives of those presently living. How are they connected to believers who may be close by (such as family and friends) and other believers of different church affiliations or who are part of other countries or cultures? Finally, consider what legacy they may be leaving for those who will come after them when they become part of the great cloud of witnesses.

9. Allow participants to ask any questions about the communion of saints they had noted previously that were not addressed in this discussion.

10. If you have people in your group who have not yet surrendered to Jesus, continue praying for the Holy Spirit to open that conversational door so you can explain the gospel. Once they receive Christ, the indwelling presence of the Holy Spirit will make the lessons in this book much more accessible to them.

CHAPTER 13
The Forgiveness of Sins

"I believe in the forgiveness of sins…"

But now God has shown us a way to be made right with him without keeping the requirements of the law, as was promised in the writings of Moses and the prophets long ago. We are made right with God by placing our faith in Jesus Christ. And this is true for everyone who believes, no matter who we are.

For everyone has sinned; we all fall short of God's glorious standard. Yet God, in his grace, freely makes us right in his sight. He did this through Christ Jesus when he freed us from the penalty for our sins. For God presented Jesus as the sacrifice for sin. People are made right with God when they believe that Jesus sacrificed his life, shedding his blood. This sacrifice shows that God was being fair when he held back and did not punish those who sinned in times past, for he was looking ahead and including them in what he would do in this present time. God did this to demonstrate his righteousness, for he himself is fair and just, and he makes sinners right in his sight when they believe in Jesus. (Romans 3:21-26)

THE HEART OF THE MATTER

In previous chapters, we have talked about God as our heavenly Father and about Jesus, who was conceived by the Holy Spirit and born of the virgin Mary, about his suffering, death, resurrection, ascension, and session. We've discussed the person and empowering work of the Holy Spirit, the universal church, and the communion of the saints. I hope each step we've taken on this journey has helped build a solid foundation for your faith as you have learned more about our incredible God and all that he has designed for our redemption and life with him.

Now we turn to the heart of our Christian Faith: the forgiveness of sin. "I believe in the forgiveness of sins…" This is what Jesus became human and died on the cross to accomplish.

DEFINING FORGIVENESS

Forgiveness is very misunderstood today. Saying, "I'm sorry," is not the same as forgiveness. Godly sorrow can lead to repentance and forgiveness (2 Corinthians 7:10), but they are not identical. In addition, forgiving an offender is not excusing their bad behavior. It is releasing your right to punish them because of it.

Biblically there are many beautiful aspects of God's complete forgiveness of our sin that all happen at the same time when we are forgiven, and I'd like to now focus on five of them.

1. *Pardon – Releasing from legal consequences.* The consequences of which we speak are those dictated by the law. The prophet Joel proclaims,

    "But Judah will be filled with people forever, and Jerusalem will endure through all generations.

    I will pardon my people's crimes, which I have not yet pardoned; and I, the Lord, will make my home in Jerusalem with my people." (Joel 3:20-21)

    Pardon is the legal component. Because of the blood of Christ, we are released from the required penalties of the Law of God. Listen to the prophet Micah as he foretells this.

Where is another God like you, who pardons the guilt of the remnant, overlooking the sins of his special people?

You will not stay angry with your people forever, because you delight in showing unfailing love.

Once again you will have compassion on us.

You will trample our sins under your feet and throw them into the depths of the ocean!

You will show us your faithfulness and unfailing love as you promised to our ancestors Abraham and Jacob long ago. (Micah 7:18-20)

And the apostle Paul explains how it was fulfilled.

Obviously, the law applies to those to whom it was given, for its purpose is to keep people from having excuses, and to show that the entire world is guilty before God. For no one can ever be made right with God by doing what the law commands. The law simply shows us how sinful we are.

But now God has shown us a way to be made right with him without keeping the requirements of the law, as was promised in the writings of Moses and the prophets long ago. We are made right with God by placing our faith in Jesus Christ. And this is true for everyone who believes, no matter who we are.

For everyone has sinned; we all fall short of God's glorious standard. Yet God, in his grace, freely makes us right in his sight. He did this through Christ Jesus when he freed us from the penalty for our sins. (Romans 3:19-24)

2. *Absolution – Releasing from guilt.* It's profound, but even our guilt is taken away. In his logical debate about the results of Jesus' resurrection, Paul writes to the Corinthians,

And if Christ has not been raised, then your faith is useless and you are still guilty of your sins. In that case, all who have died believing in Christ are lost! And if our hope in Christ is only for this life, we are more to be pitied than anyone in the world.

289

*But in fact, Christ has been raised from the dead. He is the first of
a great harvest of all who have died.* (1 Corinthians 15:16-20)

God releases us from our guilt because of the death and resurrection of Jesus. Our guilt is tied to the Law. But Christ's
sacrifice fulfilled the righteous requirements of the Law and
set us free. Paul tells the Galatians,

*But suppose we seek to be made right with God through
faith in Christ and then we are found guilty because we
have abandoned the law. Would that mean Christ has led us
into sin? Absolutely not! Rather, I am a sinner if I rebuild
the old system of law I already tore down. For when I tried
to keep the law, it condemned me.* **So I died to the law—I
stopped trying to meet all its requirements—so that I
might live for God. My old self has been crucified with
Christ. It is no longer I who live, but Christ lives in me.** *So
I live in this earthly body by trusting in the Son of God, who
loved me and gave himself for me. I do not treat the grace
of God as meaningless. For if keeping the law could make
us right with God, then there was no need for Christ to die.*
(Galatians 2:17-21, **emphasis mine**)

This is huge! Christian, because of the blood of Christ, you
and I are released from our guilt! Jesus is the Lamb of God
that takes away the sin of the world (John 1:29). Sin is no
longer covered up but removed! In Christ, we are no longer
guilty. The ongoing promise for every believer is clear.

*...if we confess our sins to him, he is faithful and just to forgive us
our sins and to cleanse us from all wickedness.* (1 John 1:9)

3. *Clemency – Granting mercy where punishment has been levied.*
Every human being is a sinner. Every human being sins because
we are all sinners. We all deserve the appropriate punishment –
death. But God is indeed rich in mercy! After Moses demanded
to see the utter glory of God (which he knew may be so glorious
that his life would be forfeit), God said "no." But he did make a
compromise with Moses.

*The Lord replied, "I will make all my goodness pass before
you, and I will call out my name, Yahweh, before you. For I*

290

will show mercy to anyone I choose, and I will show compassion to anyone I choose. But you may not look directly at my face, for no one may see me and live." The Lord continued, "Look, stand near me on this rock. As my glorious presence passes by, I will hide you in the crevice of the rock and cover you with my hand until I have passed by. Then I will remove my hand and let you see me from behind. But my face will not be seen..."

The Lord passed in front of Moses, calling out,

"Yahweh! The Lord! The God of compassion and mercy!

I am slow to anger and filled with unfailing love and faithfulness.

I lavish unfailing love to a thousand generations.

I forgive iniquity, rebellion, and sin.

But I do not excuse the guilty.

I lay the sins of the parents upon their children and grandchildren; the entire family is affected— even children in the third and fourth generations."

Moses immediately threw himself to the ground and worshiped.

(Exodus 33:19-23, 34:6-8)

God is merciful! Because of the blood of Christ that paid for our sins, we no longer have to endure the punishment those sins deserve. Christ has already taken it for us. All those who have surrendered to him have received clemency from their death sentence! We can't earn it. In fact, we can't even choose it! Paul writes to the Christians in Rome:

Are we saying, then, that God was unfair? Of course not! For God said to Moses,

"I will show mercy to anyone I choose, and I will show compassion to anyone I choose."

So it is God who decides to show mercy. We can neither choose it nor work for it. (Romans 9:14-16)

4. *Remission – Canceling the debt.* Our sin debt to God has been canceled because of the sacrificial payment made by Jesus on the cross! One of Jesus' most-famous parables teaches this lesson.

Then Peter came to him and asked, "Lord, how often should I forgive someone who sins against me? Seven times?"

"No, not seven times," Jesus replied, "but seventy times seven!

"Therefore, the Kingdom of Heaven can be compared to a king who decided to bring his accounts up to date with servants who had borrowed money from him. In the process, one of his debtors was brought in who owed him millions of dollars. He couldn't pay, so his master ordered that he be sold—along with his wife, his children, and everything he owned—to pay the debt.

"But the man fell down before his master and begged him, 'Please, be patient with me, and I will pay it all.' Then his master was filled with pity for him, and he released him and forgave his debt.

"But when the man left the king, he went to a fellow servant who owed him a few thousand dollars. He grabbed him by the throat and demanded instant payment.

"His fellow servant fell down before him and begged for a little more time. 'Be patient with me, and I will pay it,' he pleaded. But his creditor wouldn't wait. He had the man arrested and put in prison until the debt could be paid in full.

"When some of the other servants saw this, they were very upset. They went to the king and told him everything that had happened. Then the king called in the man he had forgiven and said, 'You evil servant! I forgave you that tremendous debt because you pleaded with me. Shouldn't you have mercy on your fellow servant, just as I had mercy on you?' Then the angry king sent the man to prison to be tortured until he had paid his entire debt.

"That's what my heavenly Father will do to you if you refuse to forgive your brothers and sisters from your heart." (Matthew 18:21-35)

We have been made alive with Jesus! We have been forgiven! Our Savior has disarmed all the powers of hell arrayed against us!

You were dead because of your sins and because your sinful nature was not yet cut away. Then God made you alive with Christ, for he forgave all our sins. He canceled the record of the charges against us and took it away by nailing it to the cross. In this way, he disarmed the spiritual rulers and authorities. He shamed them publicly by his victory over them on the cross. (Colossians 2:13-15)

5. *Reconciliation – Restoring a relationship; harmony.*
   Reconciliation is what we seem to talk about most in church. This is the restoration of our covenant relationship with our heavenly Father. Jesus' sacrifice on the cross paved the way. His broken body shows us that he took the penalty for our sin – he endured the cross for you and me. His shed blood cut a brand new covenant with God – a new and eternal relationship with God that cannot be broken! And those who have been reconciled have now been given the ministry of proclaiming this wonderful message of reconciliation to the rest of humanity.

And all of this is a gift from God, who brought us back to himself through Christ. And God has given us this task of reconciling people to him. For God was in Christ, reconciling the world to himself, no longer counting people's sins against them. And he gave us this wonderful message of reconciliation. So we are Christ's ambassadors; God is making his appeal through us. We speak for Christ when we plead, "Come back to God!" For God made Christ, who never sinned, to be the offering for our sin, so that we could be made right with God through Christ. (2 Corinthians 5:18-21)

We all were enemies of God – separated from him. But he took the initiative in Christ to reconcile us to himself! Paul tells the Colossians,

This includes you who were once far away from God. You were his enemies, separated from him by your evil thoughts and actions. Yet now he has reconciled you to himself through the death of Christ in his physical body. As a result, he has brought you into his own presence, and you are holy and blameless as you stand before him without a single fault.

But you must continue to believe this truth and stand firmly in it. Don't drift away from the assurance you received when you heard the Good News. The Good News has been preached all over the world, and I, Paul, have been appointed as God's servant to proclaim it. (Colossians 1:21-23)

Jesus did it. And the offer is for everyone.

There is one God and one Mediator who can reconcile God and humanity—the man Christ Jesus. He gave his life to purchase freedom for everyone. This is the message God gave to the world at just the right time. (1 Timothy 2:5-6)

Forgiveness is all five of these things simultaneously: pardon, absolution, clemency, remission, and reconciliation. And all this is ours as God forgives our sin by the blood of Christ! This is the biblical doctrine of forgiveness, and it is found in Christ's work of atonement on the cross.[29]

FORGIVENESS APPLIED

All forgiveness begins with God. Forgiveness is God's idea. Forgiveness is God's plan. So as we learn how to apply this forgiveness, we first need to learn a few things about our forgiving God.

God is a forgiving God. God has many attributes – and most of them play into the redemptive work of Jesus in some way. But for our purposes here, I want to concentrate on three attributes.

1. **God is love.** God is not just "loving"; he is love itself. God is the essence of love. He is the Source of love. The Apostle John writes,

---

29   As noted in Chapter 5, the word we use, *atonement,* is actually from Old English. It's a powerful word. Think of it this way: at-ONE-ment. It speaks of something shattered or broken that is made one, made whole again.

*Dear friends, let us continue to love one another, **for love comes from God. Anyone who loves is a child of God and knows God. But anyone who does not love does not know God, for God is love.***

God showed how much he loved us by sending his one and only Son into the world so that we might have eternal life through him. This is real love—not that we loved God, but that he loved us and sent his Son as a sacrifice to take away our sins. (1 John 4:7-10, **emphasis mine**)

God's love is perfect love. It has no ulterior motive. Because of his love, he created humanity in the first place. God wanted to share his love. It is also because of his boundless love that he established a plan to save humanity from sin. This truth is the heart and soul of the Christian faith.

"For this is how God loved the world: He gave his one and only Son, so that everyone who believes in him will not perish but have eternal life. God sent his Son into the world not to judge the world, but to save the world through him. (John 3:16-17)

But God is so rich in mercy, and he loved us so much, that even though we were dead because of our sins, he gave us life when he raised Christ from the dead. (It is only by God's grace that you have been saved!) (Ephesians 2:4-5)

God is love. But God is also *just*.

2. **God is just.** Herein is where many people run into a problem. God is not only perfectly just; he is the essence of all true justice in and of himself. He is the Source and definer of justice. This has always been true – including in the time of the Old Covenant.

"For the Lord your God is the God of gods and Lord of lords. He is the great God, the mighty and awesome God, who shows no partiality and cannot be bribed. He ensures that orphans and widows receive justice. He shows love to the foreigners living among you and gives them food and clothing. (Deuteronomy 10:17-18)

Justice demands what is right. God *requires* righteousness. God *requires* right behavior and right treatment of others. But sin has ruined all that for every single human being. Think about your own thought life, decisions you have made that do not honor God, and how you have treated others during your lifetime, and you'll confirm this truth in yourself.

Ultimately, Jesus wields God's justice. But it's important to note that Jesus also extended his grace to humanity by taking the sentence that justice requires.

Don't be so surprised! Indeed, the time is coming when all the dead in their graves will hear the voice of God's Son, and they will rise again. Those who have done good will rise to experience eternal life, and those who have continued in evil will rise to experience judgment. I can do nothing on my own. I judge as God tells me. Therefore, my judgment is just, because I carry out the will of the one who sent me, not my own will. (John 5:28-30)

But now God has shown us a way to be made right with him without keeping the requirements of the law, as was promised in the writings of Moses and the prophets long ago. We are made right with God by placing our faith in Jesus Christ. And this is true for everyone who believes, no matter who we are.

For everyone has sinned; we all fall short of God's glorious standard. Yet God, in his grace, freely makes us right in his sight. He did this through Christ Jesus when he freed us from the penalty for our sins. For God presented Jesus as the sacrifice for sin. People are made right with God when they believe that Jesus sacrificed his life, shedding his blood. This sacrifice shows that God was being fair when he held back and did not punish those who sinned in times past, for he was looking ahead and including them in what he would do in this present time. God did this to demonstrate his righteousness, for he himself is fair and just, and he makes sinners right in his sight when they believe in Jesus. (Romans 3:21-26)

God cannot neglect justice, or he would no longer be God! He cannot disregard injustice. God must satisfy his *love*. At the same time, he must satisfy his *justice*. How can God possibly satisfy both at the same time? This is where the third attribute comes in...*mercy*.

3. **God is merciful.** God doesn't just act with mercy: he is the very essence and source of mercy! Again, this has been God's nature all along. He proclaimed to Moses,

    The Lord replied, "I will make all my goodness pass before you, and I will call out my name, Yahweh, before you. For I will show mercy to anyone I choose, and I will show compassion to anyone I choose. (Exodus 33:19)

    And Moses got the message. When he re-teaches the Law to the people of Israel after they cross the Jordan River, he says,

    For the Lord your God is a merciful God; he will not abandon you or destroy you or forget the solemn covenant he made with your ancestors. (Deuteronomy 4:31)

    The Apostle Paul also came to know God's mercy in a very personal way. Writing to the Corinthian Christians, he reminds them,

    All praise to God, the Father of our Lord Jesus Christ. God is our merciful Father and the source of all comfort. He comforts us in all our troubles so that we can comfort others. When they are troubled, we will be able to give them the same comfort God has given us. (2 Corinthians 1:3-4)

    And Paul fully lays out this point about God's mercy in his letter to the Ephesians.

    But God is so rich in mercy, and he loved us so much, that even though we were dead because of our sins, he gave us life when he raised Christ from the dead. (It is only by God's grace that you have been saved!) (Ephesians 2:4-5)

    In his love, God desires a covenant relationship with us with no hindrance. But because of our sin, God wants complete and righteous justice against us. Sin must be punished! Sin must be dealt with! God cannot look the other way and still be just. And at the same time, God cannot go against his own love nature. So God himself stepped in and took our punishment. That's mercy. He loved us so much that he gave his only Son. That's love. God the Father poured out his full wrath for the sin and corruption caused by humanity's rebellion. That's justice – but it all went on Jesus.

If you have surrendered to Jesus as Lord and Savior, listen to me: God is not mad at you! He is not out to get you. He is not out to punish you in any way. It was already settled at the cross.

Forgiveness begins with God. I love Jesus' encounter with Nicodemus. Nicodemus meets the Savior at night, presumably to protect his reputation. The interchange shows that he really wants to understand, but the news is too wonderful for him to accept. Nicodemus has been faithfully waiting for the Messiah his whole life – like the faithful generations before him – and on this night, he is confronted that the Anointed One has arrived! Not only that, but he brings God's forgiveness and salvation with him!

> *Jesus replied, "I assure you, no one can enter the Kingdom of God without being born of water and the Spirit. Humans can reproduce only human life, but the Holy Spirit gives birth to spiritual life. So don't be surprised when I say, 'You must be born again.' The wind blows wherever it wants. Just as you can hear the wind but can't tell where it comes from or where it is going, so you can't explain how people are born of the Spirit."* (John 3:5-8)

Note that this critical truth is found in the section of the Creed on the Holy Spirit. That makes sense! We confess to the Father (Matthew 6:9-13). Forgiveness is the work of the Son (Ephesians 1:7; Colossians 1:13-14). But it is the Holy Spirit that works in us to convict us and make our need for repentance and forgiveness known to us. Jesus teaches his disciples,

But in fact, it is best for you that I go away, because if I don't, the Advocate won't come. If I do go away, then I will send him to you. And when he comes, he will convict the world of its sin, and of God's righteousness, and of the coming judgment. (John 16:7-8)

Our triune God is fully involved, but it is the Holy Spirit's connection with us that draws us into forgiveness.

Forgiveness comes with repentance. This is absolutely critical to understand. There can be no forgiveness without repentance from our sin. Again, repentance is not just saying we're sorry. Repentance is a change – a change of mind and a change of direction. Repentance is turning *from* our sinfulness and turning *to* Jesus! After his resurrection, Jesus meets with his disciples:

Then the two from Emmaus told their story of how Jesus had appeared to them as they were walking along the road, and how they had recognized him as he was breaking the bread. And just as they were telling about it, Jesus himself was suddenly standing there among them. "Peace be with you," he said. But the whole group was startled and frightened, thinking they were seeing a ghost!

"Why are you frightened?" he asked. "Why are your hearts filled with doubt? Look at my hands. Look at my feet. You can see that it's really me. Touch me and make sure that I am not a ghost, because ghosts don't have bodies, as you see that I do." As he spoke, he showed them his hands and his feet.

Still they stood there in disbelief, filled with joy and wonder. Then he asked them, "Do you have anything here to eat?" They gave him a piece of broiled fish, and he ate it as they watched.

*Then he said, "When I was with you before, I told you that everything written about me in the law of Moses and the prophets and in the Psalms must be fulfilled." Then he opened their minds to understand the Scriptures. And he said, "Yes, it was written long ago that the Messiah would suffer and die and rise from the dead on the third day. **It was also written that this message*** *would be proclaimed in the authority of his name to all the nations, beginning in Jerusalem: 'There is forgiveness of sins for all who repent.'* You are witnesses of all these things.

"And now I will send the Holy Spirit, just as my Father promised. But stay here in the city until the Holy Spirit comes and fills you with power from heaven." (Luke 24:35-49, **emphasis mine**)

After the Holy Spirit fell upon the disciples on the Day of Pentecost, Peter turned to the crowd and powerfully preached the good news of Jesus to them for the first time. He concludes with this message:

"So let everyone in Israel know for certain that God has made this Jesus, whom you crucified, to be both Lord and Messiah!"

Peter's words pierced their hearts, and they said to him and to the other apostles, "Brothers, what should we do?"

Peter replied, "Each of you must repent of your sins and turn to God, and be baptized in the name of Jesus Christ for the forgiveness of your sins. Then you will receive the gift of the Holy Spirit. This promise is to you, to your children, and to those far away— all who have been called by the Lord our God." (Acts 2:36-39)

Our true repentance leads to our salvation.

Repentance brings justification. We have already discussed justification in a previous chapter. Justification is God's legal and permanent declaration, as the ultimate Judge, that he finds us now innocent and righteous in Jesus Christ – made right with Him. As Paul preaches in Antioch of Pisidia, he tells the believers there,

"Brothers, listen! We are here to proclaim that through this man Jesus there is forgiveness for your sins. Everyone who believes in him is made right in God's sight—something the law of Moses could never do." (Acts 13:38-39)

When God forgives us, we are also justified in Christ.

Forgiveness brings redemption. Redemption is Jesus literally buying us back. He redeems us – paying our ransom – with his own sacrifice at Calvary. Paul declares to the Ephesians,

> *All praise to God, the Father of our Lord Jesus Christ, who has blessed us with every spiritual blessing in the heavenly realms because we are united with Christ. Even before he made the world, God loved us and chose us in Christ to be holy and without fault in his eyes. God decided in advance to adopt us into his own family by bringing us to himself through Jesus Christ. This is what he wanted to do, and it gave him great pleasure. So we praise God for the glorious grace he has poured out on us who belong to his dear Son. He is so rich in kindness and grace that he purchased our freedom with the blood of his Son and forgave our sins. He has showered his kindness on us, along with all wisdom and understanding.* (Ephesians 1:3-8)

When God forgives us, we are fully and wholly redeemed in Christ. We are fully God's children once again.

Forgiveness is the product of Christ's atonement. More than just making reparations for our sin, Jesus' atonement sets everything back the way it was meant to be. We looked at the following scripture passage in Chapter 7, but we must revisit it here. Over 700 years before the birth of Jesus, God laid out his plans for Jesus' atoning sacrifice through the ministry of Isaiah the Prophet, speaking of both the exaltation and suffering of God's Anointed Son.

> *Behold, My servant will prosper, He will be high and lifted up, and greatly exalted.*
>
> *Just as many were astonished at you, my people, So His appearance was marred more than any man, and His form more than the sons of men.*
>
> *Thus He will sprinkle many nations, kings will shut their mouths on account of Him; for what had not been told them they will see, and what they had not heard they will understand.*
>
> *Who has believed our message?*
>
> *And to whom has the arm of the Lord been revealed?*

For He grew up before Him like a tender shoot, and like a root out of parched ground;

He has no stately form or majesty that we should look upon Him,

Nor appearance that we should be attracted to Him.

He was despised and forsaken of men, a man of sorrows, and acquainted with grief; and like one from whom men hide their face, He was despised, and we did not esteem Him.

Surely our griefs He Himself bore, and our sorrows He carried; yet we ourselves esteemed Him stricken, smitten of God, and afflicted.

But He was pierced through for our transgressions, He was crushed for our iniquities; the chastening for our well-being fell upon Him, and by His scourging we are healed.

All of us like sheep have gone astray, each of us has turned to his own way; but the Lord has caused the iniquity of us all to fall on Him.

He was oppressed and He was afflicted, yet He did not open His mouth; like a lamb that is led to slaughter, and like a sheep that is silent before its shearers, so He did not open His mouth.

By oppression and judgment He was taken away; and as for His generation, who considered that He was cut off out of the land of the living, for the transgression of my people to whom the stroke was due?

His grave was assigned with wicked men, yet He was with a rich man in His death, because He had done no violence, nor was there any deceit in His mouth.

But the Lord was pleased to crush Him, putting Him to grief; if He would render Himself as a guilt offering, He will see His offspring, He will prolong His days,and the good pleasure of the Lord will prosper in His hand.

As a result of the anguish of His soul, He will see it and be satisfied; by His knowledge the Righteous One, my Servant, will justify the many, as He will bear their iniquities.

Therefore, I will allot Him a portion with the great, and He will divide the booty with the strong; because He poured out Himself to death, and was numbered with the transgressors; yet He Himself bore the sin of many, and interceded for the transgressors. (Isaiah 52:13-53-12, New American Standard Bible)[30]

Peter echoes many of these same truths in his second letter to the Church:

He never sinned, nor ever deceived anyone.

He did not retaliate when he was insulted, nor threaten revenge when he suffered.

He left his case in the hands of God, who always judges fairly.

He personally carried our sins in his body on the cross so that we can be dead to sin and live for what is right.

By his wounds you are healed.

Once you were like sheep who wandered away.

But now you have turned to your Shepherd, the Guardian of your souls. (2 Peter 2:22-25)

Yes, the atonement makes everything right again. It is essentially the fulfillment of the prayer Jesus taught us to pray, "Your kingdom (rule and reign) come, your will be done on earth as it is in heaven" (Matthew 6:10). Jesus deals with our infirmities, our illnesses, and our oppression. Jesus deals with our sorrows and our anxieties. Jesus deals with our transgressions – our sins – both those that are purposeful and those that are not. Jesus provides healing and deliverance. Jesus has moved us from death to life![31]

---

30   The *New American Standard Bible* (The Lockman Foundation, 1986) is the most literal, word-for-word English translation of the Bible we have today. It is helpful to read this long and powerful prophecy in the NASB here. Isaiah's message is such an encouragement for us even to this day!

31   Recall my footnote in Chapter 7 about this passage and how it is essentially hidden from most Jews today.

Forgiveness is the heart of our message. Forgiveness is what Jesus took on human flesh to accomplish. Forgiveness is the heart of the Christian Faith. It is a vital part of the good news that we proclaim to all of humanity.

> *And then he [Jesus] told them, "Go into all the world and preach the Good News to everyone. Anyone who believes and is baptized will be saved. But anyone who refuses to believe will be condemned. These miraculous signs will accompany those who believe: They will cast out demons in my name, and they will speak in new languages. They will be able to handle snakes with safety, and if they drink anything poisonous, it won't hurt them. They will be able to place their hands on the sick, and they will be healed."*

> *When the Lord Jesus had finished talking with them, he was taken up into heaven and sat down in the place of honor at God's right hand. And the disciples went everywhere and preached, and the Lord worked through them, confirming what they said by many miraculous signs.* (Mark 16:15-20)

> *But you will receive power when the Holy Spirit comes upon you. And you will be my witnesses, telling people about me everywhere—in Jerusalem, throughout Judea, in Samaria, and to the ends of the earth."* (Acts 1:8)

> *My dear brothers and sisters, if someone among you wanders away from the truth and is brought back, you can be sure that whoever brings the sinner back from wandering will save that person from death and bring about the forgiveness of many sins.* (James 5:19-20)

Forgiveness is the reason for the cross. Forgiveness is the pivotal point of our Christian message and mission.

Forgiveness is full and complete. David sings this truth in a most beautiful way:

> *Let all that I am praise the Lord; with my whole heart, I will praise his holy name.*

Let all that I am praise the Lord; may I never forget the good things he does for me.

He forgives all my sins and heals all my diseases.

He redeems me from death and crowns me with love and tender mercies.

He fills my life with good things.

My youth is renewed like the eagle's!

The Lord gives righteousness and justice to all who are treated unfairly.

He revealed his character to Moses and his deeds to the people of Israel.

The Lord is compassionate and merciful, slow to get angry and filled with unfailing love.

He will not constantly accuse us, nor remain angry forever.

He does not punish us for all our sins; he does not deal harshly with us, as we deserve.

For his unfailing love toward those who fear him is as great as the height of the heavens above the earth.

He has removed our sins as far from us as the east is from the west.

The Lord is like a father to his children, tender and compassionate to those who fear him.

For he knows how weak we are; he remembers we are only dust.
(Psalm 103:1-14, ***emphasis mine***)

As far as the east is from the west – that's how far God has removed our sins from us! David does not sing "As far as the north is from the south…" because these directions have limits at their respective poles. East and west are *eternally* distant from one another! Our loving, gracious, forgiving God "blots out" our sins and chooses never to remember them again. As God decries the absence of Israel's sacrifices and their refusal even to ask forgiveness, he reminds them of their inability to do anything about their plight.

"I—yes, I alone—will blot out your sins for my own sake and will never think of them again." (Isaiah 42:25)

He will do this for his own sake. He is a God of compassion.

Where is another God like you, who pardons the guilt of the remnant, overlooking the sins of his special people?

You will not stay angry with your people forever, because you delight in showing unfailing love.

Once again you will have compassion on us.

You will trample our sins under your feet and throw them into the depths of the ocean!

You will show us your faithfulness and unfailing love as you promised to our ancestors Abraham and Jacob long ago. (Micah 7:18-20)

The prophet Jeremiah also proclaims this beautiful message from God, wrapped up in the New Covenant to be established by Jesus Christ.

"The day is coming," says the Lord, "when I will make a new covenant with the people of Israel and Judah. This covenant will not be like the one I made with their ancestors when I took them by the hand and brought them out of the land of Egypt. They broke that covenant, though I loved them as a husband loves his wife," says the Lord.

"But this is the new covenant I will make with the people of Israel after those days," says the Lord. "I will put my instructions deep within them, and I will write them on their hearts. I will be their God, and they will be my people. And they will not need to teach their neighbors, nor will they need to teach their relatives, saying, 'You should know the Lord.' For everyone, from the least to the greatest, will know me already," says the Lord. "And I will forgive their wickedness, and I will never again remember their sins." (Jeremiah 31:31-34. See also Hebrews 8:10-12)

Once forgiven, God will not remember our sins. Yes! God's forgiveness is full and complete! Every time we confess our sins, God gives us a completely clean slate in life!

> *If we claim we have no sin, we are only fooling ourselves and not living in the truth. But if we confess our sins to him, he is faithful and just to forgive us our sins and to cleanse us from all wickedness.* (1 John 1:8-9)

I hope you can see just how central the biblical teaching of God's forgiveness of sins is to our life in Christ. Forgiveness is pardon. Forgiveness is absolution. Forgiveness is clemency. Forgiveness is remission. Forgiveness is reconciliation. Forgiveness begins with God – not us. Forgiveness is a mysterious and miraculous act of God where he does not compromise his character to set us free! Forgiveness brings justification and redemption. Forgiveness is complete. All of these things are wrapped up in the biblical doctrine of God's forgiveness. "I believe in the forgiveness of sins..." This is the very heart of our Christian Faith.

STUDY GUIDE

IT MAKES A DIFFERENCE

Forgiveness. It's the reason Jesus became human. It's the reason for his sacrifice. Christians who study and accept the biblical teaching on the forgiveness of sin have an incredible depth of faith. They experience the love of God more personally. They understand the fullness of God's plan of forgiveness and how it was realized in Jesus. They know God has fully granted them pardon, absolution, clemency, remission, and reconciliation. They live life justified – declared righteous by God. The love, justice, and mercy of our God blow them away. They see the mandatory link with repentance and are lovingly compelled to share the good news about God's forgiveness with the world around them. Jesus' mission is their mission.

Those who do not fully understand the forgiveness of sin are at a colossal loss. They often find God's forgiveness – and all it entails

– hard to accept. They continue to feel guilty and may even have an unhealthy fear of God. And although they may be able to describe God's justice, they fail to understand its vital connection to God's love and mercy. Many will continue trying to please God to win his favor. Those that do not grasp the forgiveness of sin rarely experience the joy and freedom of the real Christian life.

HOW DO I LIVE OUT WHAT I HAVE JUST LEARNED IN MY OWN LIFE?

1. Take a moment to stop and pray. Ask God, through the Holy Spirit, to increase your understanding of the essentials of His message to you. Ask Him to reveal and clarify any points about which have been confusing or unclear.

2. Consider how well your own understanding of forgiveness lined up with the definition given in Chapter 13. How complete was your understanding? How did reading this chapter change or expand your understanding?

3. Meditate on the role of the roles of God the Father and Jesus the Son in our forgiveness. Compare these to God's expectation of our role – true repentance. Express your gratitude to Him for this priceless gift.

4. To what extent have you tried to *earn*, rather than to *accept* God's forgiveness? Ask God to help you more fully comprehend his grace and mercy. Thank him for freeing you from the fear of punishment for your wrongdoing.

5. Consider whether there are those you need to forgive as God has forgiven you. If this is true, and you need help being ready to do so, seek counsel with your pastor, counselor or a mature church leader.

6. Take several days to consider: Who can help you apply what you learn to put it into an ongoing life's practice?

7. How are you living this out right now? How is your life reflective of your understanding of this truth?

HOW DO I IMPART WHAT I HAVE JUST LEARNED TO CHILDREN?

Preparing to teach this lesson to children: Gather the needed supplies ahead of the lesson: one large (about 12 x 18") sheet of white paper per child, several pieces of red or pink construction paper (about two – three sheets per child), scissors, a heart pattern per child, glue, and dark colored markers or crayons. A heart pattern is easily created by folding a piece of stiff paper in half and cutting a "comma" shape of the desired size, making the fold its center. It is suggested that two to four hearts per sheet of 9 x 12 paper is a realistic expectation.

1. Begin by praying with the children. Ask God, through the Holy Spirit, to help the children understand more about the Christian faith. Ask God to help them clearly understand the new things they are about to learn.

2. Continue to work on memorizing the Apostle's Creed. Be sure they have memorized through this part:

   I believe in God, the Father almighty, creator of heaven and earth.

   I believe in Jesus Christ, his only Son, our Lord, who was conceived by the Holy Spirit and born of the virgin Mary. He suffered under Pontius Pilate, was crucified, died, and was buried; he descended into hell. The third day he rose again from the dead. He ascended to heaven and is seated at the right hand of God the Father almighty. From there he will come to judge the living and the dead.

   I believe in the Holy Spirit, the holy catholic church, the communion of saints, the forgiveness of sins...

3. Talk about what forgiveness of sins means. Be sure the children understand what sins are. Also be sure the children understand that seeking forgiveness means more than just offering an apology, but involves real repentance. Remind them that Jesus' forgiveness is a free gift we receive by simply and sincerely asking for it and accepting it.

4. One illustration that may help children understand the difference between sincere repentance and simply offering an apology is to ask if they've ever had to apologize for something they did when they really weren't sorry. Ask them to compare the way that felt to a time when they realize they had been wrong, had real regret, and wanted to make things right as much as possible.

5. Explain that the forgiveness of sins is a central truth of the Christian faith. It is so important that it can be called the heart of our faith. That is why we are going to describe aspects of this truth by creating hearts.

6. Give each child a heart pattern and about two or three sheets of red and/or pink construction paper. Have them trace and then cut out hearts. You may want to show children how to optimize the number of hearts they can create from a sheet. If you don't, many children will cut one heart out of the center and declare the paper "used up". The other alternative is to cut the paper into quarter or half sheets ahead of time and give each child six pieces of cut paper.

7. Have the children write the following on the hearts – one per heart – talk about each concept as they write: 1) I repent. 2) I am forgiven. 3) Jesus took my punishment. 4) God is love. 5) God is merciful. 6) I will tell others.

8. Write "Thank you for forgiving our sins." across the top of the white paper, then glue the hearts underneath.

9. If you have children in your group who have not yet surrendered to Jesus, continue to pray for the Holy Spirit to open that conversational door so you can explain the gospel. Once they receive Christ, the indwelling presence of the Holy Spirit will make the lessons in this book much more accessible to them.

HOW DO I IMPART WHAT I HAVE JUST LEARNED TO TEENS?

1. Begin by praying with the teens. Ask God, through the Holy Spirit, to increase understanding. You can do this or ask a volunteer.

2. Read the Apostles' Creed out loud. Read it yourself, ask for a volunteer, or read it in unison.

3. Repeat these lines:

    I believe in God, the Father almighty, creator of heaven and earth.

    I believe in Jesus Christ, his only Son, our Lord, who was conceived by the Holy Spirit and born of the virgin Mary. He suffered under Pontius Pilate, was crucified, died, and was buried; he descended into hell. The third day he rose again from the dead. He ascended to heaven and is seated at the right hand of God the Father almighty. From there he will come to judge the living and the dead.

    I believe in the Holy Spirit, the holy catholic church, the communion of saints, the forgiveness of sins...

4. Have the teens pull out their Question Journals. Ask them to jot down the answers to any questions about the Creed that are answered in this session. Have them share those discoveries, giving them sufficient time to record any thoughts they wish to capture. Assure them that they can ask any remaining questions about this section at the end of the session.

5. Discuss the difference between *apologizing* (saying "I'm sorry,") and *repenting.*

6. Have the teens look through the chapter to find the characteristics of God that make forgiveness possible.

7. Have the teens consider God's part in forgiveness and then consider our part. Discuss who has the greater responsibility.

8. Ask the teens if they have heard people express doubt that they could be good enough to earn or deserve God's forgiveness. What would they say to someone who holds such a view?

9. Ask the teens why the forgiveness of sins would be considered the heart of the Christian faith.

10. Allow the teens to ask any questions about the forgiveness of sins they had noted previously that were not addressed in this discussion.

11. If you have teens in your group who have not yet surrendered to Jesus, continue to pray for the Holy Spirit to open that conversational door so you can explain the gospel. Once they receive Christ, the indwelling presence of the Holy Spirit will make the lessons in this book much more accessible to them.

HOW DO I IMPART WHAT I HAVE JUST LEARNED TO ADULTS?

1. Challenge your adults to take a moment to stop and pray, asking God, through the Holy Spirit, to increase their understanding of the essentials of the Christian Faith. Encourage them to ask Him to reveal and clarify any points which have been confusing or unclear.

2. Review the Apostle's Creed. Re-read the lines below slowly and thoughtfully:

I believe in God, the Father almighty, creator of heaven and earth.

I believe in Jesus Christ, his only Son, our Lord, who was conceived by the Holy Spirit and born of the virgin Mary. He suffered under Pontius Pilate, was crucified, died, and was buried; he descended into hell. The third day he rose again from the dead. He ascended to heaven and is seated at the right hand of God the Father almighty. From there he will come to judge the living and the dead.

I believe in the Holy Spirit, the holy catholic church, the communion of saints, the forgiveness of sins...

3. If they have not done so, encourage the participants to memorize the Creed in its entirety, reminding them that it is a summary of the essentials of the faith.

4. Have participants pull out the notes they made during previous sessions. Ask them to jot down the answers to any questions about the Creed that may be answered during this session and to share those discoveries as they happen. Provide sufficient time to record any thoughts they may wish to capture. Assure them that they will have the opportunity to ask any questions that were not answered in this session at the end of the session.

5. Ask participants to consider the view that God's forgiveness must be earned and/or that people must atone for their own sins by being "good". How do we know that is a false understanding? Why does it then persist? How does that misunderstanding trap people in fear?

6. How does a proper understanding of God's character and the nature of salvation help allay this fear and bring freedom?

7. What is the part people must play in obtaining God's forgiveness? What is our responsibility to God in gratitude for granting that forgiveness?

8. Ask participants: How did your understanding of forgiveness change or expand after reading this chapter?

9. Why might "the forgiveness of sins" be considered the heart of our message?

10. What aspects of God's forgiveness should serve as a model for our forgiveness of those who have wronged us?

11. Allow participants to ask any questions about the forgiveness of sins they had noted previously that were not addressed in this discussion.

12. If you have people in your group who have not yet surrendered to Jesus, continue to pray for the Holy Spirit to open that

conversational door so you can explain the gospel. Once they receive Christ, the indwelling presence of the Holy Spirit will make the lessons in this book much more accessible to them.

CHAPTER 14
The Resurrection of the Body

"I believe in the resurrection of the body…"

It is the same way with the resurrection of the dead. Our earthly bodies are planted in the ground when we die, but they will be raised to live forever. Our bodies are buried in brokenness, but they will be raised in glory. They are buried in weakness, but they will be raised in strength. They are buried as natural human bodies, but they will be raised as spiritual bodies. For just as there are natural bodies, there are also spiritual bodies.

The Scriptures tell us, "The first man, Adam, became a living person." But the last Adam—that is, Christ—is a life-giving Spirit. What comes first is the natural body, then the spiritual body comes later. Adam, the first man, was made from the dust of the earth, while Christ, the second man, came from heaven. Earthly people are like the earthly man, and heavenly people are like the heavenly man. Just as we are now like the earthly man, we will someday be like the heavenly man.

What I am saying, dear brothers and sisters, is that our physical bodies cannot inherit the Kingdom of God. These dying bodies cannot inherit what will last forever.

But let me reveal to you a wonderful secret. We will not all die, but we will all be transformed! It will happen in a moment, in the blink of an eye, when the last trumpet is blown. For when the trumpet sounds, those who have died will be raised to live forever. And we who are living will also be transformed. For our dying bodies must be transformed into bodies that will never die; our mortal bodies must be transformed into immortal bodies.

Then, when our dying bodies have been transformed into bodies that will never die, this Scripture will be fulfilled:

"Death is swallowed up in victory.

O death, where is your victory?

O death, where is your sting?"

For sin is the sting that results in death, and the law gives sin its power. But thank God! He gives us victory over sin and death through our Lord Jesus Christ.

So, my dear brothers and sisters, be strong and immovable. Always work enthusiastically for the Lord, for you know that nothing you do for the Lord is ever useless. (1 Corinthians 15:42-58)

EVERYONE LIVES FOREVER

I once saw a bumper sticker that gave me a sobering laugh: "Eternity: Smoking or Non-smoking?" It certainly drives the point home that there are two possible eternal destinations. Daniel, Jesus, and the Apostle John all talk about two resurrections: one to eternal life and glory, and the other to eternal condemnation and damnation. There is some kind of physical experience for those in eternal suffering. Jesus himself warns about a place where "worm does not die, and fire is not quenched" (Mark 9:48-49).

Those with faith in Jesus Christ are transformed into their new glorified, heavenly bodies when they die. Jesus' own post-resurrection body gives us some clues about what our resurrection bodies may be like. For those who have confidence in their glorious future with God, that know we stand before our heavenly Father forgiven and counted as his beloved sons and daughters, we know that all the restrictions, oppression, and aliments of this life will be gone one day and we'll live forever in a glorified body. That fact gives us great hope!

"I believe in the resurrection of the body..." It's an essential doctrine.

THE RESURRECTION BODY

As the apostle John writes his first letter to the Church, he makes this point:

> *See how very much our Father loves us, for he calls us his children, and that is what we are! But the people who belong to this world don't recognize that we are God's children because they don't know him. Dear friends, we are already God's children, but he has not yet shown us what we will be like when Christ appears. **But we do know that we will be like him, for we will see him as he really is.*** (1 John 3:1-2, **emphasis mine**)

Since we will be like Jesus, it's important to understand just what this means.

Jesus' resurrection body was the "first fruits" of a new kind of human life. The Old Testament concept of "first fruits" describes both a harvest time reality and a special feast ordained by God for the Jewish people held in the early spring at the beginning of the grain harvest. The first and best was to be brought as an offering to the Lord in remembrance of Israel's time in Egypt, her deliverance by God from Pharaoh, and her possession of the Promised Land. It essentially looks forward to the harvest of souls that will happen under the Messiah's ministry. In fact, this feast found its fulfillment in Christ's completed work for our deliverance on Calvary. Jesus' resurrection was the "first fruits" that guarantees *our* resurrection!

Paul teaches this to the Christians in Corinth.

> *But in fact, Christ has been raised from the dead. He is the first of a great harvest of all who have died...But there is an order to this resurrection: Christ was raised as the first of the harvest; then all who belong to Christ will be raised when he comes back.* (1 Corinthians 15:20, 23)

Think about it this way:

1. Jesus was perfect – and we, too, will be.

2. Jesus was no longer subject to weakness – we, too, will be blessed with heavenly strength and endurance.

3. Jesus was no longer subject to aging or death – we, too, will be free from these things.

4. Jesus was no longer subject to the limitations of space – we will also have such freedom!

Jesus' resurrection body was a physical body. The ladies who met him at the empty tomb immediately after his resurrection fell and grasped his feet.

> *And as they went, Jesus met them and greeted them. And they ran to him, grasped his feet, and worshiped him. Then Jesus said to them, "Don't be afraid! Go tell my brothers to leave for Galilee, and they will see me there." (Matthew 28:9-10)*
>
> *Mary was standing outside the tomb crying, and as she wept, she stooped and looked in. She saw two white-robed angels, one sitting at the head and the other at the foot of the place where the body of Jesus had been lying. "Dear woman, why are you crying?" the angels asked her.*
>
> *"Because they have taken away my Lord," she replied, "and I don't know where they have put him."*
>
> *She turned to leave and saw someone standing there. It was Jesus, but she didn't recognize him. "Dear woman, why are you crying?" Jesus asked her. "Who are you looking for?"*
>
> *She thought he was the gardener. "Sir," she said, "if you have taken him away, tell me where you have put him, and I will go and get him."*
>
> *"Mary!" Jesus said.*
>
> *She turned to him and cried out, "Rabboni!" (which is Hebrew for "Teacher").*
>
> **"Don't cling to me," Jesus said, "for I haven't yet ascended to the Father. But go find my brothers and tell them, 'I am ascending to my Father and your Father, to my God and your God.' "**

318

Mary Magdalene found the disciples and told them, "I have seen the Lord!" Then she gave them his message. (John 20:11-18, **emphasis mine**)

Several people sat and ate with Jesus after his resurrection. Jesus offered bread to the two men with whom he walked along the road to Emmaus.

By this time they were nearing Emmaus and the end of their journey. Jesus acted as if he were going on, but they begged him, "Stay the night with us, since it is getting late." So he went home with them. As they sat down to eat, he took the bread and blessed it. Then he broke it and gave it to them. Suddenly, their eyes were opened, and they recognized him. And at that moment he disappeared!

They said to each other, "Didn't our hearts burn within us as he talked with us on the road and explained the Scriptures to us?" (Luke 24:28-32)

He ate broiled fish with his disciples – and he showed them that he had a real body of flesh and bones, not something "ghostly."

Then the two from Emmaus told their story of how Jesus had appeared to them as they were walking along the road, and how they had recognized him as he was breaking the bread. And just as they were telling about it, Jesus himself was suddenly standing there among them. "Peace be with you," he said. But the whole group was startled and frightened, thinking they were seeing a ghost!

"Why are you frightened?" he asked. "Why are your hearts filled with doubt? **Look at my hands. Look at my feet. You can see that it's really me. Touch me and make sure that I am not a ghost, because ghosts don't have bodies, as you see that I do."** *As he spoke, he showed them his hands and his feet.*

Still they stood there in disbelief, filled with joy and wonder. Then he asked them, "Do you have anything here to eat?" They gave him a piece of broiled fish, **and he ate it as they watched**. (Luke 24:35-43, **emphasis mine**)

But perhaps the most precious example is the breakfast he cooked for his restoration encounter with Peter on the beach of the Sea of Galilee.

Simon Peter said, "I'm going fishing."

"We'll come, too," they all said. So they went out in the boat, but they caught nothing all night.

At dawn Jesus was standing on the beach, but the disciples couldn't see who he was. He called out, "Fellows, have you caught any fish?"

"No," they replied.

Then he said, "Throw out your net on the right-hand side of the boat, and you'll get some!" So they did, and they couldn't haul in the net because there were so many fish in it.

Then the disciple Jesus loved said to Peter, "It's the Lord!" When Simon Peter heard that it was the Lord, he put on his tunic (for he had stripped for work), jumped into the water, and headed to shore. The others stayed with the boat and pulled the loaded net to the shore, for they were only about a hundred yards from shore. When they got there, they found breakfast waiting for them—fish cooking over a charcoal fire, and some bread.

"Bring some of the fish you've just caught," Jesus said. So Simon Peter went aboard and dragged the net to the shore. There were 153 large fish, and yet the net hadn't torn.

"Now come and have some breakfast!" Jesus said. None of the disciples dared to ask him, "Who are you?" They knew it was the Lord. Then Jesus served them the bread and the fish. This was the third time Jesus had appeared to his disciples since he had been raised from the dead. (John 21:3-14)

Jesus' resurrection body was different than ours, but no less physical with flesh and bones.

Jesus' resurrection body was recognizably him. The two men walking down the road to Emmaus were temporarily kept from recognizing him until their eyes were opened. Mark's gospel tells us that Jesus appeared to them in a different form (Luke 24:13-32; Mark 16:12). In her extreme grief, it took Mary Magdalene a moment to recognize him (John 20:14-16). But others recognized him immediately.

And as they went, Jesus met them and greeted them. And they ran to him, grasped his feet, and worshiped him. Then Jesus said to them, "Don't be afraid! Go tell my brothers to leave for Galilee, and they will see me there." (Matthew 28:8-10)

Then the eleven disciples left for Galilee, going to the mountain where Jesus had told them to go. When they saw him, they worshiped him—but some of them doubted! (Matthew 28:16-17)

That Sunday evening the disciples were meeting behind locked doors because they were afraid of the Jewish leaders. Suddenly, Jesus was standing there among them! "Peace be with you," he said. As he spoke, he showed them the wounds in his hands and his side. They were filled with joy when they saw the Lord! (John 20:19-20)

At dawn Jesus was standing on the beach, but the disciples couldn't see who he was. He called out, "Fellows, have you caught any fish?"

"No," they replied.

Then he said, "Throw out your net on the right-hand side of the boat, and you'll get some!" So they did, and they couldn't haul in the net because there were so many fish in it.

Then the disciple Jesus loved said to Peter, "It's the Lord!" When Simon Peter heard that it was the Lord, he put on his tunic (for he had stripped for work), jumped into the water, and headed to shore. (John 21:4-7)

I passed on to you what was most important and what had also been passed on to me. Christ died for our sins, just as the Scriptures said. He was buried, and he was raised from the dead on the third day, just as the Scriptures said. He was seen by Peter and then by the Twelve. After that, he was seen by more than 500 of his followers at one time, most of whom are still alive, though some have died. Then he was seen by James and later by all the apostles. Last of all, as though I had been born at the wrong time, I also saw him. For I am the least of all the apostles. In fact, I'm not even worthy to be called an apostle after the way I persecuted God's church. (1 Corinthians 15:3-9)

Jesus' resurrection body bore the scars of his crucifixion. He showed his disciples, and specifically Thomas, the holes in his hands, his feet, and the spear hole in his side. (Luke 24:39, and John 20:20, 27)

> *"Why are you frightened?" he asked. "Why are your hearts filled with doubt? Look at my hands. Look at my feet. You can see that it's really me. Touch me and make sure that I am not a ghost, because ghosts don't have bodies, as you see that I do." As he spoke, he showed them his hands and his feet.* (Luke 24:38-40)
>
> *Eight days later the disciples were together again, and this time Thomas was with them. The doors were locked; but suddenly, as before, Jesus was standing among them. "Peace be with you," he said. Then he said to Thomas, "Put your finger here, and look at my hands. Put your hand into the wound in my side. Don't be faithless any longer. Believe!"*
>
> *"My Lord and my God!" Thomas exclaimed.* (John 20:26-28)

Jesus' resurrection body was not subject to the limits of this creation. Frankly, I don't think anyone understands the full extent of what this means. But Jesus could appear and disappear suddenly (Luke 24:31; John 20:19, 20). He is not subject to space and time.

It is essential to know what Jesus' resurrection body is like because the apostle John tells us that when Christ returns, we will be *like him* (1 John 3:2)! Paul tells the Christians in Rome that "we eagerly await the redemption of our bodies" (Romans 8:23). Finally, Paul tells the Philippians that our citizenship is actually in heaven and that we await the time when Jesus, having all things under his control, will transform our lowly bodies to be like his glorious one (Philippians 3:20-21)! Jesus' resurrection body is the prototype for the rest of us.

OUR RESURRECTION BODIES

In addition to all we know about Jesus' resurrection body, the apostle Paul gives us even more to think about when it comes to our own resurrection bodies. Let's return to the scripture passage I used to open this chapter.

It is the same way with the resurrection of the dead. Our earthly bodies are planted in the ground when we die, but they will be raised to live forever. Our bodies are buried in brokenness, but they will be raised in glory. They are buried in weakness, but they will be raised in strength. They are buried as natural human bodies, but they will be raised as spiritual bodies. For just as there are natural bodies, there are also spiritual bodies.

The Scriptures tell us, "The first man, Adam, became a living person." But the last Adam—that is, Christ—is a life-giving Spirit. What comes first is the natural body, then the spiritual body comes later. Adam, the first man, was made from the dust of the earth, while Christ, the second man, came from heaven. Earthly people are like the earthly man, and heavenly people are like the heavenly man. Just as we are now like the earthly man, we will someday be like the heavenly man.

What I am saying, dear brothers and sisters, is that our physical bodies cannot inherit the Kingdom of God. These dying bodies cannot inherit what will last forever.

But let me reveal to you a wonderful secret. We will not all die, but we will all be transformed! It will happen in a moment, in the blink of an eye, when the last trumpet is blown. For when the trumpet sounds, those who have died will be raised to live forever. And we who are living will also be transformed. For our dying bodies must be transformed into bodies that will never die; our mortal bodies must be transformed into immortal bodies.

Then, when our dying bodies have been transformed into bodies that will never die, this Scripture will be fulfilled:

"Death is swallowed up in victory.

O death, where is your victory?

O death, where is your sting?"

For sin is the sting that results in death, and the law gives sin its power. But thank God! He gives us victory over sin and death through our Lord Jesus Christ.

So, my dear brothers and sisters, be strong and immovable. Always work enthusiastically for the Lord, for you know that nothing you do for the Lord is ever useless. (1 Corinthians 15:42-58)

Jesus' resurrection ensures our promised resurrection. Earlier in his letter to the Christians in Corinth, Paul tells them, "By his power God raised the Lord from the dead, and he will raise us also" (1 Corinthians 6:14). He then underscores this truth, "But Christ has indeed been raised from the dead, the first fruits of those who have fallen asleep" (1 Corinthians 15:20). This truth about our own resurrection serves to embolden us as we fulfill our unique parts of Christ's mission – no matter what the cost. In his second letter to the Corinthians, Paul writes,

Yes, we live under constant danger of death because we serve Jesus, so that the life of Jesus will be evident in our dying bodies. So we live in the face of death, but this has resulted in eternal life for you.

But we continue to preach because we have the same kind of faith the psalmist had when he said, "I believed in God, so I spoke." **We know that God, who raised the Lord Jesus, will also raise us with Jesus and present us to himself together with you.** *All of this is for your benefit. And as God's grace reaches more and more people, there will be great thanksgiving, and God will receive more and more glory.*

That is why we never give up. Though our bodies are dying, our spirits are being renewed every day. For our present troubles are small and won't last very long. Yet they produce for us a glory that vastly outweighs them and will last forever! So we don't look at the troubles we can see now; rather, we fix our gaze on things that cannot be seen. For the things we see now will soon be gone, but the things we cannot see will last forever. (2 Corinthians 4:11-18, **emphasis mine**)

Our resurrection bodies will be transformed from death and decay to living forever. Death is the primary result of sin. When humanity rebelled against God in the garden (Genesis 3), he had already warned them that disobedience would surely bring death (Genesis 2:15-16). Death and decay are the natural outcomes of separation from the Author of Life. It makes sense, then, that these outcomes would be rendered null and void when we surrender to Christ. Jesus reminds us all, "I am the way, the truth, and the life. No one can come to the Father except through me" (John 14:6). He is the Bread of Life (John 6:35). He is the Word of Life (1 John 1:1-2). He gives life to everything in creation, and nothing exists without him (John 1:1-5). Therefore, Paul teaches,

> *But let me reveal to you a wonderful secret. We will not all die, but we will all be transformed! It will happen in a moment, in the blink of an eye, when the last trumpet is blown. For when the trumpet sounds, those who have died will be raised to live forever. And we who are living will also be transformed. For our dying bodies must be transformed into bodies that will never die; our mortal bodies must be transformed into immortal bodies.*
>
> *Then, when our dying bodies have been transformed into bodies that will never die, this Scripture will be fulfilled:*
>
> *"Death is swallowed up in victory. O death, where is your victory? O death, where is your sting?"*
>
> *For sin is the sting that results in death, and the law gives sin its power. But thank God! He gives us victory over sin and death through our Lord Jesus Christ.* (1 Corinthians 15:51-57)

Our resurrection bodies will be transformed from brokenness and dishonor to glory. In addition to Paul's message to the Corinthians, he includes an important truth in his lesson to the Ephesians on marriage.

> *For husbands, this means love your wives, just as Christ loved the church. He gave up his life for her to make her holy and clean, washed by the cleansing of God's word. He did this to present her to himself as a glorious church without a spot or wrinkle or any other blemish. Instead, she will be holy and without fault.* (Ephesians 5:25-27)

That's a strong message for all of us who are husbands! But don't miss his point. Look at what Jesus has done for us who are surrendered to him as his Church. He has made us holy (that is, separated unto God). He has made us clean, cleansed by the Word of God. He presents us as glorious. He presents us as unblemished (physically or spiritually). In Christ, we are now without fault.

The Bible says so much about our glorification in Christ.

> *For God knew his people in advance, and he chose them to become like his Son, so that his Son would be the firstborn among many brothers and sisters. And having chosen them, he called them to come to him. And having called them, he gave them right standing with himself. And having given them right standing, he gave them his glory.* (Romans 8:29-30)

> *Then the righteous will shine like the sun in their Father's Kingdom. Anyone with ears to hear should listen and understand!* (Matthew 13:43)

> *He called you to salvation when we told you the Good News; now you can share in the glory of our Lord Jesus Christ.* (2 Thessalonians 2:14)

All the damage sin has caused is undone in Christ. We move from dishonor to glory!

Our resurrection bodies will be transformed from weakness to strength. Think about this: there will be no more aging, no more illness, no more injury, no more disease, and no more weakness! Paul reminds us that our bodies are sown in dishonor but raised in glory. Our bodies are sown in weakness but are raised in power (1 Corinthians 15:43-44).

Finally, our resurrection bodies will be transformed from natural bodies to spiritual bodies. Paul writes,

> *[Our bodies] are buried as natural human bodies, but they will be raised as spiritual bodies. For just as there are natural bodies, there are also spiritual bodies.*

> *The Scriptures tell us, "The first man, Adam, became a living person." But the last Adam—that is, Christ—is a life-giving*

Spirit. What comes first is the natural body, then the spiritual body comes later. Adam, the first man, was made from the dust of the earth, while Christ, the second man, came from heaven. Earthly people are like the earthly man, and heavenly people are like the heavenly man. Just as we are now like the earthly man, we will someday be like the heavenly man. (1 Corinthians 15:43-49)

This is exciting news! There will be no more earthly limitations. If Jesus' resurrection body is any indication, our bodies also will no longer be stuck within the limits of space and time. And if we take these last two points together, we begin to see the wondrous realities of the final chapters of Revelation unveiled in our own future!

Then I saw a new heaven and a new earth, for the old heaven and the old earth had disappeared. And the sea was also gone. And I saw the holy city, the new Jerusalem, coming down from God out of heaven like a bride beautifully dressed for her husband.

I heard a loud shout from the throne, saying, "Look, God's home is now among his people! He will live with them, and they will be his people. God himself will be with them. He will wipe every tear from their eyes, and there will be no more death or sorrow or crying or pain. All these things are gone forever."

And the one sitting on the throne said, "Look, I am making everything new!" (Revelation 21:1-5)

All these incredible things are wrapped up in our understanding of the resurrection body! Our hope as followers of Jesus Christ is greatly strengthened by our knowledge of our own resurrection. Jesus' resurrection was the "first fruits," guaranteeing that all believers will also be resurrected. We will have physical bodies, recognizably us, and yet they will be transformed so we are no longer limited by time and space. We will never have to worry about death and decay again. All the garbage we have to deal with in this life – the consequences of sin, brokenness, anxiety, and dishonor – will all be transformed into glory! We will go from weakness to strength. And we will be among the multitudes of glorious resurrected saints from every nation, every tribe, every people, and every language.

After this I saw a vast crowd, too great to count, from every nation and tribe and people and language, standing in front of the throne and before the Lamb. They were clothed in white robes and held palm branches in their hands. And they were shouting with a great roar,

"Salvation comes from our God who sits on the throne and from the Lamb!"

And all the angels were standing around the throne and around the elders and the four living beings. And they fell before the throne with their faces to the ground and worshiped God. They sang,

"Amen! Blessing and glory and wisdom and thanksgiving and honor and power and strength belong to our God forever and ever! Amen."

Then one of the twenty-four elders asked me, "Who are these who are clothed in white? Where did they come from?"

And I said to him, "Sir, you are the one who knows."

Then he said to me, "These are the ones who died in the great tribulation. They have washed their robes in the blood of the Lamb and made them white.

"That is why they stand in front of God's throne and serve him day and night in his Temple.

And he who sits on the throne will give them shelter.

They will never again be hungry or thirsty; they will never be scorched by the heat of the sun.

For the Lamb on the throne will be their Shepherd.

He will lead them to springs of life-giving water.

And God will wipe every tear from their eyes." (Revelation 7:9-17)

"I believe in the resurrection of the body..." Amen!

STUDY GUIDE

IT MAKES A DIFFERENCE

Christians who follow the Creed's statement on the resurrection of the body understand that resurrection is true for everyone, but there are two possible outcomes: Some are resurrected to eternal life and glory, and others to damnation. They realize that everyone lives forever, so being consistent, loving witnesses for Christ and his gospel is critical. Such Christians also look forward to the freedom and glory of the resurrection body. They see Christ's resurrection body as the prototype, cherishing the advent of their own perfection in Christ, with no more weakness, illness, aging, or death.

It is amazing how many people today are uneducated about the biblical teaching on the resurrection. Even many Christians do not understand the glory that awaits them. Without a solid comprehension of the resurrection, some deny the existence of hell and damnation. They do not participate in spreading the good news about God's loving offer of salvation because they see no need for a divine rescue.

They may even deny that Jesus is the only way to heaven. Knowing the truth about the resurrection of the body makes an imperative difference.

HOW DO I LIVE OUT WHAT I HAVE JUST LEARNED IN MY OWN LIFE?

1. Take a moment to stop and pray. Ask God, through the Holy Spirit, to increase your understanding of the essentials of the Christian Faith. Ask Him to reveal and clarify any points which have been confusing or unclear.

2. How does it make you feel when you consider the biblical reality that we all live forever; the only difference is *where*? Are you secure in the knowledge of your own eternal destiny? If not, seek counsel with your pastor or other mature Christian. According to His promises, God wants you to be certain of your eternal destiny.

3. What response does it prompt in your heart to realize that there are those with no understanding of the need for divine rescue?

4. Consider the implications of the resurrection of the body for yourself and those you love who have embraced Christ as their Savior. Meditate on what it will mean for you and for them to have a new, glorified body free from sickness, sorrow, and pain – one similar to the resurrected body of Jesus, as described in this chapter. Thank him for that hope.

5. Think about seeing the face of Jesus, our beloved Lord. Meditate for at least a few moments about the wonder and awe of that privilege!

6. Whom will you most look forward to seeing in eternity besides Jesus? The apostles? Heroes of the faith? Friends and loved ones? Imagine the joy of that reunion.

7. Take some time to thank God for making the way to ensure our promised resurrection and the glory that awaits us.

8. Take several days to consider: Who can help you apply what you learn to put it into an ongoing life's practice?

9. How are you living this out right now? How is your life reflective of your understanding of this truth?

HOW DO I IMPART WHAT I HAVE JUST LEARNED TO CHILDREN?

Preparing to teach this lesson to children: Gather the needed supplies ahead of the lesson: One sheet of white paper, pencil, markers and/or crayons.

1. Begin by praying with the children. Ask God, through the Holy Spirit, to help the children understand more about the Christian faith. Ask God to help them clearly understand the new things they are about to learn.

2. Continue to work with the children on memorizing the Apostle's Creed. Be sure they have memorized through this part:

I believe in God, the Father almighty, creator of heaven and earth.

I believe in Jesus Christ, his only Son, our Lord, who was conceived by the Holy Spirit and born of the virgin Mary. He suffered under Pontius Pilate, was crucified, died, and was buried; he descended into hell. The third day he rose again from the dead. He ascended to heaven and is seated at the right hand of God the Father almighty. From there he will come to judge the living and the dead.

I believe in the Holy Spirit, the holy catholic church, the communion of saints, the forgiveness of sins, the resurrection of the body...

3. Ask the children to think about someone they know, perhaps a relative or friend, who is infirm or suffers in some physical way. Ask them to think about what a blessing it would be if they could have a new body free from blindness, crippling arthritis, cancer, strength-sapping heart or kidney disease, or whatever is afflicting their body and keeping them from totally enjoying this earthly life in the fullest measure. Let them know that this is what the Creed means when it refers to "the resurrection of the body." Our new bodies in the resurrection will be perfect – without pain or deformity.

4. Discuss *resurrection* in child-friendly terms such as this: if we have given our lives and hearts to Jesus, when we die, our imperfect earthly bodies are no longer needed. Instead, the inside part of us, the soul that makes us what we are, goes to live in heaven with Jesus forever, and we get a new, perfect body that will not get old, injured, or sick. We are not sure exactly how this works, but we know that we will see and recognize those we loved who went to heaven before us. These things will make us happy, grateful, and ready to praise God forever.

5. Children who have experienced the death of a close loved one or friend may ask why, if heaven is so perfect, we feel sad or cry when someone who was a believer dies. Explain that we are not sad for that person but glad; however, it is very unusual (with

very rare exceptions for a certain purpose, like Lazarus) that someone would be allowed to return to this earthly life once they have gone to live with Jesus in heaven, so the sadness is for ourselves because we miss them until it is time for us to go to heaven where we will see them again.

6. Children will often ask about what happens to pets. Don't dwell on this. The Bible does not explicitly say one way or the other. Refocus their attention to what the Bible *does* tell us – that we will be resurrected into heaven and will gain a glorious new body. We are promised that there will be no tears in heaven. We will be happy there, so we can count on that even if we do not know all of the details.[32]

7. Give each child a piece of paper and a pencil. Have them draw a light-dotted or wavy line approximately in the middle. Explain that this represents the barrier between earth and heaven. This barrier keeps us from seeing what is in heaven clearly from our side, but somehow, and we don't understand this completely until we are in heaven ourselves, those with a new heavenly body know more about what happens here on earth, and they "cheer us on." They are also thankful to and praise God with the angels.

8. On one side of the barrier, have the children draw themselves, their family members, and perhaps some friends and/or figures that represent believers from other church fellowships or countries, members of the holy, universal church we talked about in earlier chapters. They may want to include some people who are old, crippled, or have some other infirmity.

9. On the other side, have them draw figures representing believers who have passed into heaven. These figures should all be

---

32   This is John contributing this idea – My older brother is a believer (he is responsible for me being in the kingdom) and a veterinarian. He responds to the pet question this way: "I don't know if pets go to heaven or not. But here is what I think… It is sin that keeps people out of heaven. There is no indication in the Bible that animals sin. And I know that Bible books like Revelation talk about different kinds of animals in heaven. So it is very possible that God redeems our pets when he redeems all creation at Jesus' second coming." We can't build a theology on this perspective, but it can be especially helpful with kids who have lost a favorite pet. I've used it many times over the years!

whole, well, and happy. The setting should be beautiful and bright. Those in heaven might be looking at those on the earthly side and cheering them on and/or praising, thanking, and worshipping God with the angels.

10. If you have children in your group who have not yet surrendered to Jesus, continue to pray for the Holy Spirit to open that conversational door so you can explain the gospel. Once they receive Christ, the indwelling presence of the Holy Spirit will make the lessons in this book much more accessible to them.

HOW DO I IMPART WHAT I HAVE JUST LEARNED TO TEENS?

1. Begin by praying with the teens. Ask God, through the Holy Spirit, to increase understanding. You can do this or ask a volunteer.

2. Read the Apostles' Creed out loud. Read it yourself, ask for a volunteer, or read it in unison.

3. Repeat these lines:

   I believe in God, the Father almighty, creator of heaven and earth.

   I believe in Jesus Christ, his only Son, our Lord, who was conceived by the Holy Spirit and born of the virgin Mary. He suffered under Pontius Pilate, was crucified, died, and was buried; he descended into hell. The third day he rose again from the dead. He ascended to heaven and is seated at the right hand of God the Father almighty. From there he will come to judge the living and the dead.

   I believe in the Holy Spirit, the holy catholic church, the communion of saints, the forgiveness of sins, the resurrection of the body...

4. Have the teens pull out their Question Journals. Ask them to jot down the answers to any questions about the Creed that are answered in this session. Have them share those discoveries,

giving them sufficient time to record any thoughts they wish to capture. Assure them that they can ask any remaining questions about this section at the end of the session.

5. Ask the teens what they know about the resurrection. They may know considerably more about Jesus' resurrection than the promised resurrection of the saints in the Creed.

6. Have the teens read (or re-read) the section entitled *The Resurrection Body*. Ask them what was new and surprising to them about the resurrection body.

7. Ask the teens to consider people they know, or have known, whose bodies did not work perfectly in this life. Ask them to think about events here on this earth that make us disappointed or sad. Then ask them to think for a few minutes about how wonderful the new, glorified body that will not experience these things might feel. Try to imagine feeling that way forever! Thank Jesus for this coming reality.

8. Ask the teens to imagine being with Jesus among the resurrected saints from every tribe, tongue, and nation – including those they have known and loved in this life who have gone to heaven before them. Who might they be most excited to see and never be separated from again?

9. Take a few minutes to pray with the teens and thank God for the provision of his Son that allows this hope to be a reality for those of us who believe and claim Jesus as Savior.

10. Ask the teens how they might answer someone who doubts the resurrection and the reality of an afterlife that includes a heaven and a hell.

11. Allow the teens to ask any questions about the resurrection of the body they had noted previously that were not addressed in this discussion.

12. If you have teens in your group who have not yet surrendered to Jesus, continue to pray for the Holy Spirit to open that

conversational door so you can explain the gospel. Once they receive Christ, the indwelling presence of the Holy Spirit will make the lessons in this book much more accessible to them.

HOW DO I IMPART WHAT I HAVE JUST LEARNED TO ADULTS?

1. Challenge your adults to take a moment to stop and pray, asking God, through the Holy Spirit, to increase their understanding of the essentials of the Christian Faith. Encourage them to ask Him to reveal and clarify any points which have been confusing or unclear.

2. Review the Apostle's Creed. Re-read the lines below slowly and thoughtfully:

   I believe in God, the Father almighty, creator of heaven and earth.

   I believe in Jesus Christ, his only Son, our Lord, who was conceived by the Holy Spirit and born of the virgin Mary. He suffered under Pontius Pilate, was crucified, died, and was buried; he descended into hell. The third day he rose again from the dead. He ascended to heaven and is seated at the right hand of God the Father almighty. From there he will come to judge the living and the dead.

   I believe in the Holy Spirit, the holy catholic church, the communion of saints, the forgiveness of sins, the resurrection of the body...

3. If they have not done so, encourage the participants to memorize the Creed in its entirety, reminding them that it is a summary of the essentials of the faith.

4. Have participants pull out the notes they made during previous sessions. Ask them to jot down the answers to any questions about the Creed that may be answered during this session and to share those discoveries as they happen. Provide sufficient time to record any thoughts they may wish to capture. Assure them that they will have the opportunity to ask any questions that were not answered in this session at the end of the session.

5. Ask the participants: How is the concept of heaven and hell connected inseparably to the resurrection of the body?

6. Discuss with the participants the concept of resurrection of the body and the parallels drawn between Jesus' glorified and resurrected body and the one we are promised. Which of these are new perspectives? Which are they looking forward to experiencing?

7. Ask the participants to try to imagine a body free from the aches, pains, limitations, sadness, and disappointments we all experience here on earth. Then ask them to think for a few minutes about how wonderful the new, glorified body that will not experience these things might be like for themselves and their loved ones. Ask them to try to imagine experiencing that state forever!

8. Ask the participants to imagine being with Jesus among the resurrected saints from every tribe, tongue, and nation – including those they have known and loved in this life who have gone to heaven before them. Ask them who might they be most excited to see and never be separated from again?

9. Optionally, depending on your own life circumstances and those of your participants, there may be those who have been with a saint who was passing from this life to the next and was able to share a glimpse of the glory to come. What a privilege to be granted such a glimpse into the coming glory! Some may wish to share an experience that confirms the reality of the resurrection to them.

10. Take a few minutes to pray with the participants and thank God for the provision of his Son that allows the hope of the resurrection to be a reality for those of us who believe and claim Jesus as Savior.

11. Ask the participants how they might answer someone who doubts the resurrection and the reality of an afterlife that includes a heaven and a hell.

12. Allow participants to ask any questions about the resurrection of the body they had noted previously that were not addressed in this discussion.

13. If you have people in your group who have not yet surrendered to Jesus, continue to pray for the Holy Spirit to open that conversational door so you can explain the gospel. Once they receive Christ, the indwelling presence of the Holy Spirit will make the lessons in this book much more accessible to them.

CHAPTER 15
The Life Everlasting

"I believe in the life everlasting…"

Well then, since God's grace has set us free from the law, does that mean we can go on sinning? Of course not! Don't you realize that you become the slave of whatever you choose to obey? You can be a slave to sin, which leads to death, or you can choose to obey God, which leads to righteous living. Thank God! Once you were slaves of sin, but now you wholeheartedly obey this teaching we have given you. Now you are free from your slavery to sin, and you have become slaves to righteous living.

Because of the weakness of your human nature, I am using the illustration of slavery to help you understand all this. Previously, you let yourselves be slaves to impurity and lawlessness, which led ever deeper into sin. Now you must give yourselves to be slaves to righteous living so that you will become holy.

When you were slaves to sin, you were free from the obligation to do right. And what was the result? You are now ashamed of the things you used to do, things that end in eternal doom. But now you are free from the power of sin and have become slaves of God. Now you do those things that lead to holiness and result in eternal life. For the wages of sin is death, but the free gift of God is eternal life through Christ Jesus our Lord. (Romans 6:15-23)

A GIFT WE DON'T DESERVE

There is a vast difference between a wage and a gift. A wage is something one earns – something awarded for one's actions or labor. A wage is something one deserves – an expected and just payment. A gift, on the other hand, is simply given. A gift is usually given in love or at least appreciation, and is nearly always given in the context of a relationship with no strings attached. Reread the passage above with the context I've just provided.

Think about it: the wages of sin is death (Romans 6:23). What we have earned, what we deserve, what we are awarded and should rightfully expect because of our sinful state and sinful actions is death. We learned in the last chapter that death is the natural result of being separated from the Author of Life. That's the bad news. But here's the good news: the free gift of God is eternal life through Christ Jesus our Lord. We can't earn it. We don't deserve it. It's a gift lovingly given to each one who is in a relationship with Jesus the Christ.

The last stanza of the Apostles' Creed is, "I believe in the life everlasting..." It's a gift! Eternal life in heaven is not automatic. Again, in the last chapter, we learned that *everyone* lives forever. *Everyone.* There are two resurrections – one to everlasting life in glory, and one to everlasting contempt in damnation. There are two – and only two – choices. It may be helpful to remember that Jesus talked more about hell than he did about heaven. Everyone lives forever. So this everlasting life of which we speak is not just living forever, but specifically living *with Jesus* forever. This is important!

THE WAGES OF SIN

God clearly warned humanity that sin would result in death. Humanity has a bent toward sin. We can't help it. But it was not always that way – in fact, it was never God's intent for us. The Creation account tells us,

> *Then the Lord God planted a garden in Eden in the east, and there he placed the man he had made. The Lord God made all*

sorts of trees grow up from the ground—trees that were beautiful and that produced delicious fruit. In the middle of the garden he placed the tree of life and the tree of the knowledge of good and evil.

A river flowed from the land of Eden, watering the garden and then dividing into four branches. The first branch, called the Pishon, flowed around the entire land of Havilah, where gold is found. The gold of that land is exceptionally pure; aromatic resin and onyx stone are also found there. The second branch, called the Gihon, flowed around the entire land of Cush. The third branch, called the Tigris, flowed east of the land of Asshur. The fourth branch is called the Euphrates.

The Lord God placed the man in the Garden of Eden to tend and watch over it. ***But the Lord God warned him, "You may freely eat the fruit of every tree in the garden—except the tree of the knowledge of good and evil. If you eat its fruit, you are sure to die."*** *(Genesis 2:8-17,* **emphasis mine**)

God placed humanity in a beautiful garden. The first man was instructed to tend the garden and then to subdue the area outside the garden – essentially expanding its borders until it filled the whole earth (Genesis 1:26-28). God gave humanity permission to eat the seed-bearing plants and fruit from every tree throughout the garden except one. Do you see that humanity was allowed to eat from the Tree of Life? This tree was not forbidden! We learn from Genesis 3:22 that eating from that tree would have given them eternal life. God's intent for us from the beginning was a sinless, eternal life in a perfect and growing environment.

There were two trees in the middle of the garden – presumably around which the rest of the garden was planted. There was the Tree of Life which would give them eternal life, and there was the Tree of the Knowledge of Good and Evil which God warned would cause them death. In our original sin-free condition, humanity was not predisposed to go against God's instructions. There is a point now at which every human being will give in to temptation, but this was not the case in the beginning. Our first parents would not just succumb to temptation as we do. They would have to want disobedience so bad that they would *choose* to rebel against the Creator. Satan fostered that desire in them through half-truths and deceit.

Satan's deception was to cloud that specific truth about death. Satan understood the choice God had given. He knew exactly what he needed to do to deceive the first woman.

> *The serpent was the shrewdest of all the wild animals the Lord God had made. One day he asked the woman, "Did God really say you must not eat the fruit from any of the trees in the garden?"*
>
> *"Of course we may eat fruit from the trees in the garden," the woman replied. "It's only the fruit from the tree in the middle of the garden that we are not allowed to eat. God said, 'You must not eat it or even touch it; if you do, you will die.' "*
>
> *"You won't die!" the serpent replied to the woman. "God knows that your eyes will be opened as soon as you eat it, and you will be like God, knowing both good and evil."* (Genesis 3:1-5)

Did you notice that the woman did not get God's instruction right? Whose job was it to communicate that to her? She was not created until *after* God had given the man his instructions, including the critical warning about the Tree of the Knowledge of Good and Evil. It was up to the man, Adam, to make these instructions and their essential nature known to her. Apparently, he did not. Satan was aware of this and knew exactly where to strike! He had been observant enough to see where a weakness existed and had no problem exploiting it to his own advantage (and to humanity's demise). First, Satan called God's instruction into question, planting the seeds of doubt in her mind. Then he undermined her obedient trust in God's warning to humanity, saying, "You won't die!" Finally, he caused both the man and the woman (for he was standing right next to her the whole time – Genesis 3:6) to consider the possibility that God was holding out on them by making them come to him for all their needs and knowledge. By telling them they could have "open eyes" like God on their own, Satan deceived them by clouding the truth.

What happened to Adam and Eve happens to so many. They are deceived and led astray by those who cloud the truth and call God's intentions into question because they do not have a steadfast relationship with him or know what he has already said in his Word. This is the reason I'm so passionate about this book. Anyone who does not clearly understand the basic tenets of their Christian Faith can be easily deceived or at least misguided.

The "wages" of sin is indeed death. When the first man and woman *chose* to surrender to the deceiver's instructions and reject God's, they decimated their relationship with God, the Creator and Source of Life. While physiological death did not happen immediately, the death cycle was now underway. Sin now separated them from everything God intended. Sickness, injury, death, and decay were all in motion from then on. They were enslaved by their sin and their new master, Satan. Paul writes about this slavery in his letter to the Christians in Rome,

> *Well then, since God's grace has set us free from the law, does that mean we can go on sinning? Of course not! Don't you realize that you become the slave of whatever you choose to obey? You can be a slave to sin, which leads to death, or you can choose to obey God, which leads to righteous living. Thank God! Once you were slaves of sin, but now you wholeheartedly obey this teaching we have given you. Now you are free from your slavery to sin, and you have become slaves to righteous living.* (Romans 6:15-18)

We have become enslaved to sin, and it leads us to death. Period. Sin is in our very nature. It leads us to sin in thought, word, and deed. And recall how we began this chapter: "For the wages of sin is death..." (Romans 6:23). What we have earned, that which we deserve because of our sin-filled lives, is death. And it's not like God didn't warn humanity from the very beginning!

Sin always takes its slaves deeper and deeper. Sin is a slippery slope. Give in once, and it is easier to give in again. The rush and pleasure of sin have a deadening effect, wooing us to sin a little more each time for the same experience. Paul writes,

343

Because of the weakness of your human nature, I am using the illustration of slavery to help you understand all this. Previously, you let yourselves be slaves to impurity and lawlessness, which led ever deeper into sin. Now you must give yourselves to be slaves to righteous living so that you will become holy. (Romans 6:19)

Satan knew exactly what he was doing when he came directly against humanity on this specific point. Our surrendering to his deceit changed everything. But Romans 6:23 does not end with the wages of sin; it goes on to say, "...but the free gift of God is eternal life through Christ Jesus our Lord."

THE FREE GIFT OF GOD

God knew what must happen to set things right again with Creation, and specifically humanity. God speaks immediately after the first man and woman surrender themselves – and all humanity with them – to the enemy. All the way back in Genesis, the first book of the Bible, God gives the first proclamation of the gospel of Jesus Christ!

When the cool evening breezes were blowing, the man and his wife heard the Lord God walking about in the garden. So they hid from the Lord God among the trees. Then the Lord God called to the man, "Where are you?"

He replied, "I heard you walking in the garden, so I hid. I was afraid because I was naked."

"Who told you that you were naked?" the Lord God asked. "Have you eaten from the tree whose fruit I commanded you not to eat?"

The man replied, "It was the woman you gave me who gave me the fruit, and I ate it."

Then the Lord God asked the woman, "What have you done?"

"The serpent deceived me," she replied. "That's why I ate it."

Then the Lord God said to the serpent,

"Because you have done this, you are cursed more than all animals, domestic and wild.

344

You will crawl on your belly, groveling in the dust as long as you live.

And I will cause hostility between you and the woman, and between your offspring and her offspring.

He will strike your head, and you will strike his heel." (Genesis 3:8-15)

As discussed in the chapter on Christ's Virgin Birth, Genesis 3:15 is called the "protoevangelium," or the first proclamation of the gospel. Notice several things:

1. In this verse, God does not speak of Adam's offspring but of Eve's. Remember this is the only place in all of ancient Hebrew literature where the word for offspring (literally, "seed") is attributed to a woman and not a man. God is here already looking toward the Virgin Birth of Christ!

2. God refers to her offspring as *he*. As the rest of the Old Testament unfolds, we see this man is the Messiah.

3. This man, the woman's offspring, will strike or *crush* the head of the serpent. It will be a fatal blow.

4. But the serpent and his offspring will only injure the heel of the woman's offspring.

Immediately after the first man and woman surrender to Satan and rebel against God, bringing shame, death, and the decay cycle into God's creation as he warned, God speaks of his solution!

Jesus came to conquer sin and death once and for all. This statement separates the Christian Faith from all other religions and philosophies. Jesus' resurrection was a total defeat of death. Peter proclaims, "...for death could not keep him in its grip" (Acts 2:24). After Jesus' sacrifice, sin is washed away for all those who put their faith in him.

For God's will was for us to be made holy by the sacrifice of the body of Jesus Christ, once for all time.

Under the old covenant, the priest stands and ministers before the altar day after day, offering the same sacrifices again and again, which can never take away sins. But our High Priest offered himself to God as a single sacrifice for sins, good for all time. Then he sat down in the place of honor at God's right hand. There he waits until his enemies are humbled and made a footstool under his feet. For by that one offering he forever made perfect those who are being made holy.

And the Holy Spirit also testifies that this is so. For he says,

"This is the new covenant I will make with my people on that day, says the Lord:

I will put my laws in their hearts, and I will write them on their minds."

Then he says,

"I will never again remember their sins and lawless deeds."

And when sins have been forgiven, there is no need to offer any more sacrifices. (Hebrews 10:10-18)

Jesus understood that this was his purpose.

"For even the Son of Man came not to be served but to serve others and to give his life as a ransom for many." (Matthew 20:28)

Jesus gave his own life as our ransom! His life was payment for our release. Jesus ransomed us (slaves) from our master (sin). Jesus gave his life to free us from our death! This is the overarching message of the whole Bible!

He will swallow up death forever!

The Sovereign Lord will wipe away all tears.

He will remove forever all insults and mockery against his land and people.

The Lord has spoken! (Isaiah 25:8)

"For this is how God loved the world: He gave his one and only Son, so that everyone who believes in him will not perish but have eternal life. God sent his Son into the world not to judge the world, but to save the world through him. (John 3:16-17)

For the sin of this one man, Adam, caused death to rule over many. But even greater is God's wonderful grace and his gift of righteousness, for all who receive it will live in triumph over sin and death through this one man, Jesus Christ. (Romans 5:17)

For the wages of sin is death, but the free gift of God is eternal life through Christ Jesus our Lord. (Romans 6:23)

My old self has been crucified with Christ. It is no longer I who live, but Christ lives in me. So I live in this earthly body by trusting in the Son of God, who loved me and gave himself for me. (Galatians 2:20)

And now he has made all of this plain to us by the appearing of Christ Jesus, our Savior. He broke the power of death and illuminated the way to life and immortality through the Good News. (2 Timothy 1:10)

Because God's children are human beings—made of flesh and blood—the Son also became flesh and blood. For only as a human being could he die, and only by dying could he break the power of the devil, who had the power of death. (Hebrews 2:14)

He personally carried our sins in his body on the cross so that we can be dead to sin and live for what is right.

By his wounds you are healed. (1 Peter 2:24)

I heard a loud shout from the throne, saying, "Look, God's home is now among his people! He will live with them, and they will be his people. God himself will be with them. He will wipe every tear from their eyes, and there will be no more death or sorrow or crying or pain. All these things are gone forever."

And the one sitting on the throne said, "Look, I am making everything new!" And then he said to me, "Write this down, for what I tell you is trustworthy and true." And he also said, "It is finished! I am the Alpha and the Omega—the Beginning and the End. To all who are thirsty I will give freely from the springs of the water of life. All who are victorious will inherit all these blessings, and I will be their God, and they will be my children. (Revelation 21:3-7)

In Christ, we are now free from the power of sin. Humanity was utterly enslaved to sin because of what happened in the Garden of Eden. We were created without any sin or predisposition to fall into it. When we sinned, everything changed. From the moment humanity surrendered to the deceiver, rejecting the instructions of God, our tethering relationship to God was severed, and an appetite for sin overtook us. But when one surrenders to Jesus, the power and slavery to sin is eternally broken. We are no longer bound to sin. The sin within us is washed away, our record of sin is blotted out, and our appetite for sin diminishes as we grow in Christ! Hundreds of years before Christ's birth, God had Isaiah prophesy:

"Pay attention, O Jacob, for you are my servant, O Israel.

I, the Lord, made you, and I will not forget you.

I have swept away your sins like a cloud.

I have scattered your offenses like the morning mist.

Oh, return to me, for I have paid the price to set you free." (Isaiah 44:21-22)

In Christ, we are now slaves to God, leading to holiness and eternal life. We began this chapter with Paul's proclamation to the Christians in Rome:

But now you are free from the power of sin and have become slaves of God. Now you do those things that lead to holiness and result in eternal life. For the wages of sin is death, but the free gift of God is eternal life through Christ Jesus our Lord. (Romans 6:21-23)

The key words in that last sentence are "...through Christ Jesus our Lord." Paul uniquely understands this wonder. He had been steeped in Jewish theology. He surrendered to the Messiah. He had very personal encounters with Jesus that brought all of his education as a Pharisee into focus with God's actual mission (Acts 9:1-19; 2 Corinthians 12:2-3;

Galatians 1:11-12). He now lives in personal freedom in Christ and sees countless others set free by the gospel through his missionary journeys. Here's the point: We are now free from the power and bondage of sin and death; however, this is only true if we have surrendered to a new Master! If we surrender to Christ as our King and become possessed by the Holy Spirit, we do those things that lead to holiness and eternal life! This leads to our next point.

In Christ, we now have an everlasting covenant relationship with God... ***this*** *is eternal life.* Jesus' own high priestly prayer makes this clear:

> *After saying all these things, Jesus looked up to heaven and said, "Father, the hour has come. Glorify your Son so he can give glory back to you. For you have given him authority over everyone. He gives eternal life to each one you have given him.* ***And this is the way to have eternal life—to know you, the only true God, and Jesus Christ, the one you sent to earth.*** *(John 17:1-3,* **emphasis mine**)

The ultimate purpose of what Christ did at Calvary was the full and complete restoration of our relationship with God. Jesus says that eternal life is *knowing* God. Think of John 3:16-17 in this light.

> *"For this is how God* **loved** *the world: He gave his one and only Son, so that everyone who believes in him will not perish but have eternal life. God sent his Son into the world not to judge the world, but to save the world through him. (John 3:16-17,* **emphasis mine***)

God *loved* us and has wanted a restored relationship with us since the garden! So God sent his Son to save us, to rescue us, to ransom us for that purpose. Heaven is a wonderful place, but our real focus should always be on eternally dwelling with God! In Christ, God adopts us and gives us full rights as his sons and daughters (John 1:12). God restores the relationship – our connection with Himself, the Source of all life – and we dwell with him forever.

Then I saw a new heaven and a new earth, for the old heaven and the old earth had disappeared. And the sea was also gone. And I saw the holy city, the new Jerusalem, coming down from God out of heaven like a bride beautifully dressed for her husband.

I heard a loud shout from the throne, saying, "Look, God's home is now among his people! He will live with them, and they will be his people. God himself will be with them. He will wipe every tear from their eyes, and there will be no more death or sorrow or crying or pain. All these things are gone forever."

And the one sitting on the throne said, "Look, I am making everything new!" And then he said to me, "Write this down, for what I tell you is trustworthy and true." And he also said, "It is finished! I am the Alpha and the Omega—the Beginning and the End. To all who are thirsty I will give freely from the springs of the water of life. All who are victorious will inherit all these blessings, and I will be their God, and they will be my children.

"But cowards, unbelievers, the corrupt, murderers, the immoral, those who practice witchcraft, idol worshipers, and all liars—their fate is in the fiery lake of burning sulfur. This is the second death." (Revelation 21:1-8)

Surrendering to Christ makes the difference between an eternal dwelling with God and the second death.

In Christ, "life" goes from what was usurped, stolen, and destroyed by Satan to what God intended in abundance. Jesus makes this clear during his earthly ministry. Speaking specifically of Satan, he teaches,

> *The thief's purpose is to steal and kill and destroy. My purpose is to give them a rich and satisfying life.* (John 10:10)

The synoptic Gospels (Matthew, Mark, and Luke – those taking essentially the same point of view) follow a typical Jewish perspective on eternal life. They see it as the age to come – the future. But John's gospel takes the first-century Christian view that eternal life already exists in Jesus Christ!

*"I tell you the truth, **those who listen to my message and believe in God who sent me have eternal life.** They will never be condemned for their sins, but **they have already passed from death into life.***

*"And I assure you that the time is coming, **indeed it's here now,** when the dead will hear my voice—the voice of the Son of God. And those who listen will live. The Father has life in himself, and he has granted that same life-giving power to his Son. And he has given him authority to judge everyone because he is the Son of Man. Don't be so surprised! Indeed, the time is coming when all the dead in their graves will hear the voice of God's Son, and they will rise again. Those who have done good will rise to experience eternal life, and those who have continued in evil will rise to experience judgment. I can do nothing on my own. I judge as God tells me. Therefore, my judgment is just, because I carry out the will of the one who sent me, not my own will...*

"You search the Scriptures because you think they give you eternal life. But the Scriptures point to me! Yet you refuse to come to me to receive this life. (John 5:24-30, 39-40, **emphasis mine**)

Eternal life does not begin when we die; we have it already. If we have surrendered to Jesus as Lord of all, we are already experiencing the restored, everlasting covenant relationship with our God. If we are still in our sin – unforgiven and unredeemed by Christ – then we are already in our eternal state without God – eternal condemnation.

*"There is no judgment against anyone who believes in him. **But anyone who does not believe in him has already been judged for not believing in God's one and only Son.*** (John 3:18, *emphasis mine*)

Life everlasting is the free gift of God. Herein we come full circle back to Romans 6:23. Some English translations only say, "...the gift of God is eternal life in Christ Jesus our Lord." But in the best translation of the Greek here is "free gift." It is a gift solely given out of love. It cannot be earned. It is never deserved. It is freely given. When we state, "I believe in the life everlasting...", we accept all of the above!

God wanted humanity to flourish from the beginning and established parameters in Creation for a real love relationship to make that happen. God provided the Tree of Life and told humanity they were to eat its fruit! God warned humanity not to eat of one tree – the Tree of the Knowledge of Good and Evil – for such rebellion would bring death. Humanity rebelled against God and his instructions, surrendering to the Deceiver and plunging themselves and all future generations into the cycle of death and decay. But God immediately announced his plan to redeem humanity.

Jesus came to free us from the power and bondage we have to sin and death. In Christ, we are free from sin and can pursue those things that build our relationship with God again! Eternal life is *knowing God!* It is a relationship with him. And it is available now – not a future event. Eternal life is God's gift to us; however, we must accept it and surrender to the Giver to undo humanity's first surrender to the Enemy in the garden. Each of us must make that choice for ourselves.

STUDY GUIDE

IT MAKES A DIFFERENCE

Christians who embrace the Creed's statement about life everlasting have a reason for great joy. They realize their eternal life – and salvation itself – is a gift from their loving heavenly Father. They understand that the primary fruit of humanity's sin is death and that no one can escape it on their own. They realize that this life was God's intent before sin entered the world, and it is the planned outcome of his redemptive work shown in the scriptures. Those who surrender to Jesus are free from the power and bondage of sin, from the stranglehold of death, and are forever restored to a covenant relationship with God.

Many Christians say they believe in eternal life but have yet to study all that scripture teaches about this incredible gift. They cannot fully appreciate what God has accomplished on their behalf. They have not reckoned with the full ramifications of the fall in the Garden of Eden. Some of these folks have been practicing a religious form of

Christianity without surrendering to Jesus as Lord and King. They are unaware that their religious activity is worthless without that relationship.

Life everlasting is the beautiful result of our personal surrender to Jesus. All that God intended for us in the beginning is restored in that relationship.

HOW DO I LIVE OUT WHAT I HAVE JUST LEARNED IN MY OWN LIFE?

1. Take a moment to stop and pray. Ask God, through the Holy Spirit, to increase your understanding of the essentials of the Christian Faith. Ask Him to reveal and clarify any points which have been confusing or unclear.

2. If you have not committed the entire Apostle's Creed to memory, make it a priority to do so this week.

3. Meditate on the difference between a wage and a gift. Have you tried to turn God's free gift of eternal life into a wage for doing enough good deeds? Why won't this work? What wage have you actually earned?

4. Read the story of the interaction between David and Araunah the Jebusite in 2 Samuel 24: 18-25. Here David says he will not offer the Lord that which cost him nothing. Meditate on the parallels between this story and God's willingness to offer the free gift of eternal life to us at the cost of his Son.

5. Take time to offer thanks for this priceless free and everlasting gift.

6. Take several days to consider: Who can help you apply what you learn to put it into an ongoing life's practice?

7. How are you living this out right now? How is your life reflective of your understanding of this truth?

HOW DO I IMPART WHAT I HAVE JUST LEARNED TO CHILDREN?

*Preparing to teach this lesson to children: Gather the needed sup-
plies ahead of the lesson:. A skein or large ball of yarn, blank white
paper, pencils, and crayons or markers. Ahead of the lesson, stretch
out the yarn, attaching it to an object on either end, and so that the
children cannot see where it begins or ends from the room where you
will share the lesson.*

1. When the children enter the room, they will no doubt ask
    about the yarn. Tell them you will discuss its purpose in a few
    minutes.

2. Begin by praying with the children. Ask God, through the Holy
    Spirit, to help the children understand more about the Christian
    faith. Ask God to help them clearly understand the new things
    they are about to learn.

3. Let the children know that when they add the phrase from this
    chapter, they will have memorized the entire Apostle's Creed.
    Celebrate the accomplishment!

    *I believe in God, the Father almighty, creator of heaven and
    earth.*

    *I believe in Jesus Christ, his only Son, our Lord, who was
    conceived by the Holy Spirit and born of the virgin Mary.
    He suffered under Pontius Pilate, was crucified, died, and
    was buried; he descended into hell. The third day he rose
    again from the dead. He ascended to heaven and is seated
    at the right hand of God the Father almighty. From there he
    will come to judge the living and the dead.*

    *I believe in the Holy Spirit, the holy catholic church, the
    communion of saints, the forgiveness of sins, the resurrec-
    tion of the body, and the life everlasting. Amen.*

4. Discuss the meaning of the word "Amen." "Amen" has no direct
    word-for-translation, but it means "let it be so" or "truly." In this

context, it would be an affirmation that the person reciting the Creed believes the truths it contains and longs for its provisions to be realized.

5. Make sure the children have as clear an understanding of "everlasting" as they can grasp. Point out that the yarn seems to have no beginning or end. This is sort of like eternity (another word for everlasting) – although not exactly because we do know that this yarn *does* have a beginning *and* an end. Eternity does not. Eternity means lasting forever – starting before we know, including now, and going on without stopping.

6. Ask the children to imagine the most precious gift they can think of receiving. Let them share their ideas. Remind them that gifts cost the giver something, but all the receiver has to do is accept it. Discuss that God's gift of everlasting life is even more precious and expensive than any of the gifts they imagined! Jesus paid the full price for it. Remind them that if they have invited Jesus into their hearts to forgive their sins, they will spend eternity in heaven with Jesus, and that heaven is a beautiful and perfect place that lasts forever. God decides when it is time for each of us to go there, but each of us who believe in him and receive his gift will go there when he is ready for us. All we have to do is accept his gift. Remind them that though heaven is in the future, the blessings of eternal life begin now. Discuss some of these blessings.

7. Have the children draw a picture of themselves receiving a large, beautiful package from Jesus. Have them write the words, "Please accept my free gift of eternal life." near the head of Jesus, then surround the words with a speech bubble leading to Jesus' mouth.

8. Next have them write, "Thank you now and forever!" near their own head and draw a speech bubble around it leading to their own mouth.

9. It is very important to have the children write the words *before* drawing the speech bubbles. Almost inevitably, children

underestimate the space they will need to write inside the bubble if they draw the bubble first. (Advice from a 40 year veteran of teaching.)

10. If you have children in your group who have not yet surrendered to Jesus, continue to pray for the Holy Spirit to open that conversational door so you can explain the gospel. Once they receive Christ, the indwelling presence of the Holy Spirit will make the lessons in this book much more accessible to them.

HOW DO I IMPART WHAT I HAVE JUST LEARNED TO TEENS?

1. Begin by praying with the teens. Ask God, through the Holy Spirit, to increase understanding. You can do this or ask a volunteer.

2. Read the Apostles' Creed out loud. Read it yourself, ask for a volunteer, or read it in unison. Point out that after they master this line, they will have memorized the entire Apostle's Creed. Congratulate those who have done so.

3. Repeat these lines:

   I believe in God, the Father almighty, creator of heaven and earth.

   I believe in Jesus Christ, his only Son, our Lord, who was conceived by the Holy Spirit and born of the virgin Mary. He suffered under Pontius Pilate, was crucified, died, and was buried; he descended into hell. The third day he rose again from the dead. He ascended to heaven and is seated at the right hand of God the Father almighty. From there he will come to judge the living and the dead.

   I believe in the Holy Spirit, the holy catholic church, the communion of saints, the forgiveness of sins, the resurrection of the body, and the life everlasting. Amen.

4. Have the teens pull out their Question Journals. Ask them to jot down the answers to any questions about the Creed that are answered in this session. Have them share those discoveries,

giving them sufficient time to record any thoughts they wish to capture. Assure them that they can ask any remaining questions about this section at the end of the session.

5. Ask the teens to think about why Satan's tactic of deception in the Garden of Eden worked so well. Ask: "Which of these tactics does Satan still use?" Hint: Have you ever given someone a deceptive answer, maybe because you didn't want to get caught for doing something you know you shouldn't have? Why could such lies (partial truths are lies, after all) be more effective than straight out complete falsehoods?

6. Why do we need to know that eternity is not just a future destination, but has already begun?

7. Talk with the teens about gifts. How are they different from wages or paychecks? What does this say about the idea that many people have that they must earn eternal life by doing enough good things?

8. It is a fact that gifts cost the giver. Ask the teens "What price did God pay in order to offer us the gift of eternal life? What does this say about the value of this gift? What does the receiver of a gift have to do? How is this like God's promise of the gift of eternal life?"

9. Take a few minutes to pray with the teens and thank God for the gift of his Son that allows the hope of life everlasting to be reality for those of us who believe and claim Jesus as Savior.

10. Allow the teens to ask any questions about everlasting life they had noted previously that were not addressed in this discussion.

11. If you have teens in your group who have not yet surrendered to Jesus, continue to pray for the Holy Spirit to open that conversational door so you can explain the gospel. Once they receive Christ, the indwelling presence of the Holy Spirit will make the lessons in this book much more accessible to them.

HOW DO I IMPART WHAT I HAVE JUST LEARNED TO ADULTS?

1. Challenge your adults to take a moment to stop and pray, asking God, through the Holy Spirit, to increase their understanding of the essentials of the Christian Faith. Encourage them to ask Him to reveal and clarify any points which have been confusing or unclear.

2. Review the Apostle's Creed. Re-read the lines below slowly and thoughtfully. Point out that this additional line completes the entire Apostle's Creed.:

   I believe in God, the Father almighty, creator of heaven and earth.

   I believe in Jesus Christ, his only Son, our Lord, who was conceived by the Holy Spirit and born of the virgin Mary. He suffered under Pontius Pilate, was crucified, died, and was buried; he descended into hell. The third day he rose again from the dead. He ascended to heaven and is seated at the right hand of God the Father almighty. From there he will come to judge the living and the dead.

   I believe in the Holy Spirit, the holy catholic church, the communion of saints, the forgiveness of sins, the resurrection of the body, and the life everlasting. Amen.

3. Congratulate those who have memorized the Creed in its entirety, reminding them that it is a summary of the essentials of the faith.

4. Discuss Satan's tactics of deception in the Garden of Eden. Ask the participants how and when Satan uses similar tactics today.

5. Discuss the "slippery slope" of sin. Ask the participants how they have seen this lived out in the world around them.

6. Discuss the implications of the truth that eternal life has already begun and is not just a future reality.

7. Talk about gifts. How are they different from wages or paychecks? What does this say about the idea that many people have that they must earn eternal life by doing enough good

things? Think about whether you have ever treated God's gift of eternal life like a paycheck you had to earn? Why is that a temptation for many people?

8. If eternal life was equivalent to a paycheck, what wage would we have actually earned?

9. Gifts cost the giver. What price did God pay in order to offer us the gift of eternal life? What does this say about the value of God's gift? What does the receiver of a gift have to do? How is this like God's promise of the gift of eternal life?

10. Take a few minutes to pray with the participants and thank God for the gift of his Son that allows the hope of life everlasting to be reality for those of us who believe and claim Jesus as Savior.

11. Allow participants to ask any questions about everlasting life they had noted previously that were not addressed in this discussion.

12. If you have people in your group who have not yet surrendered to Jesus, continue to pray for the Holy Spirit to open that conversational door so you can explain the gospel. Once they receive Christ, the indwelling presence of the Holy Spirit will make the lessons in this book much more accessible to them.

CHAPTER 16
A Reason for the Hope You Have

Finally, all of you should be of one mind. Sympathize with each other. Love each other as brothers and sisters. Be tender-hearted, and keep a humble attitude. Don't repay evil for evil. Don't retaliate with insults when people insult you. Instead, pay them back with a blessing. That is what God has called you to do, and he will grant you his blessing. For the Scriptures say,

"If you want to enjoy life and see many happy days, keep your tongue from speaking evil and your lips from telling lies.

Turn away from evil and do good.

Search for peace, and work to maintain it.

The eyes of the Lord watch over those who do right, and his ears are open to their prayers.

But the Lord turns his face against those who do evil."

Now, who will want to harm you if you are eager to do good? But even if you suffer for doing what is right, God will reward you for it. So don't worry or be afraid of their threats. Instead, you must worship Christ as Lord of your life. And if someone asks about your hope as a believer, always be ready to explain it. But do this in a gentle and respectful way. Keep your conscience clear. Then if people speak against you, they will be ashamed

361

when they see what a good life you live because you belong to Christ. Remember, it is better to suffer for doing good, if that is what God wants, than to suffer for doing wrong! (1 Peter 3:8-17)

DEFINING HOPE

Americans typically need help understanding the biblical concept of hope. I've concluded that this is because Americanized English has altered the definition of this important term without us realizing it. We say, "I hope it doesn't rain this afternoon," or, "I hope my team wins the World Series." But these examples misuse the term because they have diluted it down to wishful thinking. May I say that the biblical concept of hope is powerfully more than that? Biblical hope is an authentic expectation. We hope for something we do not yet have but fully anticipate its arrival or reception. Biblical hope *knows* and *trusts* something on our horizon is absolutely true. We can trust in it even though we do not hold it in our hands.

Never was this more real to me than in what was, perhaps, the darkest season of my life. In 2014, just as I was beginning a new church planting work in metropolitan Orlando, Florida, I was struck with an unusually large kidney stone. We have no family history of kidney trouble. And I had never had an issue before. But before this excruciatingly painful journey was over, I had multiple kidney surgeries that traumatized my body physically and emotionally. I dealt with panic attacks, horrible anxiety, and depression for nearly three years. I had been a Christian for 30 years. I had been an ordained pastor for almost 25 years. I knew the concept of hope theologically, but I was to learn it very personally. If hope were a feeling, it had evaporated. But thankfully, I was surrounded by people – my wife, children, friends, and mentors – who helped me remain grounded in the truth. My mentor called me one day just to check in. During that conversation, I told him about the despondency I was experiencing. I'll never forget his response: "The emotions and pain you feel are real. They are really there. But they are not *true*." I sat silently on the other end of the phone and wept – a simple sentence – but so profoundly powerful in that moment. I now believe that my whole man was out of whack: my body was still reeling and healing from the intense season of surgeries (it would take over a year to physically heal), my emotions were betraying me at every turn, and I was also experiencing some targeted spiritual warfare by an enemy who knew all too well what targets to hit to keep me incapacitated.

It was in this dark season that my loved ones surrounded me and reminded me of the very real hope I had. When I could not bring myself even to open the Bible, God would *always* raise someone up to drop just the right passage into my life. One morning when I could not get out of bed, the phone rang, and dear friends from New England "just happened" to be in the area and wanted to stop by and pray with me. He is a friend and pastoral colleague; she is a professional counselor. The timing of that visit was life itself – a very real gift from God. In so many ways, I came to learn with the help of others to expect again. I hurt, but I *knew* it would not last forever. My emotional foundation had been swept away, but I could once again *trust* that Jesus was my foundation, and he was steadfast. I knew Satan and his minions were after me and my church planting team like a swarm of hornets to stop us from planting an authentic, disciple-making congregation in an area that we believe is one of his strongholds. But I also knew there was a kind of loving protection from my heavenly Father that Satan could not overcome. I'll never forget the day I woke up feeling safe again. My circumstances told one story – built on lies. My hope returned to shout another story – built on the Rock, Jesus Christ.

When it comes to our Christian Faith, it is our hope that separates us from all other religious and devoted people. In our faith walk with Jesus, we cannot rely on "wishful thinking." We need to have a hope that is steadfast expectation (remember "wheelbarrow faith"?). And when we personally waver, we need to be surrounded by others who can remind us of the powerful truth on which we stand. Christian hope is so real it is filled with anticipation. When we place our hope in Christ, we are fully trusting (relying upon) what the Scripture says he has done and what he *will* do. Hope in his return in power and glory is like anticipating a favorite holiday that is just around the corner. It hasn't happened yet, but you know it's coming. You plan for it. You prepare yourself for it. And you are so excited about it that you tell others!

The Apostle Peter tells his readers, "...if someone asks about your hope as a believer, always be ready to explain it. But do this in a gentle and respectful way. Keep your conscience clear" (1 Peter 3:15-16). The last

15 chapters have been a journey through the foundational truths of the Christian Faith based upon the framework of the Apostles' Creed. There are three reasons why I have created this tool to lead precious souls like you through this process:

1. Many Christians espouse things they say they believe but do not know where those ideas come from. They have not been taught these truths, nor have they tried to learn them on their own.

2. Many Christians really do believe in the basics of the Christian Faith, but they cannot tell you *why* they believe them or why they are important.

3. Many Christians are living in these crazy days with fear. Fear of the future. Fear of present issues in our world. They are living without the real, foundational, unshakable *hope* they should have because of their Faith!

The truth is we have incredible reasons for hope. And that's what this final chapter is all about.

THE CHRISTIAN LIFESTYLE

Want to know a secret? What you believe directly influences how you live your life. If you spend more time watching the news than reading your Bible, your life and decisions will be driven by fear and worldly wisdom. You'll have man-centered convictions about the economy, politics, crime, social ills, and other issues rather than hope in the power and plans of our Triune God. You'll be dissuaded by human agendas rather than the Immanuel Agenda. Christians everywhere are stuck in such patterns today. But suppose you have a strong Faith in our God, with immovable convictions on all the doctrinal promises we've spent the last 15 chapters unpacking together. In that case, you can live smartly and confidently in this very wayward world, and your impact on those around you will be a *kingdom* impact. People who are stuck in fear and worldly wisdom will see the hope and confidence with which you are living, and they will want to know about it (1 Peter 3:15). When you and I truly understand the essentials of our Christian Faith and we base our whole existence upon them, we can live with hope and confidence no matter what our circumstances. This foundation of Faith makes a very real difference. Our hope is one of the greatest witnesses for the reality of God we can put on display!

The foundation of faith makes us all of one mind. This is an amazing thing. The Holy Spirit takes people from very different backgrounds and experiences and builds within them the same foundation – the gospel of Christ. When God is our common Father, and Jesus is our common Savior, the Bible is our common instruction, and the mission of Jesus is our common context – we are of one mind on all that is essential. The foundation of our Faith helps us to literally be of one mind together! All of the debate and upheaval we see all over the world can be brought into alignment with our Father when we all surrender to Christ.

The foundation of faith makes us compassionate toward one another. The snarkiness and backbiting we see around us can be addressed in Jesus! When we understand our faith and how all of us are in the same position – needing forgiveness – we stop seeing each other as rivals or enemies. We start seeing each other with the eyes and heart of Jesus. We begin to sympathize with one another. We start recognizing each other's troubles and needs, and it moves us to genuine compassion. This is not mandated or some kind of welfare program, but an authentic response of the heart.

The foundation of faith makes us truly love one another. Remember the words of Jesus:

> *"So now I am giving you a new commandment: Love each other. Just as I have loved you, you should love each other. Your love for one another will prove to the world that you are my disciples."* (John 13:34-35)

The more we understand what God has done for us in Jesus Christ, the more we will respond in love to one another. The Apostle John says that we love because he first loved us (1 John 4:19). When Christ's love invades our souls, we begin to respond to those around us in love rather than with suspicion, a competitive attitude, or in hatred.

The foundation of faith makes us tender-hearted. Growing in the understanding of our Faith – coming to know how much it cost God to redeem us – makes us kind and benevolent toward one another. We stop identifying people by their flaws, sins, and brokenness and start seeing each one as a beloved, precious, and redeemed son or daughter of God in Jesus Christ. Our God-given identity as his dearly loved children shows our intrinsic value and levels the field.

The foundation of faith helps us keep a humble attitude. Humility – now there is something missing in today's world. America, in particular, could do with a good dose of relentless humility. Our humility in Christ should be genuine. It is modeled after Jesus himself. Listen to Paul's teaching to the Christians in Philippi:

> *Don't be selfish; don't try to impress others. Be humble, thinking of others as better than yourselves. Don't look out only for your own interests, but take an interest in others, too.*
>
> *You must have the same attitude that Christ Jesus had.*
>
> *Though he was God, he did not think of equality with God as something to cling to.*
>
> *Instead, he gave up his divine privileges; he took the humble position of a slave and was born as a human being.*
>
> *When he appeared in human form, he humbled himself in obedience to God and died a criminal's death on a cross.* (Philippians 2:3-8)

The foundation of faith helps us avoid evil retaliation. Whether it's in person, on social media, on television, in an email, in a meeting, or in any other form, we no longer choose retaliation. We take no personal vengeance at all (evil for evil). We do not insult people (insult for insult). We find ways to speak blessings into their lives and to be a blessing. We do not speak evil of people. We do not lie. We become instruments of peace in the Holy Spirit's hands. We have confidence that God is watching over us. Can you imagine a world where these things are true? They are only a reality in people who have a strong and hope-filled foundation to their Faith because of Jesus Christ the Messiah.

So when we face trying days – and we will – a strong Faith foundation gives us steadfast hope and changes the way we live with and relate to those around us. The Christian hope shines particularly bright in times of testing, trial, and suffering.

THE CHRISTIAN HOPE

Let's return to a portion of the Bible passage that began this chapter.

> *Now, who will want to harm you if you are eager to do good? But even if you suffer for doing what is right, God will reward you for it. So don't worry or be afraid of their threats. Instead, you must worship Christ as Lord of your life. And if someone asks about your hope as a believer, always be ready to explain it. But do this in a gentle and respectful way. Keep your conscience clear. Then if people speak against you, they will be ashamed when they see what a good life you live because you belong to Christ. Remember, it is better to suffer for doing good, if that is what God wants, than to suffer for doing wrong!* (1 Peter 3:13-17)

Peter asks an important question. Who will want to harm you if you are eager to do good? While there are evil people in this world who vehemently oppose anything and anyone that looks like Jesus, there really are only two kinds of individuals who have to regularly worry about being targeted in this world:

1. Those who do bad things and hurt people. They'll be hated and won't get away with it very long.

2. Those who hypocritically call out the evil in others. And be aware that this includes hyper-religious people who tell others how to live but don't live that way themselves.

But Peter is reflecting here on the whole lifestyle he has just described to us in the previous verses. If we live like that, it will be rare to become one of the world's targets.

Peter acknowledges evil in this world. There are some who may make us suffer. There are those who may threaten us, but we do not have to be afraid. We know that God is watching over us and that he will reward us for enduring such hardship.

Peter reminds us of our foundation. And here we are: Instead of worry or fear, we must worship Christ as the Lord of our lives! This assumes we have the faith foundation we've detailed over the last 15 chapters.

We *can* have an unshakable foundation. This also assumes we are living the lifestyle we've already discussed – one of genuine unity of mind, compassion, love, a tender heart, and absolutely no retaliation in any of our relationships. Instead of worry and fear, we worship. We give King Jesus the reverence, adoration, and glory he deserves. In fact, here is a good rule of thumb: any time we feel like worrying, we choose to worship instead! We do this because he is our Lord. He is not only our Master (which is about our work, instruction, and accountability), but also our Shepherd (the one who provides nurture, care, and protection).

Peter tells us to always be ready to explain the hope we have in Christ. And this is critical to the totality of our Christian life and witness. Let me be frank: If no one ever asks you about the hope you have in Jesus, then it's not evident in you. This is especially true in our world today. In the last several years, we have traversed a pandemic, riots, volatile political battles on the local, state, and federal levels, military movements and all-out combat around the globe, steadily increasing intensity in culture wars, and so much more. A greater number of people are living in fear, confusion, and hopelessness today than at any other time in my lifetime. People are growing more frustrated and despondent every single day because they do not see an alternative. And many Christians have decided to join the various fights rather than be resolute witnesses to the unwavering hope, truth, and peace we have in Christ. If you believe the truths we have unpacked over the last 15 chapters, and if you'll grow in the glorious lifestyle we de-scribed in the first part of this chapter, then you will be shining with real hope everywhere you go. And believe me, people will ask you about it! When they do, we all need to be ready to tell them *why* we are hopeful because of Jesus. We need to be ready to tell them about our Faith foundation and how it makes us confident and unshakable in our Faith, regardless of today's circumstances.

Peter instructs us on how to explain our hope. I absolutely love the sweet spirit Peter conveys here. It's perfectly in line with the lifestyle we've been describing. Remember: when you're talking about your Faith foundation, you're talking about your hope.

1. Be gentle. Period. Speak with real kindness. There is never an excuse for a Christ follower to be snarky, biting, or outright mean in a response. "Gotcha" Christians do not represent the Savior but their own agendas.

2. Be respectful. This is not about proving the other person wrong (that's the Holy Spirit's job). It's about answering the question about our hope. This can never be successfully done in a disrespectful way.

3. Keep a clear conscience. We should never walk away from a conversation about our Faith or our hope and feel bad about how we treated someone. Paul reminds us that our lives should demonstrate faith, hope, and love. We treat people with love.

4. Trust the Holy Spirit. When we give an explanation about the hope we have, we can expect that the conversation will ultimately be convicting to our audience (whether one or many). People will either be moved toward Christ (by the Spirit), or they will push back in some way. Their response is not your responsibility. You just answer their question about your hope and leave the rest up to God.

Finally, Peter explains that we might even suffer for doing good. That's our reality as Christians. Suffering is not always because we've done something wrong. Sometimes we suffer at the world's hands because we are doing something right. God will reward us (1 Peter 3:14). We must worship Christ (1 Peter 3:15).

WE HAVE GREAT REASON FOR HOPE!

Everything we have studied together in this book helps us build a strong foundation for our Christian Faith. And as our foundation strengthens and expands, it gives us an unshakable hope in Jesus. We are united – of one heart and mind in Christ. We are compassionate, tender-hearted, and truly love one another. We remain humble. We always have a godly response to the evil around us. We learn how to put our hope on display in even the worst of circumstances, and it becomes one of our greatest witnessing tools. We gently and respectfully explain why we are so hopeful – and this will either be used by the Holy Spirit to woo people closer to Jesus, or they will push back on their own. And even if we suffer for doing this good, we continue to worship Jesus and will seek our comfort and our reward from the heavenly Father.

Review the contents of this book regularly. This is not just information to "learn," but building blocks to the foundation of your Christian Faith. Commit these things to heart, and you'll not only experience unshakable hope and expectation in both the Lord and his promises, but you'll also be able to begin sharing these truths with others, becoming a disciple who makes disciples.

May your witness be strong. And may your kingdom fruit be plentiful. I'm praying for you.

STUDY GUIDE

IT MAKES A DIFFERENCE

If you've worked your way through all the chapters of this book – either on your own or in a group – congratulations! Even if this was your first time processing the Apostles' Creed, you still likely understand more about the love and work of God on your behalf than most of those around you. You've seen how important are the various stanzas of the Creed. And you likely now have a far greater measure of hope than many. Having such a foundation for our Christian Faith leads us toward authentic unity – being of one mind and purpose. It also makes us more compassionate toward one another – tender-hearted, humble, and loving. The hope you have provides an immovable, expectant confidence in Christ.

People who have never undertaken such an exercise will often sacrifice these traits. Their relationship with God will tend to be more shallow because their understanding of the basics of the Christian Faith is shallow. They will not have steadfast hope. They may struggle with pursuing the Immanuel agenda, with authentic unity in their relationships, with humility, and with extending genuine agape love to their family and friends, whether those folks are believers or not.

Those who have embodied the tenets of the Creed can have a profound impact for the sake of Christ's kingdom.

HOW DO I LIVE OUT WHAT I HAVE JUST LEARNED IN MY OWN LIFE?

1. Take a moment to stop and pray. Ask God, through the Holy Spirit, to increase your understanding of the essentials of the Christian Faith. Ask Him to reveal and clarify any points which have been confusing or unclear.

2. Spend time in meditation and reflection re-reading each line of the Apostle's Creed and considering what we have learned since the beginning of this study.

3. Are you ready to explain the hope you have?

4. Your "news diet" affects how you perceive your hope. How much time are you devoting to feeding your gospel hope (good news of Jesus' rule and reign) via prayer and the Word versus "gloom, doom, and fear" internet news sites, TV and radio newscasts, and social media? When you do consume what passes for the news of this world, do you balance it with biblical truth? Do you need a healthier mental and spiritual diet?

5. In what ways do your beliefs affect your life?

6. Take several days to consider: Who can help you apply what you learn to put it into an ongoing life's practice?

7. How are you living this out right now? How is your life reflective of your understanding of these truths?

HOW DO I IMPART WHAT I HAVE JUST LEARNED TO CHILDREN?

*Preparing to teach this lesson to children: Gather the needed supplies ahead of the lesson. You will need a piece of plain white paper per child, and scissors, pencils, and colored pencils and/or crayons. Markers are not suggested for this activity, as they tend to bleed

through the pages and we are using both sides. An 8 1/2 x 11 sheet of paper will work. If you want a larger book with a bigger space for illustrations, larger sized rectangular paper will work.

1. Begin by praying with the children. Ask God, through the Holy Spirit, to help the children understand more about the Christian faith. Ask God to help them clearly understand the new things they are about to learn.

2. As a review, recite the Creed with the children.

   I believe in God, the Father almighty, creator of heaven and earth.

   I believe in Jesus Christ, his only Son, our Lord, who was conceived by the Holy Spirit and born of the virgin Mary. He suffered under Pontius Pilate, was crucified, died, and was buried; he descended into hell. The third day he rose again from the dead. He ascended to heaven and is seated at the right hand of God the Father almighty. From there he will come to judge the living and the dead.

   I believe in the Holy Spirit, the holy catholic church, the communion of saints, the forgiveness of sins, the resurrection of the body, and the life everlasting. Amen.

3. In this lesson, you will be making an eight-page review book with the children. If one page is used for a title and author page and the back is left blank, there will be six pages for content. You may choose to leave other pages blank, as desired. On the content pages, have the children write and illustrate essential truths they have learned, using their own words.

   Suggested are paraphrased truths from the Creed such as:

   a. God created everything.
   b. God sent Jesus to save us from our sins.
   c. The Holy Spirit teaches and comforts us.
   d. We belong to the universal church.
   e. If we accept God's free gift, we have eternal life now and in heaven.
   f. Any other paraphrased truth from the Creed.

4. Prior to making the books, it is suggested that you discuss what you have learned about the Creed and agree on five or six sentences or phrases to include. If you skip this step with children, you may well have books that "stray" from subjects addressed in the Creed. If children want to write about pets or family, for instance, suggest they make a separate foldable book at another time. Write the agreed upon sentences or phrases so that they are displayed in such a way that the children are reminded about what they agreed to include in their books. As always, making a sample ahead of time is strongly encouraged.

5. Here is a link to an article that explains the steps to making the book with an accompanying video: *https://www.itsalwaysautumn. com/make-8-page-mini-book-one-sheet-paper-easy-foldables- idea.html* . Note: printing the template is entirely optional. You may want to create your own title and author page on the front, with a title such as *Reviewing the Creed* by *Their Name.* In that case, the template will not be useful.

6. Here are the steps in lieu of the article/video:

   a. With the paper in front of you in landscape orientation, fold the sheet in half right to left. The children will probably know this as "hamburger style'. Crease the fold.

   b. Without opening, fold again to the same side. Crease this fold.

   c. Open the second fold, then fold down from the top. Crease.

   d. Using scissors, cut the top fold (last crease, from right edge *to the center)* – not beyond!

   e. Open the paper flat. Fold longways – what the children call "hotdog style". The cut should now be at the top.

   f. Stand the paper up with the cut at the top and the long edge at the bottom.

   g. Grab the free edges and push the ends of the cut together, meeting in the middle. This will form two more pages as the cut edge bends outward.

    h.   Flatten the paper into a book shape and crease the
        uncreased edges.

    i.   Be sure children turn the book so that it is oriented to
        open from the right side before creating the title page.

    j.   Have them create a title page on the front. The rest of the
        pages should be used to write and illustrate their review
        of what they've learned about the Apostle's Creed.

7.   If you have children in your group who have not yet surrendered
     to Jesus, pray sincerely that what they've learned over the past
     weeks will allow the Holy Spirit to open their hearts to the
     gospel. Once they receive Christ, the indwelling presence of
     the Holy Spirit will make the lessons in this book much more
     accessible to them.

HOW DO I IMPART WHAT I HAVE JUST LEARNED TO TEENS?

1.   Begin by praying with the teens. Ask God, through the
     Holy Spirit, to increase understanding. You can do this or
     ask a volunteer.

2.   Read the Apostles' Creed out loud. Read it yourself, ask for a
     volunteer, or read it in unison.

*I believe in God, the Father almighty, creator of heaven and
earth.*

*I believe in Jesus Christ, his only Son, our Lord, who was
conceived by the Holy Spirit and born of the virgin Mary.
He suffered under Pontius Pilate, was crucified, died, and
was buried; he descended into hell. The third day he rose
again from the dead. He ascended to heaven and is seated
at the right hand of God the Father almighty. From there he
will come to judge the living and the dead.*

*I believe in the Holy Spirit, the holy catholic church, the
communion of saints, the forgiveness of sins, the resurrection of the body, and the life everlasting. Amen.*

3.   Ask the teens if they feel generally hopeful. Do they feel ready
     to explain the hope they have? Especially if either answer is
     "no" or "unsure", re-read the section *Defining Hope*. Ask how
     someone's definition of *hope* affects their ability to embrace it.

Suggest they re-read the italicized points from the remainder of the chapter. Discuss more in depth the explanation of any of the points they feel unsure about.

4. Read and discuss the following paragraph: Your "news diet" affects how you perceive your hope. How much time are you devoting to feeding your gospel hope (good news of Jesus' rule and reign) via prayer and the Word versus "gloom, doom, and fear" internet news sites, TV and radio newscasts, and social media? When you do consume what passes for the news of this world, do you balance it with biblical truth? What about the people you spend large amounts of time with either in person or online? Do they encourage or discourage this hope? Do you need to spend less time with the negative and/or more time with the positive to have a healthier mental and spiritual diet?

5. In what other ways do your beliefs affect your life?

6. Have the teens pull out their Question Journals. Allow teens to ask any questions about the Apostle's Creed they may still have.

7. If you have teens in your group who have not yet surrendered to Jesus, pray sincerely that what they've learned over the past weeks will allow the Holy Spirit to open their hearts to the gospel. Once they receive Christ, the indwelling presence of the Holy Spirit will make the lessons in this book much more accessible to them.

HOW DO I IMPART WHAT I HAVE JUST LEARNED TO ADULTS?

1. Challenge your adults to take a moment to stop and pray, asking God, through the Holy Spirit, to increase their understanding of the essentials of the Christian Faith. Encourage them to ask Him to reveal and clarify any points which have been confusing or unclear.

2. Review the Apostle's Creed. Re-read the lines below slowly and thoughtfully.

I believe in God, the Father almighty, creator of heaven and earth.

I believe in Jesus Christ, his only Son, our Lord, who was conceived by the Holy Spirit and born of the virgin Mary. He suffered under Pontius Pilate, was crucified, died, and was buried; he descended into hell. The third day he rose again from the dead. He ascended to heaven and is seated at the right hand of God the Father almighty. From there he will come to judge the living and the dead.

I believe in the Holy Spirit, the holy catholic church, the communion of saints, the forgiveness of sins, the resurrection of the body, and the life everlasting. Amen.

3. Congratulate those who have memorized the Creed in its entirety, reminding them that it is a summary of the essentials of the faith.

4. Ask participants if they are ready to explain the hope they have. Does the hope they have match the definition given in this chapter? Why does this definition matter?

5. Discuss this paragraph: Your "news diet" affects how you perceive your hope. How much time are you devoting to feeding your gospel hope (good news of Jesus' rule and reign) via prayer and the Word versus "gloom, doom, and fear" internet news sites, TV and radio newscasts, and social media? When you do consume what passes for the news of this world, do you balance it with biblical truth? Do you need a healthier mental and spiritual diet? If so, what steps do you need to take to do so?

6. Ask participants to explain the ways their beliefs affect their lives.

7. Discuss how embracing the hope of the gospel can help prepare the Christian to face the suffering that might come because they choose to align with biblical principles.

8. Have participants pull out the notes they made during previous sessions. Allow participants to ask any questions about the Apostles' Creed that still remain.

9. If you have people in your group who have not yet surrendered to Jesus, pray sincerely that what they've learned over the past weeks will allow the Holy Spirit to open their hearts to the gospel. Once they receive Christ, the indwelling presence of the Holy Spirit will make the lessons in this book much more accessible to them.

Printed in Great Britain
by Amazon

38837326R00225